The Future of U.S. Public Diplomacy

Diplomatic Studies

Series Editor

Jan Melissen

Netherlands Institute of International Relations 'Clingendael'

VOLUME 4

The Future of U.S. Public Diplomacy

An Uncertain Fate

By

Kathy R. Fitzpatrick

BRILL

LEIDEN • BOSTON
2010

This book is printed on acid-free paper.

Library of Congress Cataloging-in-Publication Data

Fitzpatrick, Kathy R.
The future of U.S. public diplomacy : an uncertain fate / by Kathy R. Fitzpatrick.
p. cm. — (Diplomatic studies ; v. 4)
Includes index.
ISBN 978-90-04-17720-8 (hardback : alk. paper) 1. United States—Relations—Foreign countries. I. Title. II. Title: Future of United States public diplomacy.
JZ1480.F58 2009
327.73—dc22

2009035562

ISSN 1872-8863
ISBN 978 90 04 17720 8

PRINTED IN THE NETHERLANDS

For Kurt

"Our government has lost the 'decent respect for the opinions of mankind' with which we announced our nation's birth."

Former United States Information Agency Officer

CONTENTS

PART THREE

A WAY FORWARD

ACKNOWLEDGEMENTS

I have many people to thank for their contributions to this project. My research assistant, Tamara Kosic, began this journey with me and her fingerprints are on the final product. Anthony Deos assisted in reviewing a final draft of the work. Thanks also to Herbert Levine, who copyedited the manuscript.

I am grateful to the many people who shared their time and insights on U.S. public diplomacy with me, some of whom wish to remain anonymous. I want to especially thank Amb. Kenneth Brown, Robert Callahan, Fred Coffey, Charles Dolan, Price Floyd, Gregory Franklin, Amb. Brandon Grove, Andrew Kotek, Mark Helmke, Amb. Karen Hughes, Amb. Kenton Keith, Amb. John Kordek, Matthew Lauer, Joan Mower, William Mauer, Amb. Christopher Ross, Michael McCarry, Amb. Philip Reeker, McKinney Russell, Judy Siegel, Richard Schmierer, Stanley Silverman, Amb. Pamela Smith, Sam Stratman, and Thomas Switzer.

I have benefited from the good works and comments of many others as well, particularly my colleagues in the International Studies Association, whose ideas have informed my thinking on matters related to public diplomacy. I am especially grateful for the encouragement of Philip Seib, professor of journalism and public diplomacy and director of the USC Center on Public Diplomacy. Conversations with Bruce Gregory, former director of the Public Diplomacy Institute at George Washington University, contributed both to the direction of the book and its content. His feedback on an early proposal and excellent review of the completed manuscript improved the final product.

Special thanks go to the Public Diplomacy Alumni Association (formerly the USIA Alumni Association) and its members for their support of and participation in the *USIA Alumni Study* survey. Eugene Nojek and Alan Kotok were instrumental in making the study possible. Professor Alice Kendrick of Southern Methodist University and Professor Jami Fullerton of Oklahoma State University provided valuable assistance in questionnaire development and design. Alice also contributed to the analysis of preliminary results. Prometheus Research, Inc. of New Haven, Connecticut, provided data analysis support.

The following institutions provided funding for the *USIA Alumni Study*: Quinnipiac University School of Communications, The Arthur W. Page Center at the Penn State College of Communication and the AT&T Foundation, and the DePaul University Research Council. The Wicklander Institute for Business and Professional Ethics at DePaul University provided a research fellowship that supported my work as well. Of course, the findings and views reported here are my own and should not be attributed to any of these institutions or those associated with them.

It has been a great pleasure working with Brill representatives. Hylke Faber and Irene van Rossum were wonderful in advancing the manuscript from concept through production. I want to extend special thanks to Diplomatic Studies series editor Jan Melissen for his excellent suggestions for improving the manuscript. I also want to acknowledge permission from Brill to incorporate in Chapter Four and Chapter Five excerpts from an earlier work in *The Hague Journal of Diplomacy* (Kathy R. Fitzpatrick, "Advancing the New Public Diplomacy: A Public Relations Perspective," Volume 2, Number 3, 2007, 187–211.)

Finally, I want to thank my family their continuing support of my scholarly and professional endeavors. Special thanks go to G.G. and the gang for their companionship and to Orphie for keeping me company on many an early morning, purring contentedly on my desk while I wrote. Most of all, I want to thank my husband, Kurt, for his unwavering support, encouragement, faith, and good cheer throughout this process—and for the happiness he brings into my life every day.

PREFACE

This book started with a news story. Soon after 9/11, *The Washington Post* reported that New York advertising executive Charlotte Beers had been rushed through U.S. Senate confirmation hearings to begin work as U.S. under secretary of state for public diplomacy and public affairs. According to the report, Beers would lead the nation's response to increasing hostilities toward America in the Middle East and other parts of the world. As described by then Secretary of State Colin Powell, Beers' charge was to "brand America," or "help sell America overseas."

I was stunned. At a time when anti-Americanism was escalating throughout the world, did U.S. leaders really believe that a branding campaign was the solution to the nation's deteriorating international relations?

That question led me to other questions. For example, what measures had been taken by the U.S. government *prior* to 9/11 to combat growing anti-Americanism in the Middle East? Why had U.S. public diplomacy, or government efforts to build good relations with people abroad, failed? Why had the top public diplomacy post in the U.S. government been vacant on 9/11? What was the current state of the country's public diplomacy? And, most importantly, what were the implications of a failed public diplomacy going forward?

Those questions guided the years-long study that led to this book. As it turned out, I added a few more questions along the way. During a round of interviews in May 2006 in Washington, DC, I met with Brandon Grove, then president of the American Academy of Diplomacy and a former U.S. career ambassador who had served nine presidents. As we wrapped up our conversation, which focused mostly on historical matters related to U.S. public diplomacy, Ambassador Grove looked across his desk at me and said, "I hope you'll take the extra step of not only describing the evolution of the function and how it changed through the course of history—and not only analyze its strengths and weaknesses and potential—but go beyond that and say 'Here's what is needed now.' In other words, fill in the blank pages that other studies and reports haven't filled in. What will it take to make this work? How should we be thinking differently? How long can we afford in the national interest to ignore public diplomacy in the way we do?"

This book is my response to Ambassador Grove and to others who have called on the academic and professional communities to take a serious look not just at what happened to U.S. public diplomacy and where we are now but also at what must be done to advance public diplomacy going forward.

My work on this volume has been fascinating and gratifying. Along the way, I've met some wonderful people, many of whom were also motivated by the events of 9/11 to take a closer look at the state of public diplomacy—both in the United States and other nations. Scholars and practitioners from throughout the world began to come together at conferences and meetings, in the pages of books and journals, and online to discuss and debate myriad issues associated with what had been a relatively dormant discipline and a lagging field. Suddenly, it seemed, public diplomacy mattered.

Kathy Fitzpatrick
North Haven, Connecticut, USA

INTRODUCTION

PUBLIC DIPLOMACY'S TIME?

9/11 was good for public diplomacy. The terrorist attacks in the United States, which took the lives of more than three thousand people, destroyed the World Trade Center in New York and hit the Pentagon just outside Washington, DC, demonstrated in spectacular fashion the importance of maintaining good relations among nations and peoples. And they illustrated with striking clarity the need for a robust public diplomacy operation to address ideological conflicts that could harm national interests.

This is not to say that better U.S. public diplomacy would have prevented the events of 9/11. Nor is it to suggest that the terrorist attacks were *caused* by America's failure to look after its image abroad. Rather, it is to observe that U.S. leaders' failure to recognize the importance of America's relations with ordinary people abroad *weakened* the nation's ability to stave off the strikes. In other words, increasingly hostile anti-Americanism in the Middle East unchecked by a broken public diplomacy system set the stage for the attacks.

In fact, as America scrambled to respond to the terrorist attacks, public diplomacy became front and center in discussions of U.S. national security. Unlike traditional diplomacy, which involves negotiations between national leaders, *public* diplomacy focuses on a nation's relations with foreign publics, including ordinary people, who have the ability to affect a nation's security and other interests.

In the years since 9/11, countless reports, several new books, and dozens of articles and papers on U.S. public diplomacy have been written, with most calling for America to improve public diplomacy practices. The 9/11 Commission, the independent bipartisan group established by Congress and the president in late 2002 to investigate the circumstances surrounding the terrorist attacks, made engaging "the struggle of ideas" a major recommendation for going forward.[1] Then U.S. President George W. Bush stressed the importance of

---

[1] *The 9/11 Commission Report: Final Report of the National Commission on Terrorist Attacks Upon the United States* (New York: W. W. Norton & Company, 2003), xv.

winning the war on terror, or what he called "the decisive ideological struggle of the twenty-first century."[2]

In other parts of the world, public diplomacy also took on new energy. The terrorist attacks on the United States, along with this country's widely criticized diplomatic response—notably the failed "Branding America" campaign—became the focus of scholarly and professional attention, triggering a global debate on public diplomacy in foreign ministries throughout the world that continues to this day.[3]

Although 9/11 was the catalyst for starting it, the discussion extends beyond public diplomacy's effectiveness in addressing national security matters to encompass more global concerns, including public diplomacy's expanded role and value in an increasingly interdependent, globalized world, and more practical concerns, such as public diplomacy's central function and strategic practices. As diplomacy scholar Brian Hocking observed, "A growing emphasis on the significance of communication with publics, particularly in the wake of 9/11, is preoccupying ministries of foreign affairs (MFAs) around the world and recognizes the growing significance of image in world politics and the need to develop strategies for harnessing it in the interest of policy goals."[4]

There is broad agreement among public diplomacy scholars and practitioners and other informed observers that in this new age—characterized by terrorism, globalization and the internet—the rising influence of nonstate actors in foreign affairs makes public diplomacy an increasingly important component of international relations. As diplomacy scholar Jan Melissen put it, public diplomacy has become "part of the fabric of world politics."[5] Bruce Gregory, former director of the Public Diplomacy Institute at George Washington University, also observed, "Rare is the government today that does not require its diplomats and other professionals to understand, engage and influence global publics."[6]

---

[2] George W. Bush, speech to the 88th Annual American Legion National Convention, August 31, 2006, http://www.whitehouse.gov/news/releases/2006/08/20060831-1.html (accessed November 8, 2006).

[3] See, e.g., Jan Melissen, ed., *The New Public Diplomacy: Soft Power in International Relations* (Houndmills: Palgrave MacMillan, 2005), 8.

[4] Brian Hocking, "Privatizing Public Diplomacy/" *International Studies Perspectives* 5 (2004): 149.

[5] Melissen, *The New Public Diplomacy*, 6.

[6] Bruce Gregory, "Public Diplomacy and Governance: Challenges for Scholars and Practitioners," in *Global Governance and Diplomacy: Worlds Apart?*, ed. Andrew

The growing interest in public diplomacy is based on the premise that a country's relationships with foreign publics are important in protecting and advancing political and economic, as well as security, interests. According to foreign policy scholar Philip Fiske de Gouveia, "In a globabalised world, international communications, and their impact on attitudes and behavior, have profound economic and political implications. States realize this and are acting accordingly."[7]

As evidenced by both the global conversation and the expanding body of international literature on public diplomacy, "public diplomacy is now seen as a major investment in a country's future."[8] According to Melissen, it is also "the hottest topic under discussion in the world's diplomatic services."[9] Indeed, many have argued, *public* diplomacy's time is now.[10]

Or is it?

Many who witnessed public diplomacy's rise and fall in the United States aren't so sure. Certainly, history shows that U.S. public diplomacy has been fraught with starts and stops aligned with the exigencies of the times and the political whims of national leaders. In times of war, public diplomacy has blossomed. Recall the important role of the United States Information Agency (USIA) during the U.S. struggle against communism. An independent foreign affairs agency within the executive branch, the USIA was established in 1953 to inform foreign audiences about American policies and society and to advance U.S. foreign policy objectives. At the height of the Cold War, the USIA had the most extensive presence abroad of any U.S. government agency.[11]

F. Cooper, Brian Hocking, and William Maley (Houndmills: Palgrave MacMillan, 2008), 241.

[7] Philip Fiske de Gouveia, Foreign Policy Center, paper presented at the Madrid Conference on Public Diplomacy, Madrid, Spain, October 10, 2006, http:www.realinstituteoelcano/org/documents/276.asp (accessed January 7, 2009).

[8] Standing Committee on Foreign Affairs, Defence and Trade, *Australia's Public Diplomacy: Building Our Image* (Canberra: Commonwealth of Australia, 2007), 17.

[9] Jan Melissen, "Public Diplomacy Between Theory and Practice," paper presented at the Madrid Conference on Public Diplomacy, Madrid, Spain, October 10, 2006, 1, http://www.clingendael.nl/publications/2006/20061200_cdsp_paper_melissen.pdf (accessed January 7, 2009).

[10] See, e.g., Condoleezza Rice, "Remarks with Under Secretary for Public Diplomacy and Public Affairs Karen Hughes at Town Hall for Public Diplomacy," Washington, D.C., September 8, 2005, http://www.state.gov/secretary/rm/2005/52748.htm (accessed January 7, 2009).

[11] See Wilson P. Dizard, Jr., *Inventing Public Diplomacy: The Story of the U.S. Information Agency* (Boulder, CO: Lynne Rienner Publishers, Inc., 2004).

In times of relative peace (as perceived by U.S. leaders), American public diplomacy has wilted from lack of sustenance. Consider the gutting of public diplomacy operations after the Cold War, which led to the dissolution of the USIA in 1999. By the turn of the century, U.S. public diplomacy occupied one of the lowest rungs on the U.S. diplomatic ladder. In fact, on the day the terrorists struck America in September 2001, the top public diplomacy post in the United States had been vacant for 18 months.

Thus, although elated that public diplomacy is finally being afforded the attention it deserves, public diplomacy advocates are concerned that the posttrauma infatuation with public diplomacy may dull over time. Clearly, public diplomacy's historic role both in the United States and elsewhere has been in helping to resolve existing conflicts rather than in preventing new ones. As Melissen pointed out, "Most successful public diplomacy initiatives were born out of necessity. They were reactive and not the product of forward-looking foreign services caring about relationships within foreign audiences as a new challenge in diplomatic practice."[12]

Is it likely then that in future years, public diplomacy will, once again, lose its luster and recede into the diplomatic background? Is public diplomacy merely a fad of the times—a trend that will subside as memories of 9/11 fade? Or is public diplomacy here to stay as part of a "new normal" in international relations?[13]

Of course, it is impossible to be certain of what time alone will reveal about public diplomacy's future. Yet, efforts to look beyond the present and anticipate future directions are worthwhile. As foreign affairs scholar Alan Henrikson suggested in predicting possible futures for diplomacy more broadly, "[The] exigencies of political decision-making in the world today put a premium on anticipation—on insight and foresight—as well as on reflective hindsight."[14]

Another reason such analysis is warranted now is that public diplomacy appears to have reached a crossroad in its intellectual and practical development. Looking back, we see a function widely viewed as

[12] Melissen, *The New Public Diplomacy*, 9.

[13] See, e.g., Richard Langhorne, "The Diplomacy of Non-state Actors," *Diplomacy & Statecraft* 16, no. 2, 2005, in which Langhorne discusses the need for governments to reconcile the traditional inter-state system of governance with the globalized, interconnected environment of the future.

[14] Henrikson, Alan K., "Diplomacy's Possible Futures," *The Hague Journal of Diplomacy* 1, 2006: 4.

second class in diplomatic and wider circles. Except in times of war (hot and cold), the public side of diplomacy has been treated as a secondary or frivolous undertaking, not essential—but peripheral—to protecting and advancing national interests.[15] As an example, veteran USIA officers cite a long history of prejudice against public diplomacy in the U.S. State Department, noting that the United States Information Services, which served as the public face of American public diplomacy overseas and was known as "USIS," routinely was referred to as "useless" by U.S. officials.

Looking ahead, we see a discipline emerging as a critical ingredient in the diplomatic affairs of nations. Public diplomacy scholars and practitioners refer to a "new" public diplomacy "that will be an increasingly standard component of overall diplomatic practice."[16] Former British diplomat Shaun Riordan predicted in *The New Diplomacy*, "Increasingly, in the twenty-first century, diplomacy will be public diplomacy."[17]

What changed? The answer is not just heightened concerns about terrorism. It is also that democratization and globalization, combined with advancements in communications media, have created a "new world order" in which nations have become more interdependent and cross-border networks of power have replaced traditional government structures.[18] In this new world, nations have less control over traditional spheres of politics and governance, while nonstate actors have become more prominent—and more powerful—both in raising and addressing global concerns. Witness the events of 9/11.

As borders have become more porous, domestic politics have become global politics and domestic issues have become global issues. National leaders are faced with common problems related to the environment, law enforcement, trade, finance, health, human rights and a host of other matters, including global terrorism, that require shared

[15] William Rugh, *American Encounters with Arabs: The "Soft Power" of U.S. Public Diplomacy in the Middle East* (Westport, CT: Praeger Security International, 2006), 6.

[16] Melissen, *The New Public Diplomacy*, 11.

[17] Shaun Riordan, "Dialogue-based Public Diplomacy: A New Foreign Policy "Paradigm?" In Melissen, *The New Public Diplomacy*, 187.

[18] See, e.g., Anne-Marie Slaughter, *A New World Order* (Princeton, NJ: Princeton University Press, 2004), 15, in which Slaughter describes "world order" as "a system of global governance that institutionalizes cooperation and sufficiently contains conflict such that all nationals and their peoples may achieve greater peace and prosperity, improve their stewardship of the earth, and reach minimum standards of human dignity."

solutions. At the same time, technological advancements have transformed the way people communicate within and across borders, making the international marketplace of products, services and ideas both more accessible and more transparent. New channels of interaction provide the ability to form transnational coalitions and global networks of like-minded individuals in pursuit of common interests.

These revolutionary changes have turned the practice of diplomacy on its head.[19] In days past, national leaders relied primarily on their relationships with other national leaders to navigate international waters in pursuit of their respective nations' interests. Such interactions are still important. But, as the balance of power among nations and peoples has become more diffuse,[20] foreign publics have become more important to a nation's ability to accomplish its foreign affairs objectives. Global governance has been transformed as ordinary people have acquired both the capabilities and, in many cases, the will to influence government policies and actions—both in their own nations and in others.[21] In other words, nation-states are losing their voices of authority just as nonofficial or nonstate actors are finding theirs.

As diplomats reach beyond the nation-state to engage the people who control the environment in which foreign policy is made and implemented, they "must now engage a vastly larger number of players in host countries, as the age-old 'club model' of diplomacy gives way to a less hierarchical 'network model.'"[22] Those "players" include nongovernmental organizations (NGOs), business and nonprofit corporations and other groups of individuals that are playing increasingly important roles in international relations.[23] The upshot is that public diplomacy is becoming "an integral and substantive, not just presentational, part of the policy making process."[24]

---

[19] See, e.g., Paul Sharp and Geoffrey Wiseman, ed., *The Diplomatic Corps as an Institutional Society* (Houndmills: Palgrave Macmillan, 2008).

[20] See, e.g., Joseph S. Nye, Jr., *Soft Power: The Means to Success in World Politics* (New York: Public Affairs, 2004).

[21] See, e.g., Margaret E. Keck and Kathryn Kikkink, *Activists Beyond Borders* (Ithaca, NY: Cornell University Press, 1998).

[22] Jorge Heine, *On the Manner of Practising the New Diplomacy, CIGI Working Paper No 11: Reshaping Diplomacy*, The Centre for International Governance Innovation, October 2006, www.cigionline.org (accessed April 7, 2007).

[23] See, e.g., Manuel Casteels, "Communication, Power, and Counterpower in the Network Society," *International Journal of Communication* 1 (2007): 238–266.

[24] Shaun Riordan, *The New Diplomacy* (Cambridge, UK: Polity, 2003), 123; see also Shaun Riordan, "Dialogue-based Public Diplomacy: A New Foreign Policy Paradigm?" in Melissen, *The New Public Diplomacy*, 187.

So, it would seem that the world stage is set for *public* diplomacy to play a leading role in the diplomatic affairs of nations in this new century. Before public diplomacy's promise can be realized, however, there is much work to be done. This still young field faces significant challenges that stand in the way of its advancement. Many of those challenges are grounded in historical misperceptions about public diplomacy and its role and value in national strategy. Those matters must be addressed.

As public diplomacy assumes a more prominent position in international relations, scholars and practitioners also must tackle disciplinary issues that have become the subjects of global debate and threaten to stifle public diplomacy's progress toward professional maturity. Most importantly, there is a need to better define public diplomacy's function; to develop the conceptual foundations of the discipline; to refine public diplomacy's strategic direction; to establish workable public diplomacy structures; to delineate the roles and responsibilities of new public diplomats; and to articulate principles of practice for effectively and ethically accomplishing a nation's public diplomacy objectives.[25]

This book contributes to that effort by documenting historical insights and lessons that will be useful going forward and identifying and analyzing key disciplinary challenges ahead. The purpose is to advance the debate on public diplomacy's future by examining the state of public diplomacy at this juncture and proposing new directions. Rather than have the last say, the intent is to offer some fresh perspectives on theoretical and practical matters related to public diplomacy and to raise questions that, hopefully, will spark needed discussions and future research.

The focus is on the U.S. experience in public diplomacy, which provides a good laboratory for understanding public diplomacy's past, surveying thinking and practices in public diplomacy today, and contemplating public diplomacy's future. Although public diplomacy certainly is not a uniquely American enterprise, the nation's long history in the field offers some valuable insights that suggest next steps in public diplomacy's lifecycle.

Certainly, the men and women who have served on the frontlines of American public diplomacy for more than half a century have much to

---

[25] See, e.g., Kathy R. Fitzpatrick, "Advancing the New Public Diplomacy: A Public Relations Perspective," *The Hague Journal of Diplomacy* 2, no. 3 (2007): 187–211.

contribute to the ongoing debate over U.S. public diplomacy's future. In fact, the individual views of the men and women who spent their careers working in U.S. public diplomacy, gathered through interviews and oral histories, have been integrated into histories of the USIA and other works about U.S. public diplomacy.[26] A number of the former diplomats have also written their own stories about their experiences.[27] These accounts offer significant insights into U.S. public diplomacy's history and its value.

Yet, the *collective* voice of these diplomatic experts has not yet been heard. This book helps to fill that gap by incorporating in the chapters that follow the results of the *USIA Alumni Study*, which documented the views of high-ranking veterans of American public diplomacy on a broad range of matters related to U.S. public diplomacy. The study was the first comprehensive survey of America's public diplomats since the dissolution of the USIA in 1999. More than 200 former USIA officers who conducted public diplomacy for an average of twenty-five years in all corners of the world from the 1950s to 2007 participated.[28] (See Appendix One for additional information on the study and participants.)

Of course, the limitations of relying too heavily on the views of mostly *past* public diplomacy practitioners in a book about the *future* of U.S. public diplomacy must be recognized. The global context in which public diplomacy is conducted has changed in dramatic ways, creating a need to consider new ways of thinking about and doing public diplomacy. Although the fundamental tenets of effective public diplomacy may endure, the ideas and innovations of modern observers also will be important to public diplomacy's future both in the United States and elsewhere. For that reason, this work draws on a broad range of views of public diplomacy scholars and practitioners.

---

[26] See, e.g., Association for Diplomatic Studies and Training, *Frontline Diplomacy: The U.S. Foreign Affairs Oral History Collection* (Washington, DC, 2000).

[27] See, e.g., Yale Richmond, *Practicing Public Diplomacy: A Cold War Odyssey* (New York: Berghahn Books, 2008); Wilson P. Dizard, Jr. *Inventing Public Diplomacy: The Story of the U.S. Information Agency* (Boulder, CO: Lynne Rienner Publishers, 2004); Alan L. Heil, Jr., *Voice of America: A History* (New York: Columbia University Press, 2003).

[28] Preliminary findings of this study were presented at the 2008 annual meeting of the International Studies Association; see Kathy R. Fitzpatrick, "The Collapse of American Public Diplomacy: What Diplomatic Experts Say About Rebuilding America's Image Around the World—A View from the Trenches," paper presented at the annual meeting of the International Studies Association, Chicago, IL, March 27, 2008.

On matters related specifically to U.S. public diplomacy, the scope of the work is limited by a primary focus on public diplomacy activities in the USIA and the U.S. Department of State. Although the diplomatic activities of other government agencies, as well as private sector entities, are addressed on occasion, they are afforded limited discussion. Similarly, serious study of U.S. international broadcasting, which was part of the USIA and is viewed by many to be part of U.S. public diplomacy today, is generally beyond the scope of this volume. All these matters—each of which deserves serious, book-length study—will be important to public diplomacy's future.

Overview of the Book

This book is intended for scholars and students of public diplomacy and related disciplines, public diplomacy practitioners, policy makers in positions to support public diplomacy, and others who recognize or may come to appreciate the critical importance of public diplomacy in establishing international relations that allow nations and peoples to peacefully and prosperously live and work together in an interdependent world. The hope is that by examining issues and challenges relevant to public diplomacy's future, the work will contribute to the advancement of public diplomacy in the United States and around the world.

The book is divided into three parts. Part One (Back to the Future) looks at where U.S. public diplomacy has been and where it is today. These early chapters provide historical context for the debate on public diplomacy's future by documenting the factors that influenced public diplomacy's development and identifying challenges ahead. Part Two (Advancing the Debate) examines critical issues that must be addressed as public diplomacy assumes a more prominent role in the diplomatic affairs of nations. These chapters address matters related to the conceptual and practical development of the discipline. Part Three (A Way Forward) reviews recommendations from USIA alumni for rebuilding U.S. public diplomacy and emphasizes the need for a relational approach to the study and practice of public diplomacy going forward.

The book begins with a look at the evolution and practice of public diplomacy in the United States during the pre- and post-9/11 periods. Chapter One (U.S. Public Diplomacy: Pre-9/11) documents the rise and fall of public diplomacy before, during, and after the Cold War, revealing how the nation's public diplomacy was severely diminished in the final decade of the twentieth century. This chapter shows that U.S. leaders' misperceptions regarding the importance of foreign publics to U.S. interests, combined with institutional prejudices against government "propaganda," led to the marginalization of public diplomacy over time and to the subsequent dissolution of the USIA. This chapter tells the untold story of 9/11, i.e., why America's first line of defense against ideological threats failed.

Chapter Two (U.S. Public Diplomacy: Post-9/11) examines America's diplomatic response to 9/11, revealing how public diplomacy has been approached since the terrorist attacks. This chapter shows that the nation was ill-served by the revolving door to the executive suite of U.S. public diplomacy, which has ushered in six new leaders with diverse—and in most cases troublingly narrow—perspectives on how U.S. public diplomacy should be viewed and practiced. Together, these chapters identify four distinct phases in American public diplomacy and illustrate key factors that influenced public diplomacy's growth and development over time.

Chapter Three (Insights from the U.S. Experience: Challenges Ahead) looks at how the U.S. experience in public diplomacy informs our thinking about public diplomacy's future, identifying historical insights that will be useful going forward. For example, the nation's historically conflict-driven approach to public diplomacy illustrates the perils of defining public diplomacy too narrowly. The marginalization of U.S. public diplomacy after the Cold War is particularly instructive in terms of understanding the debate over public diplomacy's worth and value. And the post-9/11 period—in which the United States turned to the private sector for help in "branding" America—illustrates how flawed assumptions can lead to flawed public diplomacy strategies.

Chapter Four (Understanding Public Diplomacy: Toward a Common Identity) begins to address the conceptual challenges in public diplomacy's future by examining one of the biggest tasks ahead: coming up with a clear, concise and generally accepted definition of public diplomacy that describes its function and value in protecting and advancing national—and international—interests. This chapter synthesizes historical and contemporary definitions of public diplomacy, demonstrating the need for a common identity and framework for the study and practice of public diplomacy.

Chapter Five (Conceptual Foundations: From Wielding Soft Power to Managing Mutual Benefit) identifies theoretical concerns that must be addressed as the public diplomacy paradigm is refined. It discusses the concept of "soft power" and the implications of approaching public diplomacy from a self-interested, political perspective. In considering whether the adoption of the soft power concept has confused rather than clarified public diplomacy's fundamental purpose, this chapter addresses the philosophical underpinnings of public diplomacy and raises a key question: What *is* the proper conceptual foundation for public diplomacy? The chapter proposes a relational approach to public diplomacy that may prove to be both more effective and more ethical than "soft power."

Chapter Six (Strategic Directions: The Branding Controversy) sorts out the "nation branding" controversy by exploring the concept of nation branding in the context of public diplomacy. The aim is to clarify the meaning of nation branding and to consider whether a marriage between nation branding and public diplomacy makes sense. The chapter concludes that, although the two disciplines share some common principles and practices, fundamental differences in worldviews, functions, and practices preclude the adoption of nation branding as a viable strategic approach to public diplomacy.

Chapter Seven (Structural Integrity: Competing Designs) addresses one of the most controversial and enduring questions in this field: How should U.S. public diplomacy be structured? In considering structural and operational factors that contribute to public diplomacy's effectiveness, this chapter examines a range of recommendations and proposals from USIA alumni and others for the design of U.S. public diplomacy.

Chapter Eight (Moving the Needle: Measures of Success) considers another age-old question: Does public diplomacy work? This chapter addresses the need for evaluations that can be used to improve public diplomacy practices and demonstrate public diplomacy's worth. It explores the meaning of "success" in public diplomacy and considers the state of evaluation in U.S. public diplomacy today, as reflected in government assessments and the national public diplomacy strategy. The chapter proposes new approaches to evaluation in public diplomacy with an emphasis on relationships.

Chapter Nine (The New Public Diplomat: Constructing a Profile) focuses on the people who do public diplomacy. This chapter examines the fundamental knowledge, skills, and traits required for success in the field and addresses the expanding role and responsibilities of public diplomats. This chapter suggests that the contemporary public diplomacy professional must combine traditional qualifications required for success in the field with new capabilities and expertise to meet new demands and challenges presented by a rapidly changing diplomatic environment.

Chapter Ten (Rebuilding U.S. Public Diplomacy: Lessons from the Field) presents recommendations from former USIA officers for rebuilding U.S. public diplomacy and restoring America's promise in the world. The findings reported here reveal fundamental tenets of public diplomacy that will be important to public diplomacy's future.

Chapter Eleven (Tempting Fate: The Future of U.S. Public Diplomacy) reflects on the intellectual and practical development of public diplomacy, concluding that a relational approach holds the most promise for public diplomacy's future. The chapter also identifies the need for attention to the "second mandate" of U.S. public diplomacy, i.e., to educate and inform *Americans* about matters related to foreign affairs, and calls on U.S. leaders to recognize public diplomacy's crucial place in twenty-first century international relations.

PART ONE

BACK TO THE FUTURE

CHAPTER ONE

U.S. PUBLIC DIPLOMACY: PRE-9/11

Americans 'discover' public diplomacy in wartime.[1]

When he entered the USIA in 1959 as a young officer, Robert L. Chatten recalled that "there were an awful lot of people in the State Department who didn't think about [public diplomacy] deeply, if at all." In fact, at his first posting in Manila, he encountered "a kind of condescension" toward the public side of diplomacy that "became standard later on—people saying things like, 'You seem like a bright young man. Why don't you get out of this Mickey Mouse peripheral thing you're doing and get into the *real* Foreign Service?' That was the roots of an abiding theme that persists to this day."[2]

Chatten made these remarks during a postretirement interview in 1994, following a successful career in U.S. public diplomacy.[3] As it turned out, during his tenure with the agency, the USIA enjoyed the heyday of its existence. The existential threat posed by communism during the Cold War dulled criticism of the international communications agency that, though not widely respected in Washington, was viewed as a necessary instrument of war—particularly one in which ideological battles could determine the outcome. As a result, the USIA received the resources it needed to carry out its mission, which was to explain and advance U.S. foreign policy and ideals overseas and build good relations for the United States with people abroad.

But when the Cold War ended, so did public diplomacy's support among American policy makers. Despite the USIA's success in helping to win the battle against the Soviet Union, many believed the agency's time had passed. The thinking was that the "peace dividend" of winning the struggle against communism allowed America to spend less

---

[1] Bruce Gregory, "Public Diplomacy and National Security: Lessons from the U.S. Experience," *Small Wars Journal*, August 15, 2008, http://smallwarsjournal.com/mag/docs-temp/82-gregory.pdf (accessed January 7, 2009).

[2] Robert L. Chatten, Oral History, July 1, 1994, *Frontline Diplomacy: The U.S. Foreign Affairs Oral History Collection* (Washington, DC: Association for Diplomatic Studies and Training, 2000).

[3] Ibid.

attention and money on foreign affairs and more on matters at home. Thus, a big investment in public diplomacy simply was no longer necessary. Of course, what U.S. leaders failed to recognize was that dramatic changes already taking place in the world would require more—not less—attention to foreign publics.

This chapter reviews the evolution of public diplomacy from its earliest days as an official government function up until the time of 9/11. The review provides important context for anticipating public diplomacy's future, illustrating the first three of four distinct phases in American public diplomacy's history. This historic review illustrates both the mercurial nature of American public diplomacy's growth and development and the uncertainty of its fate.

The first phase—"The War Phase"—took place in the first half of the 20th century during the First and Second World Wars when U.S. leaders looked to public diplomacy as a psychological weapon of war that complemented American military forces. The long second phase—"The Anti-propaganda Phase"—occurred during the Cold War, in which the nation was engaged in an ideological struggle against the Soviet Union. The third phase—"The Peace Phase"—which followed the end of the Cold War, might also be described as the "11/9 to 9/11" period. As Derek Chollet and James Goldgeier observed in *America Between the Wars*, this was "the misunderstood decade between the end of the Cold War and the start of the War on Terror."[4] Phase four—"The Terror Phase"—is discussed in Chapter Two.

Phase One: The War Phase

The first official entity to conduct public diplomacy (although not described as "public diplomacy" at the time) on behalf of the United States was the Committee on Public Information (CPI) established in 1917 by President Woodrow Wilson. CPI was widely known as the Creel Committee for its chairman George Creel, who was later credited as the founder of U.S. public diplomacy.

Although CPI's primary charge was to mobilize domestic support for America's participation in World War I, it also helped to main-

[4] See Derek Chollet and James Goldgeier, *America Between the Wars—11/9 to 9/11—The Misunderstood Decade Between the End of the Cold War and the Start of the War on Terror* (New York: Public Affairs, 2008).

tain a positive image of the United States among allies and neutral observers overseas and to undermine enemy morale through targeted information campaigns.[5] The Committee's foreign section included the Foreign Press Bureau, the Wireless and Cable Service and the Foreign Films Division.[6]

On both domestic and foreign fronts, the Creel Committee's work was recognized as an important asset in the war effort. According to public diplomacy scholar Nicholas Cull, "The cumulative effect of the CPI's international operation was palpable in the way in which newspapers around the world adopted President Wilson's rhetoric for peace."[7] But when the war ended, so did the CPI, under an executive order from the president's office.

As the country entered its next major conflict, the need for an international communications program was revisited. But it was several years before President Franklin D. Roosevelt formed the Office of War Information (OWI) in 1942 to supplement military efforts during World War II. OWI's primary objective was to help win the war through information programs designed to help domestic and international audiences understand and support the war effort. The OWI published books and magazines, created an exchange program for foreign journalists and commissioned films intended to educate foreign publics about American life and institutions.[8]

During this time, Voice of America (VOA) radio went on the air as a counter to anti-American propaganda. The station was soon broadcasting twenty-four hours a day in multiple languages, including English, German, Italian and French. VOA content included news and information, as well as commentary and cultural programming. In the VOA's first broadcast, William Harlan Hale laid out its mandate: "We bring you Voices from America. Today, and daily from now on, we shall speak to you about America and the war. The news may be good for us. The news may be bad. But we shall tell you the truth."[9]

---

[5] Nicholas Cull, *The Cold War and the United States Information Agency: American Propaganda and Public Diplomacy* (Cambridge, UK: Cambridge University Press, 2008), 6–9.

[6] Ibid.

[7] Ibid., 8.

[8] Wilson P. Dizard Jr., *Inventing Public Diplomacy: The Story of the U.S. Information Agency* (Boulder, CO: Lynne Rienner Publications, Inc., 2004), 17–36.

[9] Alan L. Heil, Jr., *Voice of America: A History* (New York: Columbia University Press, 2003), 32.

Despite its broad charge, the OWI focused mostly on foreign audiences. In his history of the USIA, agency veteran Wilson P. Dizard Jr. explained that "while there was little public opposition to propagandizing foreigners about U.S. war aims... the idea of similar operations aimed at U.S. citizens created tensions from the start."[10] As Dizard observed, U.S. officials reacted strongly to reports of Congressional investigations that documented the use of propaganda by the British and German governments to sway U.S. attitudes on participation in the war. In fact, fears of the potential influence of propaganda were so strong Congress passed the Foreign Agents Registration Act in 1938, which required representatives of foreign entities working in the United States to register with the U.S. government.

Operating overseas under the name "United States Information Service," or "USIS," the OWI managed both U.S. international broadcasting and information and advocacy efforts. The State Department contributed to the effort through cultural and educational exchanges and other programs housed in a Division of Cultural Relations and through information programs facilitated by an International Information Division. According to Cull, "the United States entered the final months of the war with a mighty global apparatus of advocacy and cultural projection."[11]

Once again, however, when the war ended, so did OWI—by an executive order of the new president Harry S. Truman. In 1945, the office was disbanded and drastically reduced VOA operations merged into the Department of State, along with a handful of the OWI's 13,000 employees, who were placed in the unit responsible for international information and cultural programs.[12] The domestic programs were phased out over the next few years.

Phase Two: The Anti-Propaganda Phase

When Congress later became concerned that communist threats were fueling anti-American sentiments in Europe and other parts of the world, U.S. leaders once again turned to public diplomacy. On August 1, 1946, Congress passed the Fulbright Act, named after Senator William

[10] Dizard, *Inventing Public Diplomacy*, 17.
[11] Cull, *The Cold War and the United States Information Agency*, 20.
[12] Dizard, *Inventing Public Diplomacy*, 37–39.

Fulbright and intended to help promote understanding between the United States and people abroad. The legislation established education and cultural exchange programs, as well as a visitors program that was created to introduce foreign citizens to American-style democracy.

Fulbright contended that "the prejudices and misconceptions that exist within every country regarding foreign people are the great barrier to any system of government." If people could just get to know each other better, he suggested, "they might develop a capacity for empathy, a distaste for killing other men, and an inclination for peace."[13]

Two years later, Congress passed the Smith-Mundt Act (named for its congressional sponsors), which created an international information and education bureau in the State Department that would be operated by the secretary of state. The mission was to "promote the better understanding of the United States among peoples of the world and to strengthen cooperative international relations."[14] The Act authorized "the preparation, and dissemination abroad, of information about the United States, its people and its policies through press, publications, radio, motion pictures, and other information media, and through information centers and instructors abroad."[15]

At the time, U.S. leaders emphasized that the new programs were, in effect, "anti-propaganda" activities intended to combat communist propaganda. In fact, American officials so feared what they perceived to be the evils of propaganda that they wrote into the legislation a prohibition on the dissemination of public diplomacy materials to domestic audiences, including the U.S. news media. (Although the law has been challenged in U.S. courts as unconstitutional, it remains in effect today.)

In 1953, President Eisenhower moved the bureau's information functions, including VOA, to the executive branch, creating the independent USIA. Although there was considerable debate about the need for a separate entity, the decision to establish the agency reportedly turned on then Secretary of State John Foster Dulles' wish to be free of the management responsibilities associated with overseeing foreign

---

[13] Jerrold Keilsen, "Public Diplomacy and Foreign Policy," *Great Decisions Briefing Book* (Washington, DC: Foreign Policy Association, 2004): 105, http://www4.uwm.edu/cie/iwa/events/event_details.cfm?event_id=884 (accessed March 10, 2004).

[14] Public Law 402, 80th Congress (Chapter 36, 2nd Session).

[15] Ibid.

communications operations.[16] However, the educational affairs functions were left behind in the State Department, reportedly in deference to Fulbright, who feared that if they became part of the USIA, their efforts would be either tainted by the "propaganda" units or become too politicized.[17] Notwithstanding this institutional arrangement, however, the USIA played a significant role in managing exchange programs overseas.

For the next forty-six years, the USIA was America's voice in the world. Its first mission was: "To submit evidence to peoples of other nations by means of communication techniques that the objectives and policies of the United States are in harmony with and will advance their legitimate aspirations for freedom, progress and peace."[18] The agency's first director was advertising executive Theodore Streibert, who initiated—with the help of the American Advertising Council—the USIA's first major campaign, which was dubbed "People's Capitalism."

By 1960, the USIA was operating at 202 posts in 85 countries, overseeing cultural and information programs, international news operations, libraries, publications, exhibits and speakers programs.[19] The agency reached a bell weather mark during the Kennedy administration with the appointment of the agency's most famous director, CBS news correspondent Edward R. Murrow, who gained fame for his war reports from Britain in the 1940s.[20] According to Dizard, when Murrow accepted the $23,000 a year job, "[m]orale within the USIA staff soared with an enthusiasm that rippled down the agency halls and out to the overseas posts."[21]

---

[16] See Hans N. Tuch, *Communicating with the World: U.S. Public Diplomacy Overseas* (New York: St Martin's Press, 1990), 18.

[17] Ibid., 20; Thomas C. Sorensen, Oral History, July 25, 1990, *Frontline Diplomacy: The U.S. Foreign Affairs Oral History Collection* (Washington, DC: Association for Diplomatic Studies and Training, 2000); see also William Rugh, *American Encounters with Arabs: The "Soft Power" of U.S. Public Diplomacy in the Middle East* (Westport, CT: Praeger Security International, 2006), 50.

[18] Quoted in Tuch, *Communicating with the World*, 21; see also Directive Approved by the President for the Guidance of the United States Information Agency, October 28, 1953, Public Papers of the Presidents of the United States—Dwight D. Eisenhower, 1953, Office of the Federal Registrar, National Archives and Record Service (Washington, DC: U.S. Government Printing Office, 1960), 728.

[19] See Cull, *The Cold War and the United States Information Agency*, 187; see also Tuch, *Communicating with the World*, 20.

[20] See, e.g., Tuch, *Communicating with the World*, 25.

[21] Dizard, *Inventing Public Diplomacy*, 85.

Murrow's relationship with the president gave him entrée and clout (and a direct telephone line to the president's office) that subsequent directors could only wish for.[22] According to Dizard, Murrow believed strongly in the need for the agency to "persuade, not just inform" and to "take an aggressive role in advising the White House on the importance of overseas public opinion in making foreign policy decisions."[23] And, according to White House officials at the time, the president agreed, frequently calling on Murrow for his counsel.[24]

In fact, Kennedy issued a presidential statement that changed the USIA's mission to reflect a more active role for public diplomacy in policy formation. The new mission was "to help achieve United States foreign policy objectives...by influencing public attitudes in other nations" and by "advising the President, his representatives abroad, and the various departments and agencies on the implications of foreign opinion for present and contemplated U.S. policies, programs and official statements."[25] Murrow later described the agency's new role to "join the other personal advisers of the president in discussions of policy while it is being formed." He said, "We are therefore no longer mere publicists grinding out our appointed quota of press releases. We have become psychological advisers to the president and, in turn, each ambassador in his individual country team."[26]

Notwithstanding this pronouncement, however, the full extent of Murrow's involvement in policy making has been questioned. For example, Cull pointed out that "the USIA had been left out of the biggest American foreign policy decision of the decade: the landings of the Bay of Pigs."[27]

When Murrow resigned soon after Kennedy's assassination, his successor (also a former foreign correspondent) Carl Rowan helped to secure the USIA's place within the Washington foreign policy community.[28] Rowan's successors, Leonard Marks and Frank Shakespeare,

---

[22] Ibid.
[23] Ibid., 87.
[24] Ibid.
[25] Tuch, *Communicating with the World*, 27; see also Ronald I. Rubin, "A New Voice for America," *International Communication Gazette* 19 (1973): 214.
[26] Quoted in Tuch, *Communicating with the World*, 287.
[27] Cull, *The Cold War and the United States Information Agency*, 191.
[28] See Dizard, *Inventing Public Diplomacy*, 87.

carried on the traditions, and by 1970, "the U.S. Information Agency had entered the high summer of its bureaucratic life."[29]

At the height of the Cold War, the USIA had thousands of public diplomacy specialists stationed in more than 175 countries operating in nearly 300 locations.[30] The impact was felt in all corners of the globe. The VOA, America's international broadcasting arm, reached 100 million people weekly. The agency was producing books and magazines in more than one-hundred languages. It was operating a global library network in 150 countries, teaching English to thousands of foreign citizens, hosting exhibits depicting American ideals that drew billions of visitors, producing films and programs widely popular in other nations, and administering cultural and educational exchange programs in which millions of world citizens participated.[31] According to Dizard, the USIA represented "the biggest information and cultural effort ever mounted by one society to influence the attitudes and actions of men and women beyond its borders."[32]

It was not long, however, before the agency became the subject of a commission chaired by CBS President Frank Stanton and charged with reviewing the USIA's mission and structure. According to Cull, the resulting report reflected "the most radical rethinking of U.S. information overseas" since the agency's founding.[33] A key issue was how the various units of U.S. public diplomacy should be configured—and particularly whether the VOA should become an independent entity. The Stanton report called for merging domestic and foreign international communications by placing the USIA's information and advocacy functions in the State Department's Office of Policy Information and moving the agency's cultural programs to a new Information and Cultural Affairs agency also under the auspices of the State Department. Although the Stanton Commission perceived a need to keep VOA independent, it wanted VOA to take a more active role in the advocacy of U.S. policies by carrying State Department-produced editorials.[34]

---

[29] Ibid., 103.
[30] See Dizard, *Inventing Public Diplomacy*, for a more detailed review of USIA's operations during this time.
[31] Ibid., 4.
[32] Ibid.
[33] Cull, *The Cold War and the United States Information Agency*, 343.
[34] Ibid.

A number of competing commissions and task forces rejected the Stanton Commission's proposal and there was no immediate action taken on any of the recommendations. But, as Cull reported, the idea of reforming the USIA had been firmly planted in the minds of U.S. officials, who would later revisit the issue.[35] Dizard also observed that the Stanton Commission was one of a number of attempts made during and after the Cold War to rearrange the public diplomacy responsibilities of the State Department and the USIA.[36]

When President Carter took office, he acted on some of the reform proposals by moving the State Department's educational and cultural affairs functions to the USIA. He also directed the agency to focus on "mutual understanding" as the objective of public diplomacy, noting that the principal function of the USIA should be to "reduce the degree to which misperceptions and misunderstanding complicate relations between the United States and other nations."[37] This new mandate, the president said, involved learning as well as informing:

> It is in the general interest of the community of nations, as well as in our own interest, that other nations and other peoples know where this great country stands, and why. We want them to understand our values, our institutions—the vitality of our culture—and how these relate to their own experience. We must make available to people of other nations facts they would not otherwise learn about ourselves and our views.
>
> It is also in our interest—and in the interest of other nations—that Americans have the opportunity to understand the histories, cultures and problems of others, so that we can come to understand their hopes, perceptions and aspirations. In doing so, the Agency will contribute to our capacity as a people and as a government to manage our foreign affairs with sensitivity, in an effective and responsible way.[38]

President Carter tasked the agency to maintain "the scholarly integrity and nonpolitical character of the exchange programs" and to undertake no "covert, manipulative or propagandistic" activities.[39] He also renamed the agency the "International Communication Agency" (USICA) although his successor later switched it back to its original name.

---

[35] Ibid., 358.

[36] Dizard, *Inventing Public Diplomacy*, 195, n. 7.

[37] See Tuch, *Communicating with the World*, 32.

[38] Quoted in Tuch, *Communicating with the World*, 32; see also The White House, Memorandum for Director, International Communication Agency, March 13, 1978.

[39] Tuch, *Communicating with the World*, 33.

Carter's choice for USIA director, John Reinhardt, was unique in that he was the first public diplomacy specialist selected to head the agency. Although the appointment pleased USIA staffers and was well received within the State Department, it did little to sustain the agency's status with the rest of the administration. Reinhardt reportedly made only one trip to the White House after his swearing in ceremony[40]—perhaps because of what Dizard called "the Carter White House's general disinterest in exploiting the agency's resources."[41]

In fact, only one other USIA director would enjoy a similar level of presidential respect as Murrow and that was California business executive Charles Wick, appointed by President Ronald Reagan in 1981. A strong advocate for public diplomacy, Wick persuaded Reagan to expand the nation's international communications initiatives, including the development of the nation's first global satellite link-up. When President Reagan spoke *directly* to the people of East Germany for the first time on live TV, it was a "watershed moment for public diplomacy," according to Thomas Switzer, former USIA officer and now director of communications for the American Foreign Service Association.[42]

During the Reagan years, the USIA continued to hone its expertise, developing a corps of professionals who had the ability to handle both long-term public diplomacy initiatives, such as educational and cultural exchanges, and to respond quickly and effectively to more time-sensitive public issues and crises as they arose. And, thanks to the leadership skills of Charles Wick, the USIA had the resources needed to get the job done. In fact, Wick (the longest-serving USIA director with eight years service) doubled USIA's budget before resigning in 1989, the same year the Berlin Wall fell.

Phase Three: The Peace Phase

After the existential threat of communism was gone, support for public diplomacy waned in Washington. As U.S. leaders turned their attention homeward, quietly celebrating a peaceful resolution to the long conflict with the Soviet Union, they began to question the nation's

[40] See Cull, *The Cold War and the United States Information Agency*, 362, n. 13.
[41] Dizard, *Inventing Public Diplomacy*, 200.
[42] Personal interview, May 3, 2006.

continued investment in public diplomacy. Many believed that the USIA had completed what was widely perceived to be its mission—i.e., to defeat communism—and, therefore, was no longer needed. Some thought a "propaganda" operation was simply improper in times of peace. Still others saw a continuing need for at least some official entity to handle U.S. relations with people abroad, particularly the educational and cultural exchanges that were widely viewed as public diplomacy's most effective tools.

As the debate over the USIA's future continued throughout the next decade, the agency had a much tougher time competing for government resources. Part of the problem, according to Ambassador Kenton Keith, a thirty-five-year USIA veteran who directed USIA operations in the Near East/South Asia/North Africa, was that despite its support during the Cold War, "Congress never really understood public diplomacy—probably not until after 9/11."[43]

The same was true of the executive branch, Keith said. Although President George (Herbert Walker) Bush cautioned against American isolationism and promoted "openness" as a key ingredient of American progress—"I see a world of open borders, open trade and, most importantly, open minds"[44]—influencing foreign public opinion was not high on the administration's foreign policy goals. "I never observed in George Bush Senior a particular understanding of or affection for public diplomacy," Keith noted.[45]

Some pointed to Wick's successor Bruce Gelb as a primary factor for the agency's difficulties during the Bush administration. A former executive at Bristol Meyers Corporation and a friend of the president, Gelb reportedly came to the USIA with high hopes of successfully applying his industry marketing expertise to U.S. public diplomacy. But his inability to gain the respect of USIA staffers, combined with a contentious and public rift between Gelb and the head of VOA, caused considerable damage to the USIA's reputation in Washington.[46] After two years of trying—and failing—to establish a credible position for himself within the foreign affairs establishment, Gelb reluctantly moved on at the White House's urging to an ambassadorship in Belgium.

---

[43] Personal interview, May 4, 2006.

[44] George Herbert Walker Bush, remarks before the 45th session of United Nations General Assembly, New York, New York, October 1, 1990.

[45] Personal interview, May 4, 2006.

[46] Cull, *The Cold War and the United States Information Agency*, 283.

Gelb's successor, Henry Catto accepted the USIA director's post in June 1991. At his swearing-in ceremony, the former ambassador to the United Kingdom reinforced the importance of public diplomacy in the post-Cold War world: "In the Information Age, public diplomacy is not only valuable, it is essential to any prolonged success in world affairs."[47] The USIA's mission, Catto said, was "to be America's information agency in the Information Age."[48] But he had little time to repair the USIA's tattered image before the Bush administration was voted out of office.

The situation changed little as the Clinton administration took over the White House. While the new president reportedly had a keen appreciation for cultural diplomacy and was widely viewed as an effective "diplomat-in-chief," his administration focused its primary attention on domestic matters, i.e., "reinventing" government and building a stronger economy. This was bad news for those who had hoped Clinton would help secure the USIA's future.

In the meantime, the agency made a valiant effort to save its place in the foreign affairs establishment by heeding Clinton's call for a leaner government and streamlining its operations. Joseph Duffy, a Clinton appointee who served as the USIA's last director, told Congress during a 1996 budget hearing that no other agency had "made as many really dramatic changes for a bureaucracy of this size as USIA."[49]

The truth, however, was that it had no choice. Every year the USIA's budget came under close scrutiny, and every year the agency walked away with less than the year before. Funding cuts continued at a dramatic pace, leading to critical staff reductions both in Washington and in the field, the closure of key overseas posts, significant cutbacks in VOA's broadcast hours, and cuts in hundreds of academic and cultural exchanges and information programs.

In 1994, Congress passed the International Broadcasting Act, which put all U.S. government international broadcasting units into a nine-

---

[47] John T. Woolley and Gerhard Peters, *The American Presidency Project* [online]. "Remarks at the Swearing-In Ceremony for Henry Catto as Director of the United States Information Agency," http://www.presidency.ucsb.edu/ws/index.php?pid=19667 (accessed January 5, 2009).

[48] Ibid.

[49] "Hearing of the U.S. Commerce, Justice, State and Judiciary Subcommittee of the House Committee," Federal News Service, April 30, 1996, http://www.fnsg.com/archive.htm?op=s&newsearch=on&catFT=on&realmCO=on&datefrom=04%2F30%2F96&dateto=04%2F30%2F96&query=duffy&fullsearch= (accessed January 9, 2009).

member Broadcasting Board of Governors (BBG).[50] The units continued to operate under the auspices of the USIA although the legislation maintained the "firewall" sacred to VOA's charter, ensuring that as Alan L. Heil, Jr., wrote in *Voice of America: A History*, VOA journalists could "pursue the facts, wherever the pursuit may lead them."[51] Although the VOA and other broadcasting units still had to fight hard for their budgets, they remained intact and the establishment of the BBG was later recognized as an important step in securing U.S. international broadcasting's place in the international marketplace of ideas.

Shortly after the establishment of the BBG, a bill to abolish the USIA was introduced into Congress.[52] Although the legislation was never enacted, the USIA's influence on "the Hill" was dwindling. Some USIA staffers blamed Duffy for the agency's falling star, seeing him as a "yes man" who didn't always have the best interests of the agency at heart. But they also acknowledged that they were partly to blame for their problems. Veteran USIA officer Robert Callahan explained, "We justified our existence on the war of ideas with international communism."[53]

So once that threat was gone, so, too, was the justification for public diplomacy—at least in the minds of U.S. policy makers, who had a long list of other priorities for post-Cold War funding. As Charles Dolan, former vice chairman of a commission that oversees public diplomacy, observed, the agency suffered from "the success of its early branding."[54]

Another problem was the inherent difficulty in proving public diplomacy's worth. Callahan explained that public diplomacy specialists are constantly asked "to prove a negative." He asked, "How can you prove that something didn't happen as a result of our actions?"[55]

With respect to demonstrating public diplomacy's effectiveness, Hans Tuch, author of *Communicating with the World: U.S. Public Diplomacy Overseas*, also pointed out that public diplomacy was only

---

[50] United States International Broadcasting Act of 1994 (Public Law 103–236).

[51] Alan L. Heil, Jr., *Voice of America: A History* (New York: Columbia University Press, 2003), 431.

[52] See, e.g., "Budget Battles Undercut U.S. Information Effort," *The New York Times*, July 7, 1995; see also Dizard, *Inventing Public Diplomacy*, 215.

[53] Personal interview, May 3, 2006.

[54] Personal interview, June 24, 2003.

[55] Personal interview, May 3, 2006.

one source of influence on the minds of people abroad. Noting the "daily onslaught of information, impressions, and perceptions to which foreign audiences are exposed through commercial or private channels such as film, television, advertising, press services and tourism," he said it was "impossible to measure accurately, except in very limited circumstances, the impact of a government's public diplomacy program on foreign audiences in the face of all the other images and signals to which they are exposed."[56]

The fact that the USIA had existed as an independent agency in the executive branch contributed to the notion that it was a temporary operation whose mission was obsolete after the end of the Cold War. Additionally, U.S. citizens who (thanks in part to the Smith-Mundt Act) didn't know much about or really understand public diplomacy had little interest in rallying to the USIA's cause. Tuch wrote in 1990 that although the USIA was widely recognized and appreciated abroad, "among the [U.S.] public and even among Washington policy makers and politicians—there is little knowledge of what it is, what it can and cannot do, how it is practiced and by whom"[57] In other words, a domestic constituency for the agency simply didn't exist.

Notably, the U.S. news media had done little to put public diplomacy on the American public's agenda. For example, researchers studying the potential impact of news coverage of public diplomacy on U.S. citizens' knowledge and understanding of the government's efforts in this area found that prior to 9/11, the function was rarely mentioned and never discussed in any detail in *The New York Times*. Additionally, when public diplomacy was referenced, "many writers were unfamiliar with the specific function of U.S. public diplomacy, possibly creating confusion on the part of readers about what public diplomacy is."[58]

In fact, when news leaders reviewed their efforts to keep Americans informed about the dangers posed by growing anti-Americanism and global terrorism in the post-Cold War period, they also recognized a failure by the media to adequately cover topics related to international

---

[56] Tuch, *Communicating with the World*, 117.

[57] Han N. Tuch, "Why Americans Don't Appreciate Public Diplomacy," *Foreign Service Journal* (January 1991): 11.

[58] Kathy Fitzpatrick and Tamara Kosic, "The Missing Public in U.S. Public Diplomacy: Exploring the News Media's Role in Developing an American Constituency," in *Media and Conflict in the Twenty-First Century*, ed. Philip Seib (New York: Palgrave MacMillan, 2005), 120–122.

relations. Former editor of the *Los Angeles Times* and a foreign correspondent for twenty-five years Michael Parks wrote, "News organizations were guilty of the same lack of judgment and neglected duty for which editorial writers have rebuked the Central Intelligence Agency and other governmental institutions."[59]

Public diplomacy did have a few champions who, in hindsight, seemed particularly prescient about the new environment the United States would face in the post-Cold War era. The U.S. Advisory Commission on U.S. Public Diplomacy (created by Congress in 1948 to provide bipartisan oversight of public diplomacy) advised in 1991 that the USIA's mission did not "depend on transitory events, on U.S. interests in a few countries, or on a single goal, such as democracy-building or anti-communism."[60] The Commission argued that public diplomacy did "not need a new mission or a major reorganization." What it needed, the Commission said, was additional resources, strategic direction and sustained commitment by America's leaders.[61]

But no one appeared to be listening. Matthew Lauer, former executive director of the Commission, recalled that before 9/11 "no more than two people showed up" to annual Commission meetings at which current initiatives in public diplomacy were reviewed and the Commission presented its recommendations for future efforts to the President, the Congress and the American people. By 1996, the USIA's staff had been reduced by more than 25 percent and funding by almost 30 percent. One former officer who joined the USIA in 1981 and later served as director of public diplomacy and public affairs for the African Bureau in the State Department explained, "They basically just starved us out."[62]

To no avail, Advisory Commission members, as well as a few other USIA proponents, continued to argue that it was a mistake to dismiss public diplomacy as no longer important—particularly when external forces were transforming the global environment. In its 1996 annual report, the Commission called for the execution of a "new" public diplomacy that recognized the "information revolution... the growing

---

[59] Michael Parks, "Foreign News: What's Next?" *Columbia Journalism Review* 40, no. 5 (January/February 2002): 52–53.

[60] United States Advisory Commission on U.S. Public Diplomacy, *Public Diplomacy in the 1990s* (Washington, DC, 1991), 16–17.

[61] Ibid.

[62] Personal interview, June 13, 2003.

power of foreign publics...the globalization of issues and the rapidly expanding reach of NGOs [that] are fundamentally changing how the U.S. pursues its interests abroad."[63]

Without a powerful insider to lobby for its cause, however, public diplomacy continued its decline. The impression among many in the USIA community was that neither USIA Director Duffy nor Madeleine Albright, Secretary of State during Clinton's second term, was a true champion of public diplomacy. Despite the fact that "public diplomacy" was one of three strategic themes Albright espoused early in her tenure as Secretary,[64] USIA insiders were unconvinced. As one put it, she simply "didn't care much" about public diplomacy.[65] Another said public diplomacy was "certainly not one of her greatest priorities."[66] Such views are supported by the fact that, according to Bruce Gregory, who served as executive director of the Advisory Commission on Public Diplomacy at the time, Albright "declined repeated invitations to attend Commission meetings."[67]

Admittedly, with a domestically-focused Congress, Albright had to fight hard for the State Department's budget. Yet, she made no special case for public diplomacy's post-Cold War mission. In fact, the USIA's most damaging budget cuts came during Albright's tenure. Callahan recalled being forced to fire embassy staff—many of whom were foreign nationals—and to substantially curtail representational responsibilities. "It was a brutal time...the most difficult time in my 27 years in Foreign Service," he said.[68]

Early in Clinton's second term, the USIA's future looked pretty bleak. In addition to funding problems and a lack of public and internal State Department support, there was serious talk about dismantling the agency as part of a complete overhaul of what some viewed as an outdated foreign affairs operation. One idea gaining support was to move public diplomacy back into the State Department.

Members of Congress were split on whether such integration made sense. Those who argued for the merger pointed to the anticipated

[63] United States Advisory Commission on Public Diplomacy, *A New Diplomacy for the Information Age* (Washington, DC, 1996), 4.

[64] Steven Erlanger, "Albright Flies Toward Vexing Issues," *The New York Times*, February 16, 1997.

[65] Personal interview, June 22, 2003.

[66] Personal interview, June 22, 2003.

[67] Personal interview, May 3, 2006.

[68] Personal interview, May 3, 2006.

efficiencies and effectiveness of a more coherent diplomatic operation that blended traditional "state-to-state" diplomacy with "state-to-people" diplomacy. Those who argued against the move noted primarily the need for the USIA to retain its independence, as well as the practical ability to shape the environment in which policy is made and implemented. Both the autonomy and flexibility needed to respond effectively to "local" issues would be severely diminished if the more open, "grass-roots" diplomatic functions involving ordinary world citizens were merged with the traditional diplomatic functions involving primarily "behind-the-scenes," sometimes secret, negotiations between state leaders, they argued. Still others thought the USIA was working just fine and should be left alone.

The decision on the agency's future was made public in late April 1997, when the Clinton administration announced plans to dissolve the USIA and fold the public diplomacy functions into the State Department.[69] Although the restructuring ostensibly was designed to put matters related to public diplomacy "at the heart of our foreign policy,"[70] many believed it was driven less by bureaucratic efficiency than by political maneuvering on the part of the Clinton administration and some members of Congress led by Republican Senator and Chairman of the Senate Foreign Relations Committee Jesse Helms, a longtime critic of the USIA.[71] According to retired USIA officer Barry Zorthian, the consolidation was a "backroom political deal between Albright and Helms."[72]

Notwithstanding the charges of political back scratching, some saw the reorganization as part of Albright's desire to reshape the nation's post-Cold War foreign policy operations in a way that would make the State Department the center of foreign policymaking.[73] When asked during a House appropriations committee hearing how the function of public diplomacy would be strengthened once it was inside State, Albright said "Public diplomacy... is something that should be integral to how the State Department operates. In an Information Age, our ability to meld what our policy is with our public message abroad is

[69] The White House Fact Sheet, "Reinventing State, ACDA, USIA and AID," April 21, 1997.

[70] Ibid.

[71] See Dizard, *Inventing Public Diplomacy*, 215.

[72] Personal interview, March 25, 2007.

[73] Serlanger, "Albright Flies Toward Vexing Issues."

very important."[74] She later explained to USIA staff members at a town hall meeting focused on the reorganization: "The current structure of our foreign affairs agencies reflects the needs of an era that no longer exists."[75]

When all was said and done, however, it appeared that the USIA had become a political pawn whose fate turned more on inside-the-beltway politics than on whether a robust public diplomacy operation was needed or on what the proper structure for such an entity should be. The deal was finalized in a bill passed by Congress the following October. As part of the reorganization, all U.S. broadcasting functions were spun off into the BBG, which became an independent entity responsible for overseeing VOA and other broadcasting units, including Radio Free Europe, Radio Liberty, Radio Free Asia, and Radio Marti.

Much of the USIA's operations were relocated to two new bureaus in the State Department—International Information Programs and Educational and Cultural Affairs—headed by the newly appointed Under secretary of State for Public Diplomacy and Public Affairs Evelyn Lieberman, who had served the Clinton administration in a variety of posts, including senior advisor to the secretary of state, director of the VOA and deputy White House chief of staff. Most of the field operations and budgets were placed under the authority of assistant secretaries who reported to the under secretary for political affairs. The foreign opinion research unit became part of the Bureau of Intelligence and Research.

It was a bad marriage from day one. On the day the merger was formalized, Albright went out of her way to assure USIA staffers that they would be welcome in their new home. In her remarks at a ceremony commemorating the consolidation, she said that "integration is not subjugation; it is an arrangement among partners.... I pledge to

[74] Hearing of the Commerce, Justice, State and Judiciary Subcommittee of the House Appropriations Committee, Federal News Service, March 10, 1999. http://www.fnsg.com/archive.htm?op=s&newsearch=on&catFT=on&catPR=on&realmCO=on&datefrom=03%2F10%2F99&dateto=03%2F10%2F99&query=albright (accessed January 7, 2009).

[75] Stephen Barr and Thomas W. Lippman, "Turf Diplomacy at State Department: Reorganization of Agencies Stirs Tensions Over Priorities," *The Washington Post*, May 28, 1997.

you that when I say you are central to American foreign policy, you will be central to American foreign policy."[76]

Or maybe not. A year later, the Advisory Commission on Public Diplomacy, in reporting on what it called the "takeover," found that former USIA employees were "demoralized" and that it would be "years before public diplomacy becomes an accepted component of the agency recognized for the value it brings to U.S. foreign policy goals and objectives."[77] Indeed, the commissioners entitled one section of their annual report "The Role of Pubic Diplomacy—In Theory," presumably in response to the lack of understanding and appreciation afforded the function.

The long history of prejudice against the public dimension of diplomacy became even more pronounced after the merger. Noting what she called "a real arrogance among the old guard" at the State Department, one veteran USIA broadcasting official said public diplomacy specialists were treated like "3rd, 4th, 5th class citizens."[78] Price Floyd, former DC-based director of media affairs at the State Department, agreed. Noting the "useless" moniker widely used in reference to USIS, he recalled, "Everyone called them that."[79] The reason, he said, was that there didn't seem to be a "comprehensible purpose" for public diplomacy. The consequence was that economic and political officers were called "substantive" officers, while public diplomacy officers were viewed as "frivolous."

In the field, public diplomacy officers encountered similar treatment both before and after the merger. Even many ambassadors shared the sentiment that USIS was "useless" in terms of its contribution to American diplomatic missions, according to former U.S. Career Ambassador Brandon Grove. "That was almost a prevalent attitude" among ambassadors, he said. "The thinking was: What do we need this for? I mean, we're diplomats. We talk to foreign ministries. We get the nation's business done. Who needs that stuff?"[80]

---

[76] Margaret Korbel Albright, "The Importance of Public Diplomacy to American Foreign Policy," *U.S. Department of State Dispatch*, 10, no. 8 (October 1999): 8–9.

[77] United States Advisory Commission on Public Diplomacy, *Consolidation of USIA Into the State Department, An Assessment After One Year* (Washington, DC, 2002), 3.

[78] Personal interview, June 22, 2003.

[79] Personal interview, June 23, 2003.

[80] Personal interview, May 8, 2006.

Stressing that such attitudes were "totally wrong," Grove explained that the problem was that people focused on all the things that USIA *did*—libraries, exchange programs, and so forth—rather on *why* they were important. Public diplomacy was "locked in functional terms," Grove said. "It lacked an underlying concept or sense of purpose."[81]

The situation worsened after the merger, as the clash of cultures between former USIA staffers and State Department officials made life difficult for all concerned. Transplanted USIA officers who were used to the autonomy of an independent agency suddenly found themselves part of a complex bureaucratic structure that required layers of paperwork to get anything done. Former USIA officer Dell Pendergrast explained in a March 2000 article in the *Foreign Service Journal* that, as an independent agency, the USIA had the ability to adapt to the "changing contours of the new global environment. The agency recognized that international relations had become an interactive process, transformed by new technologies such as the Internet and by almost instant access to news."[82] The State Department, on the other hand, "absorbed in the conventional business of government-to-government relations, lagged behind."[83] According to Pendergrast, the merger provoked "a serious concern about USIA's more open, technologically advanced, publicly-oriented style of diplomacy disappearing inside a larger, dominant culture less hospitable to organizational innovation."[84]

Those in the field particularly felt the negative effects of having to "clear" things with Washington before responding to media inquiries, for example, and acting on other matters. In many cases, by the time Washington responded, opportunities were lost. Here's how one former USIA officer described the situation:

> As a USIA spokesperson I always felt I could talk with any nationals of any country about all aspects of American culture and civilization without ever worrying about the party line. I never felt that I had to be constantly aware of what the politics between the two parties was nor did I sense that I had to always boast that we Americans are the best and the brightest. I could 'tell America's story abroad' in the most

81 Ibid.

82 Dell Pendergrast, *Foreign Service Journal* (March 2000), http://www.publicdiplomacy.org/3.htm#pender (accessed January 9, 2009).

83 Ibid.

84 Ibid.

> open, trustworthy, honest and balanced discussion with my contacts in a foreign culture. I would worry today that a State Department politico would always be looking over my shoulder to assure himself that I was spouting the party line.[85]

The disconnect between State Department officials in Washington and public diplomacy specialists in the field was exacerbated by the fact that the State Department had made little progress in defining its post-Cold War mission. When Clinton's first Secretary of State Warren Christopher came in, the idea was to promote democracy and free trade in the world. But, according to Grove, there were "no concrete strategies for accomplishing those goals," nor was there a "clear-cut definition on the type of democracy that should be advanced."[86] As a result, the State Department struggled to define its post-Cold War mission while the administration "moved on to other things," Grove said.[87]

Near the end of Clinton's first term, a report of the U.S. General Accounting Office (GAO), a Congressional oversight agency, found that U.S. leaders had made little progress in defining or supporting a new diplomatic mission since the end of the Cold War. The GAO concluded that "the needed rethinking of U.S. foreign policy objectives, requirements, and structures has not taken place at the highest levels of the foreign policy agencies."[88] While acknowledging that the full implications of the end of the Cold War were still unclear and that "the uncertainties of this post-Cold War transition period have made planning and priority-setting difficult," the report concluded that "the State Department's top management has not taken the time to focus on whether and what systemic changes may be needed in the day-to-day conduct of diplomacy."[89]

In another report, in which the GAO reviewed U.S. progress in adjusting foreign affairs functions and structures to post-Cold War realities, the GAO cited the need for a more integrated and strategic approach to U.S. activities overseas. Such changes could occur, the GAO reported, "*if* the State Department itself gained a greater appreciation of the work USIA and other agencies do [*emphasis added*]."[90]

---

85 Kathy R. Fitzpatrick, *USIA Alumni Study*, unpublished report, 2007.
86 Personal interview, May 8, 2006.
87 Ibid.
88 United States General Accounting Office, *Perspectives on Foreign Affairs Programs and Structures* (Washington, DC, November 1996), 1.
89 Ibid., 10.
90 Ibid., 5.

According to The American Academy of Diplomacy, the situation became so bad that when Secretary of State Colin Powell took office in 2000, he "inherited a faltering American diplomatic system, the consequence of a decade of neglect, inadequate appropriations, and anemic leadership."[91]

Although, by most accounts, Powell did a good job trying to reinvigorate the Foreign Service, including public diplomacy, the job was not easy—particularly given that international affairs received barely one percent of the federal budget. With respect to public diplomacy specifically, some suggested "his hands were tied because the public diplomacy structure that had been so successful for 40 years by then had been dismantled."[92] "It simply could not be resurrected by any kind of quick fix," according to Switzer.[93] Explaining that the USIA had already lost its identity, Grove too pointed out, "It was a done deal. You couldn't turn that clock back."[94]

At the same time, Powell did not move quickly to replace Lieberman, who had resigned the public diplomacy leadership post near the end of Clinton's second term. In fact, the top public diplomacy post sat vacant well into the second year of the Bush presidency—until after 9/11—creating a leadership vacuum that further diminished public diplomacy's position in Washington and left officers in the field unsure of their fate. Although Powell offered some hope for a brighter future, public diplomacy existed in a dysfunctional family that itself lacked strategic direction and treated public diplomacy like an ugly stepchild.[95]

---

[91] William C. Harrop, *Revitalizing US Diplomacy: At Long Last, Leadership*, http://www.academyofdiplomacy.org/publications/fld.html (accessed July 10, 2008).

[92] Personal interview, May 3, 2006.

[93] Ibid.

[94] Personal interview, May 8, 2006.

[95] *Consolidation of USIA into the State Department: An Assessment After One Year* (Washington, DC: United States Advisory Commission on Public Diplomacy, October 2000).

CHAPTER TWO

U.S. PUBLIC DIPLOMACY: POST-9/11

American public diplomacy is about one thing and one thing only, American national security.[1]

September 11, 2001—the day that would define George W. Bush's presidency—ushered in a new era for U.S. public diplomacy. The terrorist attacks that day shattered the illusion America was the peaceful place many thought it to be. And they illustrated with painful clarity the world's apparent affection for and understanding of America had been misjudged. The attacks also raised doubts about the ability of the United States to prevent violent acts motivated by ideological differences and carried out by nonstate actors with a common hostility toward America and the western world. As Thomas Magstadt observed in *An Empire If You Can Keep It: Power and Principle in American Foreign Policy*, "The significance of September 11 for American foreign policy is difficult to exaggerate."[2]

The president, along with most U.S. citizens, expressed surprise at the "vitriolic hatred" of the United States revealed by the attacks on American soil: "I'm amazed that there is such misunderstanding of what our country is about, that people would hate us...Like most Americans, I just can't believe it. Because I know how good we are. We've got to do a better job of making our case."[3]

Of course, the government agency that had made America's "case" in the world for nearly half a century no longer existed. And the remnants of the USIA that had been merged into the State Department lacked the ability to respond quickly and effectively to ideological

---

[1] Mark Helmke, "The Mess of Public Diplomacy," remarks presented at the Public Diplomacy Council, Washington, DC, June 3, 2003, http://www.publicdiplomacy.org/18.htm#top (accessed January 9, 2009).

[2] Thomas M. Magstadt, *An Empire If You Can Keep It: Power and Principle in American Foreign Policy* (Washington, DC: CQ Press, 2004), 221.

[3] "President Holds Prime Time News Conference," White House News Release, October 11, 2001, http://www.whitehouse.gov/news/releases/2001/10/20011011-7.html# (accessed on July 22, 2003).

threats. As the nation grieved its losses from the terrorist acts, America, once again, "discovered" public diplomacy.[4]

The last chapter reviewed the first three phases of U.S. public diplomacy—"The War Phase" during the First and Second World Wars, "The Anti-propaganda Phase" during the Cold War, and "The Peace Phase" from the end of the Cold War until 9/11. This chapter reviews phase four of U.S. public diplomacy's evolution—"The Terror Phase"—which began on 9/11. This ongoing period has been marked by the resurgence of public diplomacy as a security resource and the failed attempts of multiple public diplomacy officials to establish a viable and effective public diplomacy operation.

Phase Four: The Terror Phase

Just weeks after 9/11, *The Washington Post* reported that New York advertising executive Charlotte Beers had been rushed through Senate confirmation hearings to begin work as U.S. under secretary of state for public diplomacy and public affairs. Beers, who had been nominated for the post in June, would lead the nation's diplomatic efforts to rebuild relations with people in the Middle East and other parts of the world. Her specific task, according to then Secretary of State Colin Powell, was to "help sell America overseas," or to "brand America."[5]

Powell had told the U.S. House of Representatives Budget Committee earlier that year he intended to bring people into the public diplomacy function who could participate in "really branding foreign policy, branding the Department, marketing the Department, marketing American values to the world."[6] On September 6, 2001, just days before the terrorist attacks, Powell introduced his choice to lead U.S. public diplomacy at a NetDiplomacy Conference held at the State Department.

In explaining Beers' appointment, Powell said. "I wanted one of the world's greatest advertising experts, because what are we doing? We're selling. We're selling a product. That product we are selling is

---

[4] See Bruce Gregory, "Public Diplomacy and National Security: Lessons from the U.S. Experience," *Small Wars Journal*, August 15, 2008, http://smallwarsjournal.com/mag/docs-temp/82-gregory.pdf (accessed January 7, 2009).

[5] Peter Carlson, "The U.S.A. Account: Ad Woman Charlotte Beer's New Campaign: Getting the World to Buy America," *The Washington Post*, December 31, 2001.

[6] Ibid.

democracy. It's the free enterprise system, the American value system. It's a product very much in demand. It's a product that is very much needed. It is our job to be salespersons."[7] Weeks later, in responding to criticism that Beers might not be the right person to lead public diplomacy in the post-9/11 environment—particularly given her lack of foreign policy experience—Powell again pointed to her success in industry selling consumer products, such as Uncle Ben's rice.

As it turned out, Beers' tenure in public diplomacy was short-lived. Widely criticized for her use of marketing and advertising techniques to "win the hearts and minds" of people in Arab states, Beers' early initiatives were deemed disastrous by U.S. critics and ridiculed in many parts of the world.[8] Citing health reasons, she announced her resignation less than a year-and-a-half after she started.

Beers' troubles began soon after she arrived at the State Department. Historically resistant to "outsiders" unfamiliar with government culture and processes, Department "insiders" did not welcome Beers with open arms. In fact, her ideas for "selling" American values were met with considerable scorn. Wendy Melillo, *Adweek*'s Washington bureau chief and a fan of Beers, later described Beers' brief stint in government service: "Inside the State Department, Beers was surrounded by elitist snobs and diplomatic purists who didn't want their reputation, or the country's, sullied by marketing jargon."[9]

Beers faced criticism from outside government as well. Media reports of both her appointment and early public diplomacy initiatives were particularly harsh. Frank Rich of *The New York Times* wrote in November 2001: "Maybe we're losing the battle for Afghan hearts and minds in part because the Bush State Department appointee in charge of the propaganda effort is a CEO (from Madison Avenue) chosen not for her expertise in policy or politics but for her salesmanship on behalf of domestic products like Head & Shoulders shampoo. If we can't effectively fight anthrax, I guess it's reassuring to know we can always win the war on dandruff."[10] Citing the litany of such comments

---

[7] Colin L. Powell, "Remarks by Secretary of State Colin L. Powell," presented at the NetDiplomacy Conference, Department of State, Washington, DC, September 6, 2001.

[8] See, e.g., Farah Stockman, "Bush Aide Named to Key Diplomacy Post," *The Boston Globe*, March 15, 2005.

[9] Wendy Milillo, *Adweek* 44, no. 10 (March 10, 2003): 24.

[10] Frank Rich, "How to Lose a War," *The New York Times*, October 27, 2001, http://query.nytimes.com/gst/fullpage.html?res=9E0DE2DF1E31F934A15753C1A9679C8B63&sec=&spon=&pagewanted=3 (accessed January 28, 2009).

in the media about Beers, who was dubbed "the queen of branding," one writer noted that the "idea that Beers went from Uncle Ben to Uncle Sam has proven irresistible for media wise guys everywhere."[11]

Seemingly undeterred, Beers outlined three "strategic goals" for U.S. public diplomacy: 1) representing American values and beliefs and creating an exchange of common values; 2) demonstrating the opportunities that result from democratization, good governance, and open markets; and 3) supporting the education of the young.[12] In an interview with *Business Week Online*, she explained how she hoped to accomplish them: "The whole idea of building a brand is to create a relationship between the product and its user.... We're going to have to communicate the intangible assets of the United States—things like our belief system and our values."[13]

Beers' view of public diplomacy was decidedly narrow with respect to its role in U.S. foreign affairs. For example, when asked whether public diplomacy had any influence over policy making, her response was simply that she didn't "do policy." Speaking at a news conference at the National Press Club in December 2002, she said, "There are a number of exceptionally talented, experienced and seasoned people working virtually around the clock on the policy. Our job is to make sure that policy is delivered clearly, accurately, swiftly, in proper context.... We influence the policy in the sense that we always return the data we get from the field, we do research endlessly, we confer about the communication of the policies."[14] One of Beers' senior aides confirmed such thinking in a PBS interview in which he said, "We do not see it as our business of suggesting that policy will change."[15]

[11] Peter Carlson, "The U.S.A. Account: Ad Woman Charlotte Beers' New Campaign: Getting the World to Buy America," *The Washington Post*, December 31, 2001; see also Victoria DeGrazia, "The Selling of America, Bush Style," *The New York Times*, August 25, 2002.

[12] Charlotte Beers, "Public Diplomacy Plans for the Future," Statement before the Senate Foreign Relations Committee, Washington, DC, June 11, 2002, http://www.state.gov/r/us/12170.htm (accessed January 16, 2006).

[13] Alexandra Starr, "Charlotte Beers' Toughest Sell," *Business Week Online*, December 17, 2001, http://www.businessweek.com/magazine/content/01_51/b3762098.htm (accessed January 25, 2009).

[14] "Charlotte Beers Holds News Conference at the National Press Club," Transcript, Federal Document Clearing House, Inc., FDCH Political Transcripts, December 18, 2002.

[15] "PBS Interview with Christopher Ross on PD," *PBS Online Newshour*, January 16, 2002, http://ics.leeds.ac.uk/papers/vp01.cfm?outfit=pmt&folder=7&paper=448 (accessed January 10, 2009).

Beers' signature initiative—some would say death knell—was the "Shared Values" campaign featuring a series of television advertisements profiling the lives of Muslim Americans, speeches by diplomats and American Muslims directed at international audiences, town hall forums in selected countries, Internet communication, and a consumer lifestyle magazine called *Muslim Life in America*. According to Beers, the goal of the campaign was "to start a dialogue" between America and people in the Middle East. The campaign's message was "the U.S. is an open society, tolerant and accepting of all religions, and specifically a country where Muslims are free to practice Islam."[16]

The television ads were launched in late October 2001. *New York Times* journalist Jane Perlez, who attended a preview of the campaign at which the ads were unveiled, reported serious skepticism among both internal State Department staff who criticized them as "patronizing" and "simplistic" and nongovernmental observers who thought they had not adequately captured the complexity of being Muslim in America. Others expressed concern that the presentations "bordered on being propaganda" because they suggested "universal tolerance" in the United States.[17]

The campaign was also criticized for its affiliation with a group called The Council of American Muslims for Understanding. Although presented by Beers as an independent, nonprofit, nonpartisan organization "dedicated to providing a better understanding of Islam in America to the people in the United States and throughout the world," it was viewed by some as a front group for the State Department, which had initiated and funded the group's efforts in an attempt to gain more credibility for the government's message abroad. When the TV ads—produced by outside advertising agencies at the direction of the State Department—aired, the tagline appearing on screen at the end stated: "Presented by the Council of American Muslims for Understanding... And the American People."

One explanation for the failure of the "Shared Values" campaign was that although the ads did run in some countries with significant Muslim populations (e.g., Indonesia), critical states in the Middle

[16] Charlotte Beers, "Funding for Public Diplomacy," Statement before the Subcommittee on Commerce, Justice, and State of the House Appropriations Committee, April 24, 2002, http://www.state.gov/r/us/9778.htm (accessed January 16, 2006).

[17] Jane Perlez, "Muslim-as-Apple-Pie Videos Are Greeted with Skepticism," *The New York Times*, October 30, 2002.

East refused to run them. But even in places where the ads ran, they were not well-received, with some suggesting that they contributed to—rather than countered—anti-Americanism. In speaking before a Senate Foreign Relations Committee, for example, communications scholar Rhonda Zaharna cited the impersonal nature of advertising as particularly problematic in "a region that values people and faces, not facts and figures."[18]

When she left office, Beers claimed that her work in U.S. public diplomacy had been misjudged. Noting significant strides in the country's international communications, Beers said success should be judged on the basis of how well the State Department does in "reaching" targeted audiences. Noting too heavy an emphasis by her critics on the "Shared Values" initiative, Beers said the campaign should be viewed as part of the Department's larger efforts to reach Muslim audiences. "We have begun the dialogue" needed to explain U.S. policies, she said, but the image of the United States could not be rebuilt "in any one term, much less mine."[19]

Beers had some internal advocates who supported her efforts. One senior State Department official, who formerly served in the USIA, observed in a June 2003 interview that the "reach" of the advertising "vignettes" was "very good" and that internal research in Indonesia showed "people did notice them."[20] The "Shared Values" initiative, he said, could even provide a model for future public diplomacy initiatives because it illustrated the importance of tailoring programs to specific targeted audiences.

Powell's admiration for Beers had not cooled either. In an e-mail to State Department staff, he praised Beers' work, saying she "and her team sharpened our policy advocacy and took our values and our ideas to mass audiences in countries which hadn't heard from us in a concerted way for years.... She helped us find new ways of making our case to policy makers while expanding our outreach efforts to make connections with ordinary people, particularly in Muslim nations. Her

---

[18] Rhonda S. Zaharna, "The Network Paradigm of Strategic Public Diplomacy," Foreign Policy in Focus (April 2005), http://www.fpif.org/fpiftxt/970 (accessed September 10, 2006).

[19] Ira Teinowitz, "Beers State Dept. Program Misjudged," *Advertising Age* 74, no. 10 (March 2003): 3.

[20] Personal interview, June 24, 2003.

goal of reaching younger, broader and deeper audiences will remain with us as she departs."[21]

Following Beers' departure, Patricia Harrison, who was in charge of the State Department's cultural and educational affairs units, served as acting head of public diplomacy for several months before Margaret Tutwiler, a veteran of foreign affairs who had most recently been U.S. ambassador to Morocco, was tapped to fill the post. News reports at the time indicated that Tutwiler was less than enthusiastic about her new assignment, with one source noting she "has let the word out that she comes reluctantly."[22] Another reported that Tutwiler offered "only a terse comment" about her new post: "I hope that I am able to contribute to the overall public diplomacy efforts of our government."[23]

Tutwiler's apparent reticence could have reflected the pervasive view both in and outside Washington at the time that U.S. public diplomacy was broken—perhaps beyond repair. Citing "Republican and Democratic lawmakers, State Department officials and independent experts," *The New York Times* reported in December 2003, the same month Tutwiler took office, "The government's public relations drive to build a favorable impression abroad—particularly among Muslim nations—is a shambles."[24]

In her confirmation hearings, Tutwiler said that if confirmed, she would "do what I can to contribute to the overall effort of trying to prevent any further deterioration of our nation's image, of trying to find a way to more forcibly articulate and defend our policies, of trying to find focused and effective ways to explain ourselves to foreign audiences, and, finally, to trying to find ways to insure that the activities we undertake are measurable."[25] In testimony before the Senate Relations Committee two months later, Tutwiler emphasized the long-term nature of America's public diplomacy challenge: "[O]ur country has a problem in far too many parts of the world today, especially in the Middle East and South East Asia, a problem we have regrettably

[21] Ira Teinowitz, "Beers State Dept. Program Misjudged," 3.

[22] Wendy Melillo, "No Brand USA Expected from New Diplomacy Chief: Unlike Ex-Ad Executive Beers, Tutwiler in a Political Insider," *Adweek* 44, no. 41 (October 20, 2003): 9.

[23] Christopher Marquis, "Effort to Promote U.S. Falls Short, Critics Say," *The New York Times*, December 29, 2003.

[24] Ibid.

[25] Margaret DeB. Tutwiler, Opening Statement before Senate Foreign Relations Committee, October 29, 2003, www.state.gov/r/us/27372.htm (accessed June 3, 2007).

developed over many years through both Republican and Democratic administrations, and a problem that does not lend itself to a quick fix or a single solution of a simple plan. Just as it has taken us years to get into this situation, so too will it take many years of hard focused work to get out of it."[26]

Public diplomacy's strategic goals were clear, according to Tutwiler: "Focus on those areas of the world where there has been a deterioration of the view of our nation...listen more, not only to foreign audiences, but to our own public diplomacy personnel overseas...do a better job of reaching beyond the traditional elites and government officials...pursue new initiatives and improve older ones in the hopes of reaching younger, broader and deeper audiences."[27]

But Tutwiler made little progress on any of these initiatives before resigning six months later for a private sector post. It would be more than a year before her replacement was named.

In the meantime, U.S. officials had stopped asking *why* the terrorist attacks had occurred and had started asking *how*—how they happened and how such attacks could be prevented in the future. The primary focus was on determining who and what was to blame for U.S. leaders' failure to "connect the dots" that would have prevented the strikes and on identifying critical breakdowns that should be addressed going forward.

In late November 2002, the U.S. Congress and the president appointed a "9/11 Commission" to examine the causes of the terrorist attacks. The commission was given the broad mandate to investigate the "facts and circumstances relating to the terrorist attacks" and to report back to the American people on what happened in the years preceding 9/11 that might have contributed to the attacks. The commission's report was to address issues related to U.S. intelligence agencies, law enforcement agencies, diplomacy, immigration issues and border control, the flow of assets to terrorist organizations, commercial aviation, the role of congressional oversight and resource allocation, and other areas determined relevant by the commission.[28]

---

[26] Margaret DeB. Tutwiler Opening Statement before the Senate Foreign Relations Committee, February 26, 2004, http://foreign.senate.gov/testimony/2004/TutwilerTestimony040226.pdf (accessed January 22, 2009).

[27] Ibid.

[28] *The 9/11 Commission Report: Final Report of the National Commission on Terrorist Attacks Upon the United States* (New York: W. W. Norton & Company, 2003), xv.

When the commission issued its final report, it had much to say on most of these matters. But, curiously, it had virtually nothing to say on America's diplomatic preparedness to combat ideological threats to U.S. interests. The primary focus of the report was on breakdowns in intelligence, border security, federal aviation, and law enforcement. Certainly, all of these elements are critical to any government's counter-terrorism program. With respect to diplomacy, however, the report simply cited the State Department's diminished role in U.S. international relations, concluding: "The diplomatic efforts of the State Department were largely ineffective."[29]

Why were breakdowns in diplomacy generally and public diplomacy specifically—supposedly the nation's first line of defense against ideological threats to national interests—ignored? Although the answer is unclear, the gap seems to provide a sense of how "Washington" viewed the importance of foreign public opinion to national security interests. What is clear is that public diplomacy was not top of mind for those charged with identifying defects in the country's ability to forestall hostile attacks on Americans prior to 9/11.

At the same time, in its recommendations for going forward, the 9/11 Commission highlighted the need to "engage the struggle of ideas" in the Middle East, noting the important role of public diplomacy in doing so. Apparently, the terrorist attacks had served as a wake-up call that the nation should be paying more attention to its relations with people abroad. As Armin Meyer, a thirty-year U.S. diplomat, wrote in his memoir, the events of 9/11 "emphasized dramatically the crucial importance of anticipating hostile action, identifying and dealing with root causes, and nipping disasters in the bud."[30]

The U.S. Congress responded to calls from the 9/11 Commission and others for more attention to public diplomacy with supplemental funding for special initiatives in the Middle East, including money for information programs, international exchanges and international broadcasting. Following the invasion of Iraq—and the resulting dramatic increase in anti-Americanism in the Middle East and elsewhere—Congress provided additional funding for public diplomacy through the Intelligence Reform and Terrorism Prevention Act

[29] Ibid., 349.

[30] Armin Meyer, *Quiet Diplomacy: From Cairo to Tokyo in the Twilight of Imperialism* (New York: iUniverse, Inc., 2003).

of 2004, which recognized "the importance of how America and its policies are perceived abroad" and called for the expansion of public diplomacy activities in the Middle East.[31]

The new law provided for the promotion of free media in Islamic countries, scholarships for Muslims to attend American-sponsored schools, public diplomacy training in the Department of State, and an International Youth Opportunity Fund. The BBG also received funding for expanded programming in the Middle East, including a new radio station, Radio Sawa, and a new television network, the Middle East Television Network.

However, the supplements were meager in comparison to the infusions provided the military and other government functions. While the government had invested *hundreds of billions* of dollars to rebuild military and intelligence agencies and other functions important to America's ability to meet the security challenges of the new century, it had invested only pennies (about *half a million*) by comparison in public diplomacy.

The White House also took steps to shore up America's international communications capabilities. Under an executive order from the president, the White House Office of Global Communications (OCG) was established in late January 2003 and charged with the mission "to advise the President, the heads of appropriate offices within the Executive Office of the President, and the heads of executive departments and agencies on utilization of the most effective means for the United States Government to ensure consistency in messages that will promote the interests of the United States abroad, prevent misunderstanding, build support for and among coalition partners of the United States, and inform international audiences."[32] Then White House Press Secretary Ari Fleischer said the new effort reflected the importance the President "places on conveying America's message to the world."[33]

The OCG issued daily briefings to U.S. spokespersons throughout the world in an effort to coordinate the messages coming out of

[31] See Susan B. Epstein, *U.S. Public Diplomacy: Background and the 9/11 Commission Recommendations, CRS Report for Congress* (Washington, DC: Congressional Research Service, 2005).

[32] Executive Order 13283—"Establishing the Office of Global Communications," George W. Bush, *Weekly Compilation of Presidential Documents* (05114187) 39, no. 4, January 27, 2003.

[33] "Bush Signs Order Formalizing Role of White House Global Communications Office," *The White House Bulletin*, January 21, 2003.

Washington and to enhance the United States' presence in foreign media. In responding to criticism that the office was set up to handle White House "propaganda," Tucker Eskew, the new director of the Office, explained: "In part, our mission is to shine a light on others' disinformation, such as that of the Iraqi regime. We are here to use accurate, truthful and overt communications to advance American and coalition interests."[34]

In its 2004 final report—which concluded that "U.S. strategic communications must be transformed"—the Defense Task Force on Strategic Communication criticized the OCG for failing to engage in strategic direction, coordination and evaluation. According to the Task Force, the OCG had "evolved into a second tier organization devoted principally to tactical public affairs.[35] The office was closed in March 2005.

The Pentagon also got involved in public diplomacy with the establishment of the Office of Strategic Influence, whose mission was to influence public sentiment abroad about the war on terrorism, especially in Islamic regions.[36] After word began to spread that the office proposed to engage in "disinformation" campaigns with foreign media, however, it was closed down.[37] But the Defense Department remained keenly interested in information as a strategic resource and later incorporated an ideological component into its strategic military plan for winning the war on terrorism. Although reportedly intended to help get America's message out and to counter the terrorists' effective use of media channels, it also was viewed as an effort to make up for the failure of the State Department to develop an effective public diplomacy operation. Speaking at the Army War College, then Defense Secretary Donald Rumsfeld said, "If I were grading, I would say we probably deserve a D or D plus as a country as to how well we're doing in the battle of ideas that's taking place in the world today.... We have not found the formula as a country."[38]

---

[34] Ibid.; see also Bob Kemper, "Agency Wages Media Battle; Team Makes Sure Message Is Unified, Positive," *Chicago Tribune*, April 7, 2003.

[35] *Report of the Defense Science Board Task Force on Strategic Communication* (Washington, DC: Department of Defense, September 2004), 25.

[36] See Eric Schmitt and James Dao, "A 'Damaged' Information Office Is Declared Closed by Rumsfeld," *The New York Times*, February 27, 2002.

[37] Ibid.

[38] Quoted in Linda Robinson, "The Propaganda War: The Pentagon's Brand-New Plan for Winning the Battle of Ideas Against Terrorists," *U.S. News & World Report*,

Rumsfeld's successor Robert Gates would later express similar interest in improving the country's public diplomacy capabilities. Acknowledging that the U.S. had made a mistake in dismantling the USIA, Gates emphasized the importance of "soft power" in going forward.[39] He said, "We are miserable at communicating to the rest of the world what we are as a society and a culture, about freedom and democracy, about our policies and our goals."[40]

Renewed interest in public diplomacy was also evident in the growing number of public and private organizations studying the issue, as well as increased scholarly and professional attention. The American business community became particularly concerned about the impact of rising anti-Americanism on U.S. business' ability to compete in overseas markets. In a special issue of the *Journal of Business Strategy*, Michael Goodman, wrote that "[t]he role of business now includes public diplomacy."[41] Goodman observed that businesses have been called to respond to the eroding global trust in American businesses brought about by "global scandals, the perception of globalization as an American initiative, and a widespread disagreement with U.S. policy abroad."[42]

Such thinking was manifested in entities such as Business for Diplomatic Action (BDA), a private sector task force formed by U.S. advertising executive Keith Reinhard. Recognizing that "[a]nti-Americanism is bad for business," BDA's mission is "to enlist the U.S. business community in actions to improve the standing of America in the world with the goal of, once again, seeing America admired as a global leader and respected as a courier of progress and prosperity for all people."[43] Toward that end, BDA brings together professionals in media, political science, marketing, communications and global development to offer guidance to the U.S. government on "communication and perception issues that U.S. businesses are uniquely positioned

May 21, 2006, http://www.usnews.com/usnews/news/articles/060529/29propaganda_2.htm (accessed January 7, 2009).

[39] See David Brooks, "The Education of Robert Gates," *The New York Times*, September 19, 2007.

[40] Quoted in Thom Shanker, "Defense Secretary Urges More Spending for U.S. Diplomacy," *The New York Times*, November 27, 2007.

[41] Michael B. Goodman, The Role of Business in Public Diplomacy," *Journal of Business Strategy* 27, no. 3 (2006): 5.

[42] Ibid.

[43] "Who We Are," Business for Diplomatic Action, http://www.businessfordiplomaticaction.org/who/ (accessed January 9, 2009).

to address."[44] The group characterizes its work as "A New Brand of American Diplomacy."[45]

By the 4th anniversary of 9/11, some thirty reports and dozens of articles on the topic of U.S. public diplomacy had been published. Although no consensus had emerged on the specific solutions required to reverse America's negative image in the world, there was broad agreement that U.S. public diplomacy needed to be "fixed." By then, there was also broad agreement that the public diplomacy initiatives undertaken in the years since 9/11 had not fixed it. The revolving door to the executive suite, combined with the lack of an overall strategic plan and a lack of sustained support for public diplomacy among government leaders, were widely cited as contributing to the problem.

A 2003 study by the Council on Foreign Relations concluded that although "growing anti-Americanism is increasingly compromising America's safety," not enough resources had been allocated to public diplomacy, which had been treated as an "afterthought."[46] Another 2003 study initiated by Frank Wolf, then Chairman of the House Subcommittee on State Department Appropriations, reported that "at a critical time in our nation's history, the apparatus of public diplomacy has proven inadequate, especially in the Arab and Muslim world."[47]

An investigation by the GAO in the same year also found that public diplomacy had been impeded because "an interagency public diplomacy strategy has not been completed that would help State and other federal agencies convey consistent messages and achieve mutually reinforcing benefits overseas."[48] Two years later, another GAO report showed little progress. At a time when "anti-Americanism is spreading and deepening around the world," it stated, the U.S. "government does not yet have a national public communications strategy."[49] An independent assessment of the leadership and management

---

[44] Ibid.

[45] Fact Sheet, Business for Diplomatic Action, undated.

[46] Council on Foreign Relations, *Finding America's Voice: A Strategy for Reinvigorating U.S. Public Diplomacy* (Washington, DC, 2003), 5–6.

[47] The Advisory Group on Public Diplomacy for the Arab and Muslim World, *Changing Minds, Winning Peace: A New Strategic Direction for U.S. Public Diplomacy in the Arab and Muslim World* (Washington, DC, 2003).

[48] U.S. Government Accountability Office *U.S. Public Diplomacy: State Department Expands Efforts but Faces Significant Challenges* (Washington, DC, September 2003).

[49] United States Government Accountability Office, *Interagency Coordination Efforts Hampered by the Lack of a National Communication Strategy* (Washington, DC: April 2005).

of the State Department conducted by the Foreign Affairs Council concluded, "Public diplomacy (PD) was arguably the Department of State's weakest program in January 2005."[50]

In March 2005, President Bush nominated his long-time political advisor Karen Hughes to serve as the next under secretary of state for public diplomacy and public affairs. In reporting on Hughes' nomination, the media noted that she would not begin her post until nearly five months later—sometime after she got her son off to college. Unsurprisingly, the apparent lack of urgency with which Hughes' viewed her new assignment led some to question whether she really wanted the job.

Whether she wanted it or not, however, Hughes had her work cut out for her as she assumed what was described in *The Washington Post* as the "least noticed, least respected, and most important job in the State Department."[51] By the time she took office, most informed observers agreed that dismantling the USIA had been a mistake. And they agreed that the hodge-podge of initiatives attempted by Hughes' predecessors had not made a dent in increasing hostilities toward the United States in the Middle East or elsewhere.

Perhaps because of such concerns, reactions to Hughes' nomination were mostly positive. While some questioned her lack of foreign policy credentials, many saw her appointment as an acknowledgement that the president was taking public diplomacy more seriously and hoped that, because of her personal relationship with him, she would have more success than her predecessors in elevating public diplomacy in the foreign affairs establishment. In fact, the president said that Hughes' appointment "signifies my personal commitment to the international diplomacy that is needed."[52]

Because Hughes "had the ear" of the president, many hoped she also would be able to integrate public diplomacy more fully into the foreign policy making process. Given her reported commitment to stay on throughout Bush's second term, many also believed she would provide sustained and sorely needed leadership for the function.

Additionally, Hughes had the strong support of Bush's new Secretary of State Condoleezza Rice, who seemed to recognize a need to

[50] Foreign Affairs Council, *Managing Secretary Rice's State Department: An Independent Assessment*, (New York, June 2007), 20.

[51] Anne Applebaum, "Think Again Karen Hughes" *Washington Post*, July 27, 2005.

[52] "Another Lady with a Tough Job," *Economist* 374, no. 8418 (2005): 36.

improve U.S. public diplomacy. Shortly after Hughes' arrival at the State Department, Rice emphasized the importance of public diplomacy in a Department town hall meeting. "Public diplomacy has to be a priority for this government," she said. "I am a very strong believer in the integration of public diplomacy, of message, of communication, and of policy... Karen will be part of my policy team."[53]

Yet, when Rice announced a new strategic plan for U.S. diplomacy in the new century, it included little proof of public diplomacy's heightened role in diplomatic affairs. The new plan, called "Transformational Diplomacy," was described as an effort to "secure a future of freedom for all people." The objective, according to Rice, was "to work with our many partners around the world, to build and sustain democratic, well-governed states that will respond to the needs of their people and conduct themselves responsibly in the international system."[54] Emphasizing that "transformational diplomacy" was rooted "in partnership, not in paternalism," she explained, "In doing things with people, not for them, we seek to use America's diplomatic power to help foreign citizens better their own lives and to build their own nations and to transform their own futures."[55]

The State Department's fact sheet on "Transformational Diplomacy" mentioned public diplomacy twice. It stated that public diplomacy would play a key role in advancing the Department's new regional focus through public diplomacy centers that would "take America's story directly to the people and regional television media in real time and in the appropriate language." Public diplomacy also was listed as one of the skills all U.S. diplomats would need going forward: "As always, public diplomacy is an important part of every diplomat's job description."[56]

When Hughes first arrived at the State Department, she approached her new job with evangelical zeal. Quickly announcing a "listening tour" to the Middle East, which would allow her to experience public

[53] Condoleezza Rice, "Remarks with Under Secretary for Public Diplomacy and Public Affairs Karen Hughes at Town Hall for Public Diplomacy," Washington, DC, September 8, 2005.

[54] Condoleezza Rice, "Transformational Diplomacy," speech at Georgetown University, January 18, 2006, http://www.unc.edu/depts/diplomat/item/2006/0103/rice/rice_georgetown.html (accessed January 22, 2009).

[55] Ibid.

[56] Fact Sheet, "Transformational Diplomacy," Office of the Spokesman, State Department, January 18, 2006.

diplomacy's challenges firsthand, she laid out an ambitious plan for turning U.S. public diplomacy around. In her confirmation hearing she had defined her challenge as "the urgent need to foster greater understanding, more respect and a sense of common ideals among Americans and people of different countries, cultures and faiths around the world."[57]

The president, Hughes said, "has charged me with developing a long-term strategy to make sure that our ideals prevail—ideals, by the way, which belong not only to America, but are shared by civilized people the world over."[58] Throughout her tenure, she would re-emphasize this idea, reiterating the need to "create the conditions and the climate that allow people to give our ideas a fair hearing.... We are confident, if they are able to think for themselves, if they're able to give that fair hearing, that people will choose the power of our ideals."[59]

The strategic framework for accomplishing this mission included three "pillars": to foster a vision of hope and opportunity rooted in the president's freedom agenda; to isolate and marginalize extremists; and to foster a sense of common interests and values among diverse cultures and faiths. These "pillars" would be built on four "Es," Hughes said—education, exchanges, empowerment, and engagement. "We must engage more vigorously, and that's first. We can't expect people to give a fair hearing to our ideas if we don't advocate them very aggressively."[60]

The other side of "engagement," according to Hughes, was a more rapid and aggressive response to misinformation—"rumors, inaccuracies, and hate speech whenever—wherever they are engaged in around the world."[61] She said that when she arrived at the State Department, "I found that what had happened in 2003 and 2004 was we hadn't been engaging in debates in Europe, attending the conferences, we hadn't been appearing on the TV shows."[62]

---

[57] Karen Hughes, Opening Statement before the Senate Foreign Relations Committee, July 22, 2005, http://www.state.gov/r/us/2005/49967.htm (accessed January 17, 2007).

[58] Karen Hughes, "America's Dialogue with the World: A Comprehensive Strategy for Public Diplomacy," remarks at Women's Foreign Policy Group 10th Anniversary Luncheon Event, Washington, DC, November 4, 2005.

[59] Condoleezza Rice, "Remarks with Under Secretary for Public Diplomacy and Public Affairs Karen Hughes at Town Hall for Public Diplomacy."

[60] Ibid.

[61] Ibid.

[62] James Blitz, "US Faces 'Long Struggle' to Overcome Worldwide Hostility,"

Hughes' response was to develop a twenty-four-hour "rapid response unit" intended to improve U.S. officials' ability to respond quickly and effectively to negative reports about America in the foreign media. Staff members in the Washington, D.C.-based unit monitored and translated major world media reports in real-time and prepared daily "Rapid Response" reports that were dispatched to U.S. officials throughout the world, giving them U.S. positions on various issues. The idea was to provide those in the field with the administration's key messages on various matters so that they would more actively engage with foreign journalists. Toward that end, Hughes also created regional public diplomacy hubs in targeted media markets, placing U.S. spokespersons there to advocate U.S. policies in regional media.

Hughes viewed cultural and educational exchange programs as "the single most valuable public diplomacy tool."[63] Exchanges, she said, have "been the most effective over the last 50 years, because we can prove that they make a lasting difference, not only in people's lives, but also in their attitudes."[64] Her exchange initiatives focused mostly on expanding existing programs and developing new programs to support women and youth—for example, the *Fortune*/State Department International Women Mentoring Program was created to help women develop management and business skills. Another example was the Iraqi Young Leaders Exchange Program, which brought high school and university students to the United States in an effort to engender the good will of future world leaders toward America.

Hughes' education initiatives addressed perceived needs both to educate Americans about other cultures—to "be better citizens of the world"—and to educate people abroad about America and its values. She sought the support of the private sector for these efforts—for example, a University Presidents Summit on International Education was held to enlist the help of U.S. university leaders to strengthen international education and emphasize its importance to national interests.[65]

Financial Times, November 6, 2007, http://www.ft.com/cms/s/0/b1fdd5f8-8c8f-11dc-b887-0000779fd2ac.html (accessed January 26, 2009).

[63] Condoleezza Rice, "Remarks with Under Secretary for Public Diplomacy and Public Affairs Karen Hughes at Town Hall for Public Diplomacy."

[64] Nicholas Kralev, "Foreign Ministration; Hughes Takes Long View on Image of U.S.," *The Washington Times*, July 15, 2007.

[65] "Major Public Diplomacy Accomplishments 2005–2006," U.S. Office of Public Diplomacy and Public Affairs, undated.

Empowerment, Hughes said, meant empowering individual American citizens to serve as U.S. ambassadors throughout the world. "Empowerment is critical because we have to recognize that in some of this work, the voice of a government official may not be the most effective or the most credible voice." For that reason, Hughes said, she would work closely with the private sector "to marshal its enormous creativity" and resources.[66]

Hughes later added a fifth "E"—evaluation—to her strategy "to improve our ability to measure success or failure." She said, "We want to direct our resources to what works."[67]

In June 2007, Hughes laid out the strategies for accomplishing public diplomacy's long-term mission—i.e., "making sure that our ideals prevail"—in the National Strategy for Public Diplomacy and Strategic Communication. The plan outlined the strategic priorities of U.S. public diplomacy and provided an "action plan" for going forward. According to the plan, "Public diplomacy is, at its core, about making America's diplomacy public and communicating America's views, values and policies in effective ways to audiences across the world. Public diplomacy promotes linkages between the American people and the rest of the world by reminding diverse populations of our common interests and values."[68] Notably, the plan addressed only the communication and promotional aspects of public diplomacy. There was no mention of public diplomacy's policy role. (See Appendix Two for the full text of the plan.)

Hughes' approach to public diplomacy was criticized by some as too self-interested and ideologically driven. Price Floyd, for example, observed that Hughes and her post-9/11 predecessors all were too focused on selling foreign policy when they should have focused on promoting American values. "People in other countries have understood all too well what this administration's policies are. They simply don't agree with them," he said.[69]

---

[66] Condoleezza Rice, "Remarks with Under Secretary for Public Diplomacy and Public Affairs Karen Hughes at Town Hall for Public Diplomacy."

[67] Karen Hughes, "Remarks by Karen Hughes," remarks at Shell Distinguished Lecture Series, Baker Institute for Public Policy, Houston, TX, March 29, 2006, www.state.gov/r/us/64106.htm (accessed October 21, 2007).

[68] U.S. Department of State, National Plan for Public Diplomacy and Strategic Communication (Washington, DC: June 2007): 12.

[69] Price Floyd, "Try Policy Instead of PR," *Los Angeles Times*, November 19, 2007, A21.

In fact, Hughes learned this first-hand on her first trip to the Middle East—her "listening tour"—where she encountered considerable pushback in her efforts to promote women's rights, to explain the U.S. invasion of Iraq, and to defend the nation's support for Israel. Hughes was taken aback when people reacted harshly, suggesting that Americans did not understand their traditions and should not attempt to impose their views on other countries.[70] *The New York Times* later called Hughes' visit to the Middle East "embarrassing."[71]

When asked in a March 2007 interview whether she thought an approach to public diplomacy based on "making sure that our ideals prevail" could be interpreted by people abroad as an attempt to convert them to U.S. ways of thinking, she said, "That's an interesting point—I don't—that's certainly not my intent—and I think you can find a lot of places where I've talked about our common ideals and our shared values.... What I do try to convey is that they are shared views.... When I say our ideals I then define them. Freedom. Respect for the rule of law. Respect for the value of each individual. I think it's more a matter of explaining that the ideals that we do hold most dear in America are in fact ideals that are universal the world over."[72]

Two years after taking the helm of U.S. public diplomacy, Hughes resigned. At the end of her term, she received mixed marks for her efforts, praised mostly for securing new funding for public diplomacy, raising the budget to nearly $1 billion a year, and for institutional changes that improved public diplomacy processes, including the government's ability to respond quickly to misinformation in foreign media.[73] Her efforts to increase international exchanges and expand the government's diplomatic partnerships with the private sector were also acknowledged.[74] Although Hughes also claimed credit for

---

[70] See, e.g., Steven R. Weisman, "Bush Confidante Finds Latest Role to Be Uphill Battle," *The New York Times*, December 6, 2005; Guy Dinmore, "Saudi Students Rebuff US Communications Guru," *Financial Times Online*, September 27, 2005, http://www.ft.com/cms/s/0/ebe0f15c-2fa2-11da-8b51-00000e2511c8.html (accessed January 27, 2009); Lucy Jones and Fawaz Turki, "Karen Hughes' 'Listening' Tour and Its Aftermath," *Washington Report on Middle East Affairs* 24, no. 9 (December 2005): 24–26.

[71] "Selling America," *The New York Times*, November 4, 2007.

[72] Personal interview, March 23, 2007.

[73] See, e.g., Foreign Affairs Council, *Task Force Report: Managing Secretary Rice's State Department: An Independent Assessment* (Washington, DC, June 2007): 20–23.

[74] See, e.g., Glenn Kessler and Robin Wright, "Hughes to Leave State Dept. After Mixed Results in Outreach Post," *The Washington Post*, November 1, 2007.

"knitting together public diplomacy and policy"[75]—and she reportedly did sit in on State Department policy meetings while in office[76]—there was considerable skepticism that any long-term gains had been made in that regard.

At the announcement of her resignation, Hughes said she had accomplished her mission: "I feel that I've done what Secretary Rice and President Bush asked me to do by transforming public diplomacy and making it a national security priority central to everything we do in government."[77] Rice said Hughes had exceeded expectations, doing a "remarkable job" and making public diplomacy "strong and central" to U.S. foreign policy.[78]

Notably, Hughes described her accomplishments in terms of "output," rather than "impact." Before her departure, on November 1, 2007, her office released a list of 18 "innovations" that illustrated her success. "Under the direction of Under Secretary for Public Diplomacy and Public Affairs," the statement read, "Public diplomacy has become a national security priority that is now viewed as central to the work of America's diplomats worldwide. Under Secretary Hughes aggressively expanded public diplomacy and international communication programs, won increased funding for them, and initiated numerous innovations and institutional changes."[79]

Some discredited Hughes work by pointing to the findings of a new study of world public opinion that found "the United States' image abroad is bad and getting worse."[80] In its 2007 Global Attitudes Project, the Pew Research Center reported that "[o]ver the past five years, America's image has plummeted throughout much of the world"[81] and is "abysmal" in the Middle East and Asia. The poll pointed out that

---

[75] Karen Hughes, "Remarks by Karen Hughes."

[76] Foreign Affairs Council, *Task Force Report: Managing Secretary Rice's State Department: An Independent Assessment* (Washington, DC, June 2007): 21.

[77] Daniel Dombey and Andrew Ward, "Bush Ally Resigned to Head Home to Texas," *Financial Times*, November 1, 2007.

[78] Associated Press, "Hughes, a Bush Confidante, is Resigning; Aide's Last Job: Boosting U.S. Image in Islamic World," *The Wall Street Journal*, November 1, 2007.

[79] "Changing the Nature and Scope of Public Diplomacy," News Release, Office of the Under Secretary for Public Diplomacy and Public Affairs, November 1, 2007.

[80] The Chicago Council on Global Affairs, *World Public Opinion 2007* (Chicago, IL, 2007): 28.

[81] Pew Research Center, *Global Unease with Major World Powers: Rising Environmental Concern in 47-Nation Survey*, The Pew Global Attitudes Project (Washington, DC, 2007): 13.

America's image "continues to decline [even] among the publics of many of America's oldest allies."[82]

Others contended that increasing levels of anti-Americanism weren't Hughes' fault. For example, Andrew Kohut, executive director of the group that conducted the study, suggested that the drop in America's image "may not be a measure of [Hughes'] lack of competence, but how little, in the end, public diplomacy can do when the issue, in the end, is big events."[83]

The *Los Angeles Times* wrote, "Hughes' inability to solve anti-Americanism was less a reflection on her talents than on the impossibility of her job."[84] Rather, the *Times* pointed to the need for "rational argument" over policy disputes, blaming the State Department for its failure to provide it. Similarly, *The New York Times* reported upon Hughes' retirement that some of her "initiatives may have a beneficial effect. But it should be clear to anyone who is paying attention that the issue is not who has the job of public diplomat. The best hope of defusing anti-Americanism and restoring our country's international standing lies in a renewed commitment to the values that make it great, including respect for civil liberties and international law. That will require a change of attitude, as well as personnel, much higher up—in the Oval Office."[85]

Hughes' successor, James K. Glassman, was quietly nominated by the president in December 2007. Glassman, a former journalist who just eight months earlier had been named chairman of the BBG, which oversees U.S. international broadcasting, assumed the public diplomacy position in an acting capacity while awaiting Senate confirmation of his appointment. Notwithstanding the fact that his time in the post would be brief, i.e., until the end of the Bush presidency, Glassman expressed his intention to focus on three areas: "1) leading the war of ideas, 2) building on our current public diplomacy strengths in educational and cultural exchanges, and 3) bringing fresh and vital technologies to bear on all our efforts."[86]

---

[82] Ibid., 3.

[83] Brian Knowlton, "Karen Hughes Leaving U.S. Post; She's One of the Last of Bush's Texas Aides," *The International Herald Tribune*, November 1, 2007.

[84] "America's Tough Sell; Hughes Tenure at State Reminds that Even the Most Vigorous Diplomacy Does Little to Popularize Unwanted Policies," *Los Angeles Times*, November 3, 2007.

[85] "Selling America," *The New York Times*, November 4, 2007.

[86] Opening Statement of James K. Glassman, Senate Foreign Relations Committee Hearing on Nomination of Under Secretary of State for Public Diplomacy and Public Affairs,

In his confirmation hearing, Glassman indicated that his main focus would be "the war of ideas—perhaps better expressed as global ideological engagement." The emphasis of public diplomacy, Glassman stressed, should be on the need "to counter and defeat the violent extremists who threaten America and the freedom of people around the world."[87] His view that public diplomacy's primary purpose was to combat terrorism mirrored those of other post-9/11 public diplomacy officials. However, Glassman rejected strategies based on what he saw as his predecessors' attempts to "[make] people like us" in favor of efforts designed to discredit the extreme ideologies of would-be terrorists.[88]

Shortly after his swearing-in in June 2008, Glassman launched what he called a "new" approach to U.S. public diplomacy with the "desired end state" being "a world in which the use of violence to achieve political, religious, or social objectives is no longer considered acceptable.... Efforts to radicalize and recruit new members are no longer successful, and the perpetrators of violent extremism are condemned and isolated."[89] Speaking to the Council on Foreign Relations, Glassman announced what he called the new mission of twenty-first century public diplomacy: "to tell the world of a good and compassionate nation and at the same time to engage in the most important ideological contest of our time—a contest that we will win."[90]

One aspect of Glassman's appointment that stands out is the fact that he was the first man to lead U.S. public diplomacy after the dissolution of the USIA. Although possibly just a coincidence that the first five individuals in both the Clinton and Bush administrations to serve as under secretary of state for public diplomacy and public affairs were all women, one former USIA officer who now serves as a senior public diplomacy specialist in the State Department didn't see it that way. When asked what it meant that only women had been nominated,

---

January 30, 2008, http://foreign.senate.gov/testimony/2008/GlassmanTestimony080130.pdf (accessed January 22, 2009).

[87] Ibid.

[88] Spencer Ackerman, "Future of Public Diplomacy Unsettled at State," *The Washington Independent*, February 17, 2009. Retrieved on May 15, 2009, from http://washingtonindependent.com/30404/future-publicd-diplomacy--unsettled-at-state.

[89] James K. Glassman, "Public Diplomacy in the Twenty First Century," speech to the Council of Foreign Relations, Washington, DC, June 30, 2008, http://www.cfr.org/publication/16719/public_diplomacy_in_the_twentyfirst_century.html (accessed January 28, 2009).

[90] Ibid.

she said, "It means that public diplomacy is considered by many of the very most senior decision makers [in government] as a facilitative service." As a result, she said, "They would like to choose people who are convincing, who can be charming on cue, who are smart and can implement and can make things happen within their sphere—but who will take direction."[91]

Such comments suggest that despite public diplomacy's "official" policy function—that is, to counsel and advise the president and other government leaders on the public implications of foreign policy decisions—public diplomacy is viewed and used primarily as a technical communication function. In fact, there is considerable evidence to demonstrate that, despite contemporary rhetoric from U.S. officials to the contrary, public diplomacy remains isolated from the core of the nation's policy processes.

As an example, in 2008, the U.S. Advisory Commission on Public Diplomacy released the results of an intensive study of the "human resources dimension" of U.S. public diplomacy that revealed both an enduring prejudice against public diplomacy and a lack of understanding and/or regard within the State Department for the special expertise of public diplomacy professionals. The report also documented a clear "glass ceiling" for U.S. Foreign Service officers who choose to work in public diplomacy.[92] (See Chapter Nine for more discussion of this report.)

With respect to public diplomacy's policy role, the Commission reported that although it is difficult to judge the extent to which public diplomacy concerns are taken into consideration in actual foreign policy decision-making, an important "proxy" for gauging public diplomacy's role in policy formulation is whether public diplomacy specialists are serving in the senior-most levels of the State Department bureaucracy. In this regard, the findings were disappointing.

Nearly nine years after the integration of public diplomacy into the State Department, the Commission reported, public diplomacy "remains the most under-represented" of the five career tracks in the Department, which includes officers in the areas of politics, economics,

---

[91] Personal interview, March 22, 2007.

[92] The United States Advisory Commission on U.S. Public Diplomacy, *Getting the People Part Right: A Report on the Human Resources Dimension of U.S. Public Diplomacy* (Washington, DC, 2008).

public diplomacy, consular affairs, and management.[93] In 1999, the Commission pointed out, there were no public diplomacy specialists at the assistant secretary level and only two at the ambassador level, representing 1% overall. In 2007, the Commission found, there was one assistant-secretary with public diplomacy expertise and four ambassadors, representing 3% overall. According to the report, "no career track has yielded fewer ambassadors than PD in any year from 1999 to 2007."[94] Also during this period, "no PD officer has ever risen to the Foreign Service rank of career ambassador, the Service's top rung."[95]

Noting the importance of these findings "as a matter of equity and morale," the report continued, "the more fundamental point is that the relative lack of success on this front suggests a lack of progress on the overarching issue of the integration of PD into the core work of the department."[96] Thus, the Commission concluded, "the PD track is no longer 'separate,' but it is certainly not yet 'equal.'"[97] According to the commission, "True integration of public diplomacy considerations into the policy process will be achieved only when PD officers are in the policy-makers' seats."[98]

On April 14, 2009—within the first 100 days of the Obama administration—the White House announced President Barack Obama's intention to nominate Judith A. McHale, then Discovery Communications President and CEO, to serve as under secretary of state for public diplomacy and public affairs. She was described in the announcement as "a leading media and communications executive whose career has been devoted to building companies and non-profit organizations dedicated to reaching out to and connecting people around the world."[99] She was described by others as a "longtime friend"[100] to the

[93] Ibid., 34.

[94] Ibid., 35.

[95] Ibid.

[96] Ibid.

[97] Ibid., 28.

[98] Ibid., 8.

[99] The White Office of the Press Secretary, *News Release*, "White House Announces More Key Administrative Posts," April 14, 2009, http://www.whitehouse.gov/the_press_office/President-Obama-Anounces-More Key-Administration Posts-4/14/09 (accessed May 1, 2009).

[100] Al Kamen, A Lovely Consolation Prize for Ms. Kennedy?" *The Washington Post*, January 23, 2009, http://www.washingtonpost.com/wp-dyn/content/article/2009/01/22/AR2009012203621.html (accessed June 2, 2009).

new Secretary of State Hillary Clinton, a "Democratic mega-donor"[101] and a "foreign affairs neophyte"[102] with "no diplomatic experience."[103]

At her confirmation hearing before the U.S. Senate, McHale laid out six "core principles" that she said provided the "foundation for a new framework for public diplomacy in the 21st Century" and that would guide her work. Those principles emphasized that 1) "public diplomacy is an essential component of foreign policy and must be integrated into the policy process at every level"; 2) "public diplomacy must be run strategically"; 3) "results require resources"; 4) "rewards require risks"; 5) "new technology, used effectively and creatively, can be a game changer"; and 6) "public diplomacy is not something the government can or should do alone."[104]

Her work, McHale said, would focus on "rebuilding our network of American Centers and strengthening our cultural diplomacy"; "ensuring a public diplomacy structure with clear lines of authority and accountability"; "striking an appropriate balance between the Departments of Defense and State and maintaining a coherent interagency process"; and "ensuring that public diplomacy receives the resources and support it needs."[105]

Notwithstanding the significance of such efforts, those hoping for bold actions or big ideas for revitalizing U.S. public diplomacy were disappointed—particularly after noting that Clinton had offered few specifics regarding any possible changes in public diplomacy at her own confirmation hearing. While both clearly recognized the importance of America's reengagement in the world—as Clinton said, "America is back"—neither McHale nor Clinton provided any early signals that a new public diplomacy agency was being contemplated or that other big changes were in store.

In reflecting on Clinton's testimony, former U.S. diplomat John Brown predicted, "What is most likely is that public diplomacy, qua

---

[101] Ibid.

[102] Patricia H. Kushlis, "The Good, the Bad and the Questionable," *Foreign.Policy .com*, April 17, 2009. Retrieved on May 1, 1009, from http://whirlview.typepad.com/whirledview/2009/04/the-good-the-bad-and-the-questionable.html.

[103] Helle Dale, "Obama's Arab-TV Interview," February 5, 2009. Retrieved on May 1, 2009, from http://www.heritage.org/press/commentary/ed020409b.cfm.

[104] Judith A. McHale, "Testimony as Nominee for Under Secretary for Public Diplomacy and Public Affairs," Senate Foreign Relations Committee, Washington, DC, May 13, 2009, http://www.state.gov/r/remarks/124155.html (accessed June 2, 2009).

[105] Ibid.

public diplomacy, will muddle through at the State Department for the next few—if not many—years" without the "highly hyped 'innovative' programs" of the Hughes era.[106]

As this book went into production, the jury was still out on U.S. public diplomacy's fate under the Obama administration, with McHale's confirmation pending and Clinton's long-range plans for public diplomacy undefined.

Toward The Policy Phase

Veteran USIA officer Hans Tuch wrote in 1990 that it was clear that "public diplomacy [had] become an imperative of a nation's international life."[107] But, he said, it had not become a priority for the U.S. government. According to Tuch, "the gauging of public opinion abroad and the consideration of these public attitudes and perceptions... [are] not sufficiently recognized as integral elements in the formulation and execution of U.S. foreign policy."[108]

Nearly twenty years later, foreign public opinion is still not a critical component of U.S. foreign policy—and public diplomacy is still not a priority for the U.S. government. Although 9/11 highlighted the need for the nation to tend to its international relations, little progress has been made in defining public diplomacy's role in national strategy and in rebuilding a public diplomacy entity capable of addressing the ideological challenges of the twenty-first century.

Only when these things happen will the next phase—"The Policy Phase"—of public diplomacy begin. Although there are some hints of its coming, this period cannot be officially documented until U.S. leaders accept—and adequately support—public diplomacy's critical role in protecting and advancing national interests, which include— but are not limited to—national security. The Policy Phase will be marked by broad recognition of public diplomacy's unique contributions to the nation's ability to establish beneficial relations with foreign publics and to regain—and sustain—the respect and support of world citizens who, to great degree, will determine *America's* fate in the world.

---

[106] John Brown, "Smart Power In, Public Diplomacy Out,?" *John Brown's Notes and Essays*, March 2, 2009, http://johnbrownnotesandessays.blogspot.com/2009/03/smart-power-in-public-diplomacy-out.html (accessed June 2, 2009).

[107] Hans N. Tuch, *Communicating with the World: U.S. Public Diplomacy Overseas* (New York: St Martin's Press, 1990), 3.

[108] Ibid., 9–10.

CHAPTER THREE

INSIGHTS FROM THE U.S. EXPERIENCE: CHALLENGES AHEAD

Public diplomacy is not a luxury, nor is it a temporary factor in our diplomacy. It is vital to our national interest and has to be a permanent element in our structure and activities abroad.[1]

Over the course of half a century, the United States built one of the most sophisticated and successful public diplomacy operations in the world—and then destroyed it. What have we learned in the process? How can the U.S. experience in public diplomacy inform contemporary thinking and practices in public diplomacy?

This chapter offers ten observations concerning the evolution of American public diplomacy that help to answer these questions.

Evolutionary insights

1. *An episodic commitment to public diplomacy reflects a failure by national leaders to recognize the importance of foreign* publics *in international relations and public diplomacy's unique and critical role in the protection and advancement of national and international interests*

Public diplomacy's fortune in the United States can be tied directly to the nation's involvement in international conflicts in which U.S. leaders perceived a need to influence foreign public opinion for the advancement of U.S. "war" interests. As Bruce Gregory observed, although American diplomats throughout history "were expected to engage foreign publics as well as their governments in wartime…in peacetime ambassadors focused their attention on other governments, not their citizens."[2]

---

[1] Former USIA officer; see Kathy R. Fitzpatrick, *USIA Alumni Study*, unpublished report, 2007.

[2] Bruce Gregory, "Public Diplomacy and Strategic Communication: Cultures, Firewalls, and Imported Norms," paper presented at the American Political Science Association Conference on International Communication and Conflict, Washington, DC, August 31, 2005.

The decline of public diplomacy after the end of the Cold War is most telling in this regard. Once the Berlin Wall fell—ending the conflict with the Soviet Union and making the United States the world's sole superpower—government leaders had little use for public diplomacy. Foreign public opinion seemed of little consequence to the "indispensable nation." As a result, the U.S. public diplomacy apparatus was dismantled and the nation's preparedness to deal with ideological threats was severely diminished—along with much of the goodwill the country had spent decades cultivating with people abroad.

A similarly narrow view of public diplomacy as a "security" resource has been evident in post-9/11 public diplomacy initiatives. U.S. officials have concentrated on "winning hearts and minds" in the Arab world, while neglecting U.S. relationships with important constituents outside the Middle East. This emphasis on public diplomacy's role in the "war on terror" suggests that national leaders do not fully appreciate public diplomacy's broader role in promoting and advancing non-security-related interests.

Placing public diplomacy in the context of war perpetuates the historic myth that public diplomacy is an instrument of war no longer needed when wars end. It should go without saying that good relations with the people of other countries and a positive image of America help to both prevent conflicts that can escalate into new wars and contribute to America's ability to achieve its foreign policy objectives. Certainly, the consequences of discounting public diplomacy's value after the Cold War demonstrated the importance of maintaining a robust public diplomacy operation in times of war *and* peace. But it took 9/11 for U.S. leaders to begin to acknowledge it.

When compared to other countries' approaches to public diplomacy, the U.S. view of the function as primarily a wartime resource is troublingly parochial. As Jan Melissen has pointed out, "The strong emphasis in the United States on homeland security, the 'war on terror' and 'winning hearts and minds' in the Islamic world does not mirror the concerns and interests in public diplomacy that are articulated in many other countries."[3] Although 9/11 was "an important trigger for the present debate on public diplomacy throughout the global diplomatic community," he said, "for many countries it was not the

[3] Jan Melissen, *The New Public Diplomacy: Soft Power in International Relations* (Houndmills: Palgrave MacMillan, 2005), xx.

beginning, nor did the US experience set the terms for thinking on this issue outside North America."[4]

Of course, U.S. public diplomacy leaders are partly to blame for justifying public diplomacy's worth primarily on the basis of national security concerns. During the Cold War, for example, rather than attempt to demonstrate to Congressional and other U.S. leaders public diplomacy's important role in shaping the global environment in which a range of U.S. interests could be effectively advanced, public diplomacy officials based funding requests primarily on the need to defeat communism. More recently, public diplomacy officials have emphasized public diplomacy's role in combating terrorism.

As Nicholas Cull observed, the USIA was "never fully accepted on Capitol Hill, and rather than fighting the battle to establish public diplomacy as an essential dimension of foreign relations, the agency sold itself as a crisis tool, and was hence hostage to the end of the Cold War and a victim of its own success."[5] Cull pointed out that, while the USIA emphasized its role in the conflict between the United States and the Soviet Union for budgetary reasons, the agency's operations "fell disproportionately into the realm of maintaining relations with America's allies. Arguably its true achievement lies here also."[6]

Certainly, USIA officers viewed the agency's mission as extending beyond the context of the Cold War. As one veteran public diplomacy officer put it, "I never considered USIA just a Cold War agency. It was an organization dedicated to increasing international understanding of the U.S. and its policies."[7] Another observed that "the information work as well as the educational and cultural exchanges carried out by USIA had a value in and of themselves, independent of the Cold War."[8] Another noted, "I did not see USIA as a 'Cold War' agency. I was talking to foreign audiences about the U.S., its society, culture, institutions, policies, etc. 'Fighting' the Cold War was incidental to that."[9]

---

[4] Ibid.

[5] Nicholas J. Cull, *The Cold War and the United States Information Agency: American Propaganda and Public Diplomacy, 1945–1989* (Cambridge, UK: Cambridge University Press, 2008), 500.

[6] Cull, *The Cold War and the United States Information Agency*, 494.

[7] Former USIA officer; see Kathy R. Fitzpatrick, *USIA Alumni Study*, unpublished report, 2007.

[8] Ibid.

[9] Ibid.

Had U.S. policy makers fully recognized the USIA's critical role in combating disinformation promulgated by America's enemies *and* in establishing and sustaining good relations with America's allies and friends throughout the world, the story of the USIA might have had a different ending. So, too might post-9/11 public diplomacy efforts been more effective in repairing U.S. relations with people abroad. Going forward, public diplomacy's broad role and value in national strategy must be better understood and appreciated by U.S. officials.

2. *The lack of a coherent and consistent definition has stifled public diplomacy's advancement.*

U.S. public diplomacy's mission, principles and practices have shifted with the priorities of successive administrations and the political whims of U.S. leaders in the White House, in the State Department and in the Congress. According to Hans Tuch, "Among those who directed public diplomacy within the U.S. government and who predominated in legislating its policies and resources, more have favored one or another direction dictated by their own experience, political predilection, and dedication to having their ideas prevail."[10] As a result, there has been no "permanent consensus as to what public diplomacy consists of and what direction it should take."[11]

One of the most fundamental—and most critical—issues that must be addressed going forward is the lack of a clear and consistent definition of public diplomacy that articulates its scope and function and demonstrates its worth and value in protecting and advancing national interests. Another issue that must be resolved is the conceptual foundation of the discipline. When the USIA existed, public diplomacy was mission-driven with a focus on the establishment of long-term relationships that would generate the goodwill and support needed for the United States to advance its policies, ideals and values in the world. Following the terrorist attacks on 9/11, public diplomacy became almost exclusively crisis-driven with re-active message campaigns and activities seemingly designed to "sell" or impose U.S. policies, ideals and values on people abroad.

This shift from a more symmetric, dialogic, relational approach to a more asymmetric, self-interested, political approach to public diplo-

[10] Hans N. Tuch, *Communicating with the World: U.S. Public Diplomacy Overseas* (New York: St. Martin's Press, 1990), 13.

[11] Ibid.

macy demonstrates that the United States has not settled on a generally accepted worldview of public diplomacy. Going forward, public diplomacy's function must be clearly articulated and the conceptual foundation of the discipline must be established.

Toward that end, it will be important to consider the conceptual, as well as the practical, dimensions of public diplomacy. As public relations scholar Jacquie L'Etang has observed, efforts to advance diplomacy "must go beyond practical ['how to do it'] guidance and consider the motivations, values, beliefs and conventions of the practice, its organizational and social effects, as well as the underlying assumptions and political configurations that go along with these practices."[12]

In this respect, there is much work to be done. Notwithstanding America's long history in conducting public diplomacy, the conceptual development of the discipline remains in the embryonic stage. As media scholar Etyan Gilboa has observed, there is no unifying framework for the study and practice of public diplomacy.[13] As a result, matters related to how public diplomacy should be viewed, valued, and practiced continue to be debated.

3. *Historically-based misperceptions of public diplomacy as government "propaganda" are detrimental to public diplomacy's future*

Despite significant efforts to distance public diplomacy from propaganda, which is widely viewed as inherently deceptive and manipulative, the idea that public diplomacy is simply a euphemism for propaganda still lingers in the minds of many, including government officials. As an example, soon after 9/11, in discussing public diplomacy's role in the "war on terror," former U.S. Ambassador and Assistant Secretary of State Richard Holbrooke said, "Call it public diplomacy, or public affairs, or psychological warfare, or—if you really want to be blunt—propaganda."[14]

The news media have contributed to such perceptions. For example, in a study of *The New York Times* coverage of public diplomacy from 1993

---

[12] Jacquie L'Etang, "Public Relations as Diplomacy," in *Critical Perspectives in Public Relations,* ed. Jacquie L'Etang and Magda Pieczka (London: International Thomson Business Press, 1996), 24.

[13] Etyan Gilboa, "Searching for a Theory of Public Diplomacy," *The Annals of the American Academy of Political and Social Science* 616 (March 2008): 55–56.

[14] Richard Holbrooke, "Get the Message Out," *The Washington Post,* October 28, 2003.

to 2003, researchers found that the newspaper's post-9/11 coverage of public diplomacy—which focused almost exclusively on matters related to the terrorist attacks and the wars in Afghanistan and Iraq—the newspaper critically portrayed U.S. diplomatic efforts as "putting a new spin on old-fashioned American propaganda."[15] The reports described public diplomacy as "psychological warfare" designed to "get the upper hand in the propaganda war" and included references to "the Bush administration's message masters" who were "selling images and ideas" and "slick advertisements." According to the study, such coverage may have suggested to readers that the government's public diplomacy efforts "were designed to create false images rather than present an accurate picture of the United States and its policies."[16]

At the same time, it should be noted that U.S. public diplomacy initiatives undertaken in the post-9/11 period may have exacerbated perceptions that the American government engages in "propaganda" campaigns. As an example, in evaluating the "Shared Values" initiative—which featured happy Muslims living good lives in America—for propaganda characteristics, media ethics scholar Patrick Plaisance identified three "ethical shortcomings." First, he said, the truthfulness of the claims made in the ads was called into question by the suggestion that persecution of minorities does not exist in America. Second, the strategy could be seen as "treating people as means rather than as ends—of pursuing a goal of changing the opinions that Muslims have of the United States because it benefits the United States to do so—rather than seeking genuine, more comprehensive mutual understanding." Third, he suggested, the campaign could be seen as designed to affect the "evaluative narrowing" of its receivers by "presenting an unargued and idyllic vision that ignores fundamental truths of historical and continuing inequality and discrimination."[17]

Similar concerns were raised about later efforts designed to explain—as Karen Hughes put it—"that the ideals that we do hold most dear in America are in fact ideals that are universal the world over."[18] Both

---

[15] Kathy Fitzpatrick and Tamara Kosic, "The Missing Public in Public Diplomacy: Exploring the News Media's Role in Developing an American Constituency," in *Media and Conflict in the Twenty-First Century*, ed. Philip Seib (New York: Palgrave Macmillan, 2005), 120.

[16] Ibid., 120–121.

[17] Patrick Lee Plaisance, "The Propaganda War on Terrorism: An Analysis of the United States' 'Shared Values' Public-Diplomacy Campaign After September 11, 2001," *Journal of Mass Media Ethics* 20, no. 4 (2005): 263–264.

[18] Personal interview, March 23, 2007.

Condoleezza Rice and Colin Powell made similar arguments. Notwithstanding the sincerity of U.S. officials' belief that the adoption of American ideals and values would improve the lives of people throughout the world, such statements suggest that U.S. public diplomacy is intended to get people abroad to accept American ideals and values rather that to engage in a true dialogue in which the views and actions of American officials also might be adjusted.

So perhaps it should not be surprising that strong perceptual links between public diplomacy and propaganda endure. But the implications of allowing public diplomacy to continue to be equated with propaganda are significant. Before public diplomacy is fully accepted as a legitimate and indispensable national resource, ties—both rhetorical and real—between public diplomacy and its disfavored cousin "propaganda" must be severed.

4. *Prejudices against public diplomacy both in the diplomatic community and outside undermine public diplomacy efforts*

One of the biggest curiosities in American public diplomacy's history is the long-standing and pervasive lack of regard for the public dimensions of diplomacy among other diplomats. Even during the USIA's most successful era, the work of the agency was widely and routinely characterized as "useless" in the diplomatic community. When the public diplomacy functions were merged into the State Department in 1999, the situation did not improve. The U.S. Advisory Commission on Public Diplomacy's 2008 report clearly revealed both an enduring prejudice against public diplomacy and limited opportunities for career advancement for public diplomacy specialists within the U.S. government.

In fact, for some of the USIA officers who were transferred to the State Department, the situation became intolerable. In the words of one who made the transition, "I quit the job in frustration... and will never work in public diplomacy again. I view public diplomacy in the State Department as irreparably broken. State doesn't 'get' public diplomacy other than dealing with the press." Among several reasons the officer cited for leaving public diplomacy was that "working in public diplomacy was definitely perceived as less important than 'real' State Department work."[19]

[19] Former USIA officer; see Kathy R. Fitzpatrick, *USIA Alumni Study*, unpublished report, 2007.

Looking ahead, broad scale changes in diplomacy may help ease such tensions. Transformational shifts in global society are such that *all* diplomats must rethink their roles in the diplomatic affairs of nations and address the increasing importance of diplomacy's public role. As Paul Sharp and Geoffrey Wiseman observed in *The Diplomatic Corps as an Institution of International Society*, "As globalization gathers pace, diplomats and diplomacy are said to become irrelevant. International relations increasingly involve peoples and, indeed, people, rather than states. They are increasingly focused on what people as a whole care about, and every important technological development in the last century or so reinforces trends in this direction."[20]

As diplomats in the United States and elsewhere sort out their new roles and responsibilities in international relations, *public* diplomacy undoubtedly will be viewed as more important to a nation's ability to accomplish its foreign affairs objectives. But old prejudices die hard and it will take time for positive impressions of public diplomacy to form. For that reason, going forward, the roles and responsibilities of public diplomats must be clearly delineated.

If public diplomacy specialists are to be recognized as "professionals" and valued accordingly, then is it imperative that public diplomacy be recognized as a professional function requiring unique skills and special expertise. It also must be recognized that the retirements of hundreds of U.S. veteran practitioners in the years leading up to and after the dissolution of the USIA—many with decades of experience and multiple language capabilities—left a skeletal public diplomacy corps that will take years—if not decades—to replace. This significant loss of talent makes recruitment and retention of qualified public diplomacy professionals an even greater priority.

5. *Public diplomacy's policy advisory role is undervalued and underutilized*

A primary reason cited by U.S. officials for dissolving the USIA was to move public diplomacy closer to the heart of foreign policy making in the State Department.[21] But this move did little to secure a place for public diplomacy in policy formulation. In fact, government officials

[20] Paul Sharp and Geoffrey Wiseman, ed., *The Diplomatic Corps as an Institution of International Society* (Houndmills: Palgrave MacMillan), 270.

[21] See, e.g., White House Fact Sheet, December 30, 1998, http://www.fas.org/news/usa/1998/12/98123003_tlt.html (accessed January 10, 2009).

have been curiously slow in warming up to the idea that the (foreign) public implications of policy decisions and actions should be considered *before* decisions are made and actions are taken. This seems somewhat inexplicable given U.S. policy makers' keen awareness of the importance of cultivating domestic public support for policy agendas. Indeed, political operatives routinely counsel presidents and other officials on such matters.

But only two directors of the USIA—Edward R. Murrow and Charles A. Wick—played significant roles in advising U.S. leaders on the implications of U.S. decisions and actions among people abroad. And only one under secretary of public diplomacy—Karen Hughes—has been involved to a great extent in policy discussions after the dissolution of the agency. In each case, a close relationship with the president was cited as the reason for the involvement of public diplomacy in policy matters. The fact that their respective successors found themselves more excluded from policy making processes supports such thinking.

The sporadic involvement of public diplomacy in policy discussions does not bode well for either public diplomacy or the nation. As USIA veteran Walter Roberts observed, "The history of public diplomacy has conclusively shown that its success depended upon a country's policies. Even finely attuned public diplomacy programs would not and could not make much headway if they were accompanied by policies that are rejected by foreign publics."[22]

By silencing the voice of public diplomacy in policy matters, government leaders are effectively silencing the voices of foreign publics whose influence on the global environment is rapidly rising. As 9/11 tragically demonstrated, one way or another, they will make their views known. If public diplomacy is to fully contribute to national strategy, the policy advisory role of public diplomacy must be recognized and permanently built in to the foreign policy-making process.

At the same time, reluctance on the part of public diplomacy officials to become involved in policy making also must be addressed. Post-9/11 public diplomacy officials' narrow view of public diplomacy as primarily a promotional, communication function—rather than a policy advisement function—has limited opportunities for public diplomacy to play a significant role in policy matters. Future leaders

[22] Walter R. Roberts, "What Is Public Diplomacy? Past Practices, Present Conduct, Possible Future," *Mediterranean Quarterly* 18, no. 4 (2007): 51.

must recognize that for the nation to fully benefit from its public diplomacy resources, they must "do policy."

6. *Public diplomacy requires a permanent infrastructure that will support and sustain a robust public diplomacy operation over time; provide the flexibility and autonomy required to effectively conduct public diplomacy in the field; and be guided by long-term national (as opposed to short-term political) ideals and interests*

U.S. leaders have never been able to agree on an ideal structure for public diplomacy. For more than 50 years, public diplomacy functions have been shifted between the State Department, various government offices and the USIA. Indeed, the decision to dissolve the agency in 1999—which resulted in moving the information/advocacy and cultural/education functions back to the State Department (their original home) and spinning off international broadcasting into a quasi-independent entity—was the culmination of decades of debate over public diplomacy's proper place in foreign affairs. It quickly became apparent, however, that the merger didn't end the debate; rather, it simply set off a new debate that intensified in the wake of 9/11.

Numerous proposals have been offered for the restructuring of U.S. public diplomacy. Options range from rebuilding the USIA to outsourcing significant aspects of public diplomacy operations to private parties to reforming public diplomacy in the State Department. Such proposals illustrate the lack of consensus on what an ideal public diplomacy structure would look like.

The fact that public diplomacy's place in the national strategy—along with its component parts and strategic direction—have been revisited with successive administrations and successive public diplomacy leaders suggests that one of the most important aspects of advancing the nation's public diplomacy will be developing the infrastructure required to support and sustain a robust public diplomacy operation over time. This will require that the public diplomacy entity be focused on advancing *national* interests—rather than the ideals and values of successive administrations.

7. *A domestic constituency for public diplomacy is critical to securing public diplomacy's place in the foreign affairs establishment*

For nearly half a century, while the USIA was busy telling America's story abroad, no one was telling the USIA's story at home. As a result, when the future of the agency was being debated in Washington, the USIA had no domestic constituency to support its cause.

The U.S. State Department holds the official responsibility "to help Americans understand the importance of foreign affairs."[23] Yet, few resources have been committed to educating citizens about the role of public diplomacy in establishing and sustaining good relations for the United States with people abroad. Of course, the State Department historically has not been a champion of public diplomacy. At the same time, the Smith-Mundt Act passed in 1948, which prohibited the dissemination of U.S. public diplomacy materials directed at foreign publics within the United States, virtually guaranteed that U.S. citizens would be ignorant of both their country's efforts to engage with foreign publics and the reasons for doing so.

The national news media, which play a critical role in educating U.S. citizens about foreign affairs and the country's efforts in international relations, have been little help. The *New York Times* study cited above found that "U.S. public diplomacy may have been among the most under-reported stories of the past decade."[24] In examining the newspaper's reports on American public diplomacy, researchers found that prior to 9/11, public diplomacy "was rarely mentioned and never discussed in any detail."[25] Although post-9/11 coverage suggested an increased interest in public diplomacy as a news subject, "in-depth coverage was still lacking."[26] Overall, the study's authors concluded, the reports "likely had little influence on either the public diplomacy agenda or public understanding of the function."[27]

Going forward, a more ambitious effort to inform U.S. citizens about the importance of international relations generally and public diplomacy specifically will be needed. Efforts to involve American citizens in public diplomacy initiatives also must be improved. But before this can happen, government leaders themselves must be convinced that America's ability to advance its national interests requires the support of people beyond the country's borders.

8. *Public diplomacy's effectiveness is diminished by the lack of clearly defined principles of practice*

The U.S. government's post-9/11 efforts to "brand America" raised important questions about the strategic direction of public diplomacy

---

[23] See, e.g., U.S. Department of Public Affairs Overview, http://www.state.gov (accessed January 10, 2009).

[24] Fitzpatrick and Kosic, "The Missing Public in Public Diplomacy," 119.

[25] Ibid.

[26] Ibid.

[27] Ibid.

in the United States and other nations. Both the appropriateness and effectiveness of applying commercial marketing techniques to nations has since been the subject of global debate. At the heart of the matter is whether "nation branding" provides a sound strategic approach for public diplomacy initiatives. Although America's post-9/11 branding efforts suggest not, the relationship between nation branding and public diplomacy has not been fully explored.

As practitioners and scholars continue to investigate strategic options, the beliefs and assumptions that guide public diplomacy policies and practices require serious study. For example, principles of "mutuality," which were fundamental to the USIA's mission and are emphasized in discussions of the "new" public diplomacy (see Chapter Four), were virtually abandoned by U.S. public diplomacy officials in the post-9/11 environment in favor of more one-way, asymmetric approaches. As international relations scholar Alison Holmes observed about America's post-9/11 efforts, "Public diplomacy has become a by-word for defending the US against the views of others rather than engaging in discussion that might change the views of all those involved."[28]

Such shifts in strategic direction reveal a lack of consistency that could hinder future U.S. public diplomacy efforts. The emphasis on "messaging" and "American" interests also suggests a troublingly narrow view of public diplomacy as primarily an "information" function designed to get people abroad to adopt U.S. views and values. Clearly, correcting the public record and explaining U.S policies and actions to foreign publics are important. But a reliance on mass-mediated messages designed to advocate U.S. positions both undermines public diplomacy's mission and diminishes its effectiveness. Going forward, as public diplomacy principles of practice are refined, the focus should be on relational strategies that reflect the human dimensions of international relations and the need for "mutual" understanding and benefit.

9. *Public diplomacy's achievements must be documented*

History offers numerous examples—albeit mostly anecdotal—of situations in which public diplomacy helped to positively influence the

[28] Alison Holmes, "The Shifting Subtleties of 'Special': Differences in US and UK Approaches to Public Diplomacy in Business," *Journal of Business Strategy* 27, no. 3 (2006): 24.

attitudes of people abroad toward America.[29] Often cited are the international exchanges that brought today's foreign leaders to America in their youth and helped shape their views of the United States, its ideals and its values.

But empirical evidence of public diplomacy's effectiveness is lacking. Certainly, output—measured by tasks performed—is not a true measure of a public diplomacy program's impact. At the same time, only miniscule resources have been dedicated to research that could help demonstrate public diplomacy's success—about $3 million annually in recent years. These dollars historically have been used on public opinion polling and, while such polls are helpful in identifying public sentiment in various parts of the world,[30] additional research methods are needed to better understand not only what public opinion is but also *why* public opinion is what it is in specific locations. Additionally, the question of whether such polling provides adequate measures of public diplomacy's success in establishing and sustaining beneficial relationships with people abroad has not been seriously addressed.

A well-funded research program would allow public diplomacy officials to gather the data needed for both developing effective public diplomacy programs and for evaluating the success of those programs. In the absence of clear evidence of public diplomacy's effectiveness, government leaders are less likely to support the function. For example, during the Cold War, the existential threat was such that U.S. leaders *wanted* to believe it worked and, therefore, provided funding for public diplomacy efforts.[31] But once that existential threat was gone, support dwindled.

A similar cycle was evident after 9/11 when fears of additional terrorist attacks prompted Congress to provide supplemental resources for public diplomacy initiatives in the Middle East. Going forward, however, the meager funds earmarked for public diplomacy suggest little confidence on the part of U.S. policy makers in public diplomacy's ability to protect and advance the country's interests.

---

[29] See, e.g., Jarol B. Manheim, *Strategic Public Diplomacy and American Foreign Policy* (New York: Oxford University Press, 1994).

[30] See, e.g., *Public Diplomacy: Practitioners, Policy Makers, and Public Opinion, A Report of the Public Diplomacy and World Public Opinion Forum* (Los Angeles: USC Center on Public Diplomacy and Washington, DC: Pew Research Center, 2006).

[31] Personal interview with Thomas Switzer, May 3, 2006.

10. *Public diplomacy must be recognized as an integral part of a nation's broader diplomatic mission*

The U.S. State Department's inability to chart a coherent post-Cold War course significantly influenced the development and direction of U.S. public diplomacy and contributed to its decline in the period leading up to 9/11. The lack of a national diplomatic strategy, particularly at a time when the world was rapidly changing in ways that required more attention to diplomacy, was particularly harmful not only to public diplomacy but to the nation.

The failure of U.S. leaders to redefine foreign affairs objectives, requirements and processes in the post-Cold War period indicated a lack of appreciation for the important and expanding role of diplomacy in the "Information Age." In ignoring calls to adjust foreign affairs functions, strategies, and structures to the realities of a new time—and to respond to the increasing influence of nonstate actors in global affairs—U.S. leaders displayed a costly short-sightedness that has not yet been corrected.

Going forward, it should be recognized that public diplomacy plays an important role in advising government leaders on the public implications of decisions and actions and directing efforts to help nations develop beneficial relations with foreign publics. Public diplomacy also helps to prevent and/or diminish conflicts with people abroad and shape a global environment that is hospitable to the pursuit of national interests. But it also must be recognized that public diplomacy is only one cog in a nation's diplomatic machine. To be most effective, public diplomacy must be part of a national diplomatic mission that is clear and consistent—and reflective of a nation's fundamental ideals and values.

PART TWO

ADVANCING THE DEBATE

CHAPTER FOUR

UNDERSTANDING PUBLIC DIPLOMACY: TOWARD A COMMON IDENTITY

Public diplomacy is not providing information. It is building relationships.[1]

How is it, at a time when nations and peoples have become more interconnected and interdependent than at any time in the nation's history and America's image throughout the world has reached an all-time low, the U.S. government has not made public diplomacy a priority in the national strategy? Is it because U.S. leaders simply don't believe international relations—particularly relations with foreign *publics*—are important? Is it because U.S. leaders don't see the potential for public diplomacy to have any real effect on America's relations with people abroad—perhaps because of poorly conceptualized post-9/11 public diplomacy initiatives?

Or is it because public diplomacy advocates—practitioners, scholars, and others—have not made a persuasive case for public diplomacy's place in twenty-first century diplomacy? In other words, is it because those most interested in seeing public diplomacy succeed have been unable to convince government leaders and others that public diplomacy is important—even crucial—to determining a nation's fate in this new world?

The truth (as earlier chapters indicate) is that the state of U.S. public diplomacy today may be attributed to many factors—including the seeming inability of those who study and practice public diplomacy to adequately explain what public diplomacy is, how it works, and why it is important. But, if this emerging profession is to reach its full potential—both as a discipline and a diplomatic resource—it's time to start thinking more about such matters.

Of course, many aspects of public diplomacy have been examined. In fact, in discussing the many recommendations offered since 9/11 on

---

[1] Former USIA officer; see Kathy R. Fitzpatrick, *USIA Alumni Study*, unpublished report, 2007.

how to improve U.S. public diplomacy, Bruce Gregory suggested that the nation had reached the point of "report fatigue" on the subject.[2] However, little attention has been paid to the conceptual foundations of public diplomacy. Most researchers and writers—particularly post 9/11—have approached the topic from a practical perspective with a focus on strategic and tactical elements, looking at how to "fix" U.S. public diplomacy.[3] These are important matters. But few have examined the topic from a conceptual perspective, addressing the beliefs and assumptions that guide public diplomacy policies and practices.[4] As media scholar Robert Entman observed, "The literature on public diplomacy lacks a theoretical infrastructure."[5]

The lack of attention to the theoretical underpinnings of public diplomacy is not unique to the United States nor to U.S. writers. As the editors of *The Hague Journal of Diplomacy* observed in the first issue, diplomacy generally has been "under-theorized."[6] In *The Dynamics of Diplomacy*, Jean-Robert Leguey-Feilleux made a similar observation, noting that "there is no general theory of diplomacy or theoretical framework to facilitate systematic analysis." In fact, Leguey-Feilleux suggested, "The significant changes taking place in contemporary diplomatic practice are probably making the development of a general theory more difficult."[7]

---

[2] Bruce Gregory, "Not Your Grandparents' Public Diplomacy," paper presented at the Public Diplomacy Retreat, Department of Foreign Affairs, Ottawa, Canada, November 30, 2005.

[3] See, e.g., Anthony J. Blinken, "Winning the War of Ideas," *The Washington Quarterly* 25 (2002): 101–114; Peter G. Petersen, "Public Diplomacy and the War on Terrorism," *Foreign Affairs* 81 (2002): 74–94; Rosaleen Smyth, "Mapping U.S. Public Diplomacy in the 21st Century," *Australian Journal of International Affairs* 55 (2001): 421–444; Christopher Ross, "Public Diplomacy Comes of Age" *The Washington Quarterly* 25 (2002): 75–83; and Barry Fulton, "Taking the Pulse of American Public Diplomacy in a Post 9/11 World," paper presented at the Public Diplomacy Institute, Washington, DC, March 18, 2004.

[4] One notable exception is Getinet Belay, "Ethics in International Interaction: Perspectives on Diplomacy and Negotiation," in *Ethics in Intercultural and International Communication*, ed. Fred L. Casmir (Mahwah, NJ: Lawrence Erlbaum Publishers, 1997), 227–265.

[5] Robert M. Entman, "Theorizing Mediated Public Diplomacy: The U.S. Case," *The International Journal of Press/Politics* 13, no. 2 (2008): 87.

[6] Jan Melissen and Paul Sharp, "Editorial," The *Hague Journal of Diplomacy* 1 (2006): 1.

[7] Jean-Robert Leguey-Feilleux, *The Dynamics of Diplomacy* (Boulder, CO: Lynne Rienner Publishers, 2009), 11.

As public diplomacy assumes a more prominent role in international relations, however, there is a growing need to "clarify the essence and uniqueness of public diplomacy" in a country's diplomatic affairs.[8] In virtually every substantive work about public diplomacy, the authors observe the lack of a clear, concise, and generally accepted definition of public diplomacy.[9] Yet, as the proceedings of a recent international public diplomacy conference indicate, "[p]ublic diplomacy has entered the lexicon of twenty-first century diplomacy without clear definition of what it is or how the tools it offers might best be used."[10]

This chapter examines the confusion surrounding the concept of public diplomacy, looking at the factors that have contributed to the lack of conceptual clarity in the field and questions that must be addressed as the definition of public diplomacy is refined. It identifies the need for a common vocabulary that would contribute to the advancement of public diplomacy research and professional practice and considers the implications of diverse functional perspectives on public diplomacy practices.

An elusive concept

Admittedly, public diplomacy is not easily explained or understood. Even those who do public diplomacy have a hard time describing their work. For example, in commenting on the expanded interest in public diplomacy after 9/11, former U.S. State Department spokesperson Philip T. Reeker said that although U.S. public diplomacy specialists "had always bemoaned the fact that nobody knew what we were doing...suddenly there was this great interest and we were sort of stymied on how to describe what we were doing."[11]

In fact, public diplomacy practitioners are not alone in their struggle to define this unique instrument of statecraft.[12] Scholars and students

---

[8] Etyan Gilboa, "Searching for a Theory of Public Diplomacy," *The Annals of the American Academy of Political and Social Science* 616 (March 2008): 56.

[9] See, e.g., John Robert Kelley, "Between 'Take-Offs' and 'Crash Landings': Situational Aspects of Public Diplomacy," in *Routledge Handbook of Public Diplomacy*, ed. Nancy Snow and Philip M. Taylor (New York: Routledge, 2009), 72–85.

[10] Ann Lane, "Public Diplomacy: Key Challenges and Priorities," *Report on Wilton Park Conference* (West Sussex, UK: April 2006): 2.

[11] Personal interview, June 20, 2003.

[12] See Carnes Lord, *Losing Hearts and Minds? Public Diplomacy and Strategic Influence in the Age of Terror* (Westport, CT: Praeger Security International, 2006), 6–8.

of the discipline, as well as practitioners and government leaders, have been unable to agree on a universally accepted definition since the term was adopted in the 1970s in an effort to distance the work of the USIA from what historically had been known as "government propaganda." As Gregory observed, "Public diplomacy's meaning is evolving and contested" with no consensus on its analytical boundaries.[13]

Partly for this reason, most people don't really understand what public diplomacy is or why it is important. Another reason is that the nation's efforts in public diplomacy are barely visible to U.S. citizens and policymakers, thanks in part to a federal law that prohibits the dissemination of American public diplomacy materials within the United States.[14] As Hans Tuch pointed out, "Congress early on insisted on immunizing the American people from its own government's foreign information programs by limiting the government to telling its story abroad."[15] Finally, neither the State Department nor the U.S. news media has made any significant attempts to increase public understanding of the growing importance of foreign relations generally or public diplomacy specifically.[16]

Why does this matter? Because the absence of a clearly articulated—and widely understood and appreciated—function for public diplomacy in international relations stymies public diplomacy's professional and academic growth and development and threatens public diplomacy's future. Without clarity and agreement on public diplomacy's function and value, it is difficult to standardize policies and principles of practice; to determine effective operational structures, processes and strategies; to develop education and training programs designed to turn out qualified public diplomacy professionals; and to gain the institutional support needed to carry out the public diplomacy mission. As U.S. Foreign Service Officer Kenneth Wimmel advised more than four decades ago, "in the absence of a convincing and logically consistent explanation of what public diplomacy is, those who practice it risk

[13] Bruce Gregory, "Public Diplomacy: Sunrise of an Academic Field," *The Annals of the American Academy of Political and Social Science* 616 (March 2008): 274.

[14] United States Information and Educational Exchange (Smith-Mundt) Act, Public Law 90–4–02, ch. 36, 62 Stat. 9 (1948).

[15] Hans S. Tuch, "Why Americans Don't Appreciate Public Diplomacy," *Foreign Service Journal* (January 1991): 11.

[16] See Kathy Fitzpatrick and Tamara Kosic, "The Missing Public in Public Diplomacy, in *Media and Conflict in the Twenty-First Century*, ed. Philip Seib (New York: Palgrave MacMillan, 2005), 106–125.

being regarded as propagandists—in the worst sense of the word—on the one hand, or on the other hand as people engaged in an undertaking of questionable futility which fulfills no demonstrated need and lacks any legitimate purpose."[17]

More importantly, the lack of widespread understanding of public diplomacy diminishes the nation's ability to accomplish its foreign affairs objectives. By relying primarily on the military to advance American foreign policy and interests in the post-9/11 environment, for example, the United States has failed to fully tap one of its most important strategic resources.

What to call it

Even the descriptor itself—"public diplomacy"—is the subject of some debate, illustrating that "naming is part of a struggle over meaning."[18] Though prominent in discussions of government efforts to burnish national reputations and images abroad, the term "public diplomacy" is not universally loved or accepted. For example, when the USIA Alumni Association changed its name to the Public Diplomacy Alumni Association in 2008 in an effort to attract more members, it encountered considerable resistance from some of its long-time associates.[19]

A number of alternatives to "public diplomacy" have been suggested, including "political communication," "political advocacy," "international communication," "intercultural communication," "international public relations," "international information," "cultural diplomacy," "media diplomacy," and "nation branding." Another term that has gained some popularity is "strategic communication," which many see as encompassing the full range of a government's efforts to communicate with foreign publics. For example, in *Joint Forces Quarterly*, Jeffrey Jones defined "strategic communication" as the "synchronized coordination of statecraft, public affairs, public diplomacy, military

---

[17] Kenneth Wimmel, "What Is Public Diplomacy?," *Foreign Service Journal* (October 1978): 31–44; quoted in "Comments and Correspondence," *Foreign Affairs* 60, no. 1 (Fall 1981): 190.

[18] Bruce Gregory, "Public Diplomacy and Strategic Communication: Cultures, Firewalls, and Imported Norms," paper presented at the American Political Science Association Conference on International Communication and Conflict, Washington, DC, August 31, 2005.

[19] Personal interview with Eugene Nojek, March 7, 2008.

information operations, and other activities, reinforced by political, economic, military, and other actions, to advance U.S. foreign policy interests."[20]

In proposing that "strategic communication" is analogous to public diplomacy, Gregory defined "strategic communication" as "a variety of instruments used by governments...to *understand* global attitudes and cultures, *engage* in a dialogue of ideas between people and institutions, *advise* policymakers, diplomats, and military leaders on the public opinion implications of policy choices, and *influence* attitudes and behaviors through communication strategies."[21]

Creating some confusion on the potential for "strategic communication" to replace "public diplomacy," the editor of a recently published handbook of public diplomacy stated that U.S. public diplomacy had been "renamed" "strategic communication" in 2006–2007 and indicated that the two terms may be used interchangeably.[22]

According to Jan Melissen, a reason to stay with the term "public diplomacy" is that it "reinforces the view that the public is part of the wider process by which states and others represent themselves and their interests to one another. PD is in other words not a stand alone phenomenon, and by now means not the mere application of new techniques of marketing, advertising, media management or spin doctoring to the conduct of international relations, but is an expression of broader patterns of change in diplomacy."[23]

The important point here is that continuing debate over the descriptor "public diplomacy"—and the fact that many other terms are viewed as analogous to "public diplomacy" and used accordingly—contributes to the confusion surrounding the function, further hindering efforts to enhance understanding of public diplomacy.

---

[20] Jeffrey Jones, "Strategic Communications: A Mandate for the United States," *Joint Forces Quarterly*, no. 39, May 29, 2008, www.dtic.mil/doctrine/jel/jfq_pubs/1839.pdf (accessed June 6, 2006); see also Ken S. Heller and Liza M. Persson, "The Distinction Between Public Affairs and Public Diplomacy," in Snow and Taylor, ed. *Routledge Handbook of Public Diplomacy*, 225.

[21] Bruce Gregory, "Now That It's a Part of a Global Conversation, Should We Keep the Term Public Diplomacy?," paper presented at the Centre for International Governance Innovation Conference, Wilton Park, Sussex, UK, June 23–24, 2006.

[22] See Philip M. Taylor, "Public Diplomacy and Strategic Communication," in Snow and Taylor, ed. *Routledge Handbook of Public Diplomacy*, 15–16.

[23] Jan Melissen, "Public Diplomacy Between Theory and Practice, The Present and Future of Public Diplomacy: A European Perspective," paper presented at the Madrid Conference on Public Diplomacy, Madrid, Spain, October 10, 2006.

Interdisciplinary perspectives

Scholars and practitioners approach public diplomacy from diverse perspectives. According to Etyan Gilboa, "This field is probably one of the most multidisciplinary areas in modern scholarship."[24] Diplomatic studies, political science, international relations, public relations, international communication, media studies, marketing and advertising are all represented in the public diplomacy literature. In each case, scholars and practitioners see public diplomacy through the lens with which they are most familiar. For example, political scientists and politicians see public diplomacy through a political lens. Public relations scholars and practitioners see public diplomacy through a relational lens. Marketing and advertising scholars see public diplomacy through a promotional lens. Diplomacy scholars see public diplomacy through a foreign policy lens.

Certainly, interdisciplinary study of public diplomacy is a good thing. The public diplomacy literature is enriched by diverse perspectives on matters of common interest. However, the wide-ranging perspectives make reaching agreement on even the most fundamental aspects of public diplomacy difficult.

"Old" versus "new" public diplomacy

Complicating the definitional picture further is the emergence of what some public diplomacy scholars and practitioners call a "new" public diplomacy that is distinguished from its historical counterpart. The "new" public diplomacy incorporates what are widely viewed as the diplomatic imperatives of an increasingly interdependent global society in which events occurring in one nation reverberate across borders, and nonstate actors have become more prominent and powerful in world affairs. In such an environment, a nation's ability to establish and sustain supportive relationships with nonstate actors is a critical component of its diplomatic strategy for protecting and advancing national interests.

The new public diplomacy reflects a perceived need for greater collaboration and cooperation among nations and peoples by emphasizing

---

[24] Eytan Gilboa, "Media Diplomacy: Conceptual Divergence and Applications," *The Harvard International Journal of Press/Politics* 3, no. 3 (1998): 56.

principles of mutuality and dialogue. Traditionally, it is suggested, public diplomacy has been viewed and used as "an attempt at manipulation of foreign publics"[25] through communication designed to garner support among people abroad for a particular nation's foreign policies, ideals, and values. The communication taking place under the old public diplomacy paradigm is described as one-way and asymmetric in the sense that it is designed to influence the attitudes of foreign publics but not necessarily those of the sponsoring nation. According to communications scholar Mohan J. Dutta-Bergman, "Central to [traditional] public diplomacy is the objective of influencing the receiver countries without being open to persuasion."[26]

Gilboa pointed out that traditional public diplomacy, which he suggested has been used primarily in antagonistic relationships, "seeks to create a favorable image for a country's policies, actions, and political and economic system, assuming that if public opinion in the target society is persuaded to accept that image, it will exert pressure on its government to alter existing hostile attitudes and policy."[27] According to Gilboa, the goal of "classic" public diplomacy in most cases is "to create a favourable image of a nation's policies, actions, and political and economic system." In other cases, goals might be to encourage domestic pressure on a government to alter its policies and/or, in extreme cases, produce regime change.[28]

Under the old public diplomacy paradigm, such programs are explained as being "pushed out to target audiences."[29] According to Shaun Riordan, there is "no space" in this approach for the engagement of foreign publics in genuine debate.[30] Public diplomacy professionals operating under the "old" approach essentially serve as mouthpieces of their respective governments, and foreign publics are viewed as "targets" of public diplomacy efforts.

---

[25] Jan Melissen, *The New Public Diplomacy: Soft Power in International Relations* (Houndmills: Palgrave MacMillan, 2005), 11.

[26] Mohan J. Dutta-Bergman, "U.S. Public Diplomacy in the Middle East: A Critical Cultural Approach," *Journal of Communication Inquiry* 30, no. 2 (April 2006): 109.

[27] Gilboa, "Media Diplomacy," 56.

[28] Eytan Gilboa, "Public Diplomacy: The Missing Component in Israel's Foreign Policy," *Israel Affairs* 12, no. 4 (October 2006): 717.

[29] Christopher Ross, "Public Diplomacy Comes of Age," *The Washington Quarterly* 25, no. 2 (Spring 2002): 82.

[30] Shaun Riordan, *The New Diplomacy* (Cambridge, UK: Polity, 2003), 121.

"Messages, in so far as they exist," said Riordan, "are simply exercises in propaganda, designed to demonstrate the superiority of a given nation's position."[31] The intent is to develop positive views of the sponsoring nation among people abroad and to persuade them to support the sponsoring nation's views and interests. According to Riordan, the basic premise is "that by engaging in a country's political and social debates, you can create the intellectual and political climate in which your specific policies can flourish."[32]

The new public diplomacy is explained as "[moving] away from—to put it crudely—peddling information to foreigners and keeping the foreign press at bay, towards engaging with foreign audiences."[33] In that respect, Melissen suggested, the new public diplomacy is not only about promoting policy but is also about involving and consulting other players in the policy development process. According to the University of Southern California (USC) Center on Public Diplomacy, the new public diplomacy "starts from the premise that dialogue, rather than a sales pitch, is often central to achieving the goals of foreign policy."[34] As Gilboa described it, the new public diplomacy is "a communication system designed to create a dialogue with both foes and allies."[35]

While some equate the old public diplomacy with propaganda campaigns intended to manipulate public opinion or "narrow people's minds,"[36] Melissen contended that the new public diplomacy is different: "It is similar to propaganda in that it tries to persuade people what to think, but it is fundamentally different from it in the sense that public diplomacy also listens to what people have to say."[37]

Another aspect of the "new" public diplomacy that distinguishes it from the "old" public diplomacy is the view that public diplomacy is not an inherently government enterprise. "New" public diplomacy advocates reject the idea that public diplomacy is a uniquely

[31] Ibid.

[32] Ibid., 122.

[33] Melissen, *The New Public Diplomacy*, 13.

[34] *Center Overview* (Los Angeles, CA: USC Center for Public Diplomacy, 2006).

[35] Gilboa, Public Diplomacy," 718.

[36] See, e.g., Mohan J. Bergman, "U.S. Public Diplomacy in the Middle East," 116, in which Dutta-Bergman argued that "traditional public diplomacy efforts that are theorized and practiced with the domain of influencing the members of the receiver culture through the manipulation of symbols constitute propaganda."

[37] Melissen, *The New Public Diplomacy*, 18.

state activity, citing the active participation of nonstate international actors, e.g., NGOs and corporations, in efforts to burnish the images of nations abroad. In contemplating the inclusion of nonstate actors in the definition of public diplomacy going forward, USIA veteran Walter R. Roberts pointed out that it would be the second time the definition of "diplomacy" has been expanded since "public diplomacy" was included to describe official contacts with foreign publics.[38]

To some degree, discussions of "old" and "new" public diplomacy have interfered with efforts to bring conceptual clarity to the field. Although descriptions of the "new" public diplomacy—particularly the greater emphasis on mutuality and dialogue—accurately reflect the changing nature of diplomatic requirements, both advocacy and engagement are important components of contemporary public diplomacy. In noting the perceived need to move from a monologue to a dialogue-based public diplomacy, for example, Geoffrey Cowan and Amelia Arsenault identified three "layers" of public diplomacy—monologue, dialogue, and collaboration—that, they contended, are *all* required to accomplish public diplomacy objectives. Acknowledging that each layer has strengths and limitations, they contended, "In a world of economic, political, and cultural interdependence, monologue, dialogue, and collaboration, when appropriately practiced, are all essential tools for public diplomacy, both online and offline."[39]

Additionally, there is some question about whether historic public diplomacy practices fall neatly into the "old" public diplomacy category and—notwithstanding the normative nature of "new" public diplomacy discussions—whether contemporary practices fall neatly into the "new" public diplomacy category. For example, the *USIA Alumni Study* provided considerable evidence that USIA officers viewed dialogue and engagement as central to their work. Post-9/11 U.S. public diplomacy initiatives, on the other hand, have been primarily focused on one-way messaging activities.

[38] Walter R. Roberts, "What Is Public Diplomacy?, Past Practices, Present Conduct, Possible Future," *Mediterranean Quarterly* 18, no. 4 (Fall 2007): 46.

[39] Geoffrey Cowan and Amelia Arsenault, "Moving from Monologue to Dialogue to Collaboration: The Three Layers of Public Diplomacy," *The Annals of the American Academy of Political and Social Science* 616 (March 2008): 27.

Functional perspectives

A recent review of the scholarly and professional public diplomacy literature showed that scholars and practitioners hold diverse perspectives on the primary function of public diplomacy.[40] The study, which involved the review of more than 150 definitional statements of public diplomacy, identified six functional categories, which represent distinct ways of thinking about and practicing public diplomacy: 1) advocacy/influence, 2) communication/informational, 3) relational, 4) promotional, 5) warfare/propaganda, and 6) political.

Notably, these categories are not mutually exclusive, meaning that some definitions of public diplomacy incorporate multiple perspectives. Additionally, while the categories help to distinguish among different approaches to public diplomacy, a definitional emphasis on one aspect of public diplomacy does not necessarily preclude recognition of the importance of other aspects. Thus, the value of such study lies not in an effort to quantify the definitions in various categories, but rather in the discovery of conceptual distinctions that have implications for the study and practice of public diplomacy.

The advocacy/influence perspective of public diplomacy rests on the assumption that public diplomacy's function is to influence the attitudes, opinions, and behaviors of foreign publics. As an example, Ben Mor wrote that public diplomacy "seeks to persuade foreign elites and publics that the values, policies, and actions of the state deserve their—and their government's—support."[41]

Those who approach public diplomacy from a communication/informational perspective see public diplomacy as a nation's communication with citizens of other nations to inform and educate them about a nation and its policies, ideals, and values. As an example, a widely-quoted definition offered by Tuch is: "a government's process of communicating with foreign publics."[42]

A relational perspective of public diplomacy rests on the belief that public diplomacy's function is to establish and sustain beneficial

---

[40] See Kathy R. Fitzpatrick, "Understanding Public Diplomacy: Toward a Common Identity." Paper presented at the annual conference of the International Studies Association, New York, New York, February 17, 2009.

[41] Ben D. Mor, "Public Diplomacy in Grand Strategy," *Foreign Policy Analysis* 2 (2006): 157.

[42] Hans S. Tuch, *Communicating with the World: U.S. Public Diplomacy Overseas* (New York: St. Martin's Press, 1990), 3.

relations with people in other countries. As an example, British diplomat Mark Leonard emphasized that "[p]ublic diplomacy should be about building relationships."[43]

A promotional perspective of public diplomacy suggests that public diplomacy's function is to promote or "sell" particular aspects of a nation to foreign publics. Often, a promotional view deals with matters related to tourism, trade and investment. But it also applies to promotion of a country's ideas, ideals, values, culture, and policies. As an example, public diplomacy scholar Nancy Snow described public diplomacy as efforts "to market a more positive image of America to the world."[44] The Business for Diplomatic Action, a group that supports a role for business in public diplomacy, also depicted public diplomacy as a promotional function, indicating that public diplomacy is a means "to promote positive, credible perceptions of the United States in the minds of the world's citizens."[45]

A political perspective of public diplomacy reflects a view of public diplomacy as a political instrument. For example, former USIA officer Donna Marie Oglesby described public diplomacy as "the way in which [a] nation engages in international politics."[46]

Those adopting a warfare/propaganda perspective of public diplomacy view it as an instrument of national security used to support and/or complement military efforts. For example, in *Losing Hearts and Minds? Public Diplomacy and Strategic Influence in the Age of Terror*, Carnes Lord defined public diplomacy as "psychological, political warfare."[47]

The practical implications of these functional distinctions may be significant. For example, public diplomacy programs guided by an advocacy/influence perspective may be more likely to emphasize

[43] Mark Leonard, "Diplomacy by Other Means," *Foreign Policy*, no. 132 (September/October 2002): 48–56.

[44] Nancy Snow, *The Arrogance of American Power: What U.S. Leaders Are Doing Wrong and Why It's Our Duty to Dissent* (Lanham, MD: Rowman & Littlefield Publishers, Inc., 2007), 209.

[45] Business for Diplomatic Action, *America's Role in the World: A Business Perspective on Public Diplomacy* (San Francisco, October 2007), http://74.125.45.132/search?q=cache:b1qu0TC1ZX0J:www.businessfordiplomaticaction.org/action/a_business_perspective_on_public_diplomacy_10_2007_approvedfinal.pdf+business+for+diplomatic+action+and+america%27s+role+in+the+world&hl=en&ct=clnk&cd=1&gl=us (accessed January 10, 2009).

[46] Donna Marie Oglesby, "A Pox on Both Our Houses," paper presented at the Political Communication Pre-conference on International Communication and Conflict, Washington, DC, August 31, 2005.

[47] Lord, *Losing Hearts and Minds?*, 8.

self-interested, political objectives, rather than relational objectives designed to address common concerns and shared interests. Similarly, those who approach public diplomacy from a promotional perspective may recommend media campaigns designed to "sell" national policies, ideals and/or values to foreign publics. The objective in both cases likely would be to get people abroad to adopt the sponsoring nation's ideas, views, and values rather than to accommodate others' ideas, views, and values.

On the other hand, those who approach public diplomacy from a relational perspective may be more likely to recognize the need for dialogue and engagement with foreign publics, as well as the importance of negotiation and compromise, in efforts to advance mutual interests. Programs based on a relational perspective also may be more likely to emphasize interactive, people-to-people communication initiatives and stress mutual understanding and benefits in policies and practices.

Those who approach public diplomacy from a communication/informational perspective may be more likely to accept technical responsibilities than to seek a professional advisory role. Finally, those who view public diplomacy through a political lens or a warfare/propaganda lens may over-emphasize "war" objectives at the expense of other objectives. In such cases, the marginalization of a nation's public diplomacy resources likely would occur, as was the case in the United States after the end of the Cold War.

Definitional chaos

The definitional analysis cited here also demonstrated considerable confusion about how public diplomacy's function, purpose, and strategies are distinguished. What some view as the function of public diplomacy, others see as either a strategy or purpose. As an example, the following statements illustrate the use of "communication" as a function, strategy and purpose, respectively:

Function: "Public diplomacy is the communication of U.S. interests and ideals beyond governments to foreign publics."[48]

Strategy: "[Public diplomacy] supplements and reinforces traditional intergovernmental diplomacy, seeking to strengthen mutual

[48] U.S. Advisory Commission on Public Diplomacy, *Public Diplomacy for the 21st Century* (Washington, DC, 1995): 4.

understanding between peoples through a wide variety of international communication and educational and cultural exchange programs."[49]

Purpose: "[T]he goal of public diplomacy is to achieve communication between nation-states."[50]

Such examples illustrate the confusion caused by definitions suggesting that public diplomacy *is* communication rather than *uses* communication to accomplish its goals and objectives. They also demonstrate that public diplomacy should not be defined either by its objectives or by the strategies it employs. Given the diverse needs and interests of nations, and the particular circumstances in various parts of the world, public diplomacy objectives will encompass a range of desired outcomes and require multiple strategies.

Toward a common identity

It seems clear that an important step in the advancement of public diplomacy will be the development of a clear and concise—and enduring—framework for understanding public diplomacy that is relevant and meaningful for all those involved in the study and practice of public diplomacy. At the same time, some have questioned whether the development of a universal definition of public diplomacy is either possible or desirable given the nature of the function and the youth of the discipline.

In debating this matter, scholars and practitioners must weigh any perceived advantages of continuing to operate without definitional clarity against the need for a workable and generally accepted definition that would guide systematic research and professional development of the field and its practitioners. They also must consider the consequences of allowing public diplomacy to continue to be widely misunderstood—and redefined by the shifting priorities and ambitions of successive administrations. The U.S. experience in public diplomacy is case in point here.

While it may be premature to attempt consensus on a single statement that precisely defines the parameters of public diplomacy, it is

[49] U.S. Advisory Commission on Public Diplomacy, *Report 1980* (Washington, DC, 1980): inside front cover.

[50] Mohan J. Dutta-Bergman, "U.S. Public Diplomacy in the Middle East, 104.

time to address important definitional issues that will influence public diplomacy's future growth and development. Toward that end, in addition to clarifying the central function of public diplomacy, the following four questions should be considered:

What is/are the purpose(s) of public diplomacy?

Although the public diplomacy literature indicates a range of views on this matter, the majority view appears to be that public diplomacy's purpose is the advance national interests and values. As an example, James Glassman said that public diplomacy's mission is "the achievement of the national interest."[51]

Others have suggested that public diplomacy's purpose is to influence the knowledge, attitudes, and actions of foreign publics. For example, former U.S. Ambassador Christopher Ross described public diplomacy as government efforts "to shape mindsets abroad."[52] In providing what he called a European perspective on public diplomacy, Philip Fiske de Gouveia offered a similar view: "The purpose of this, ideally two-way, engagement is generally to influence attitudes towards the government's country so as to encourage tourism and inward investment, and to facilitate, for example, closer political ties or alliances."[53]

Still others have suggested that the purpose of public diplomacy is to enhance international understanding and/or relations. As an example, Tuch wrote that the purpose of public diplomacy is "to bring about understanding for its nation's ideas and ideals, its institutions and culture, as well as its national goals and current policies."[54] Social scientist Daniel Yankelovich similarly observed that U.S. public diplomacy's goal "is to improve perceptions and understanding between the people of the United States and the people of other countries."[55]

---

[51] James Glassman, speech at the Council on Foreign Relations, Washington, DC, July 2, 2008, http://www.america.gov/st/texttrans-english/2008/July/20080702123054xjsnommis0.3188745.html (accessed January 10, 2009).

[52] Christopher Ross, "Pillars of Public Diplomacy," *Harvard International Review* (Summer 2003): 22.

[53] Philip Fiske de Gouveia, "The Future of Public Diplomacy," paper presented at Madrid Conference on Public Diplomacy, Madrid, Spain, October 10, 2006.

[54] Tuch, *Communicating with the World*, 3.

[55] Daniel Yankelovich, *Making Public Diplomacy Work* (1977): 4, unpublished report quoted in Allen C. Hansen, *USIA: Public Diplomacy in the Computer Age* (Second Edition) (New York: Praeger, 1989), 2.

The purpose of public diplomacy also has been described as being to influence the policies and actions of foreign governments and/or to advance foreign policy. For example, In *Organizing the Nation's Public Diplomacy*, Gifford Malone wrote, "The objective, in most cases, is to influence the behavior of a foreign government."[56] The 2005 report of the U.S. Advisory Commission identified a single "core goal" for public diplomacy: "to advance policies."[57]

Still others have suggested that public diplomacy's purpose is to influence the international environment of opinion. For example, Wilson Dizard stated that public diplomacy is intended "to influence world public opinion."[58]

Others view public diplomacy's purpose as being the advancement of national security. For example, former U.S. Ambassador Edward P. Djerejian defined public diplomacy as "the way the U.S. communicates its values and policies to enhance our national security."[59]

According to others, public diplomacy's purpose is to enhance national image. As an example, public diplomacy scholar Javier Noya stated that public diplomacy is "aimed at impacting positively on a country's image and perception abroad."[60]

Still others have suggested that the purpose of public diplomacy is to increase "soft power." Former U.S. Ambassador Pamela Hyde Smith, for example, stated that public diplomacy "succeeds when it accurately reflects and advocates a government's policies and amplifies a nation's soft power"[61]

Finally, public diplomacy's purpose also has been defined as to promote democracy. According to the 1990 annual report of the U.S.

---

[56] Gifford Malone, *Organizing the Nation's Public Diplomacy* (Lanham, MD: University Press of America, 1988), 3.

[57] U.S. Advisory Commission on U.S. Public Diplomacy, Report of the Advisory Commission on Public Diplomacy (Washington, DC, 2005), www.state.gov/r/adcompd/rls/55903.htm (accessed January 9, 2008).

[58] Wilson P. Dizard Jr., *Inventing Public Diplomacy: The Story of the U.S. Information Agency* (Boulder: Lynne Rienner Publishers, 2004), 4.

[59] Edward P. Djerejian "A New Strategic Direction for U.S. Public Diplomacy in the Arab & Muslim World," (Washington, DC: Advisory Group on Public Diplomacy for the Arab and Muslim World, 2003): 8.

[60] Javier Noya, "The United States and Europe: Convergence or Divergence in Public Diplomacy?," paper presented at the Madrid Conference on Public Diplomacy, Madrid, Spain, October 10, 2006.

[61] Pamela Hyde Smith, "The Hard Road Back to Soft Power," *Georgetown Journal of International Affairs* (Winter/Spring 2007): 3.

Advisory Commission on Public Diplomacy, public diplomacy supports one fundamental policy goal—"to promote democracy."[62]

What actors are/should be included in/excluded from the list of entities/ individuals that/who engage in the conduct of public diplomacy?

A central issue here is whether public diplomacy is an inherently government function, as some have argued, or whether it includes the "diplomatic" actions of nonstate actors, as others have contended. Reflecting the "government" perspective, the U.S. Department of State *Dictionary of International Relations Terms* defined public diplomacy as "government-sponsored programs intended to inform or influence public opinion in other countries."[63]

On the other hand, Cowan and Cull suggested that public diplomacy involves "an international actor's attempt to advance the ends of policy by engaging with foreign publics."[64] Business scholar Michael Goodman similarly indicated that public diplomacy includes "the country to country interaction and intercultural communication of private groups such as businesses."[65] Notably, the first usage of the term "public diplomacy" by Edward Gullion at Tufts University in 1965 incorporated private parties in its definition of the term, stating that public diplomacy includes "the interaction of private groups and interests in one country with those of another."[66]

Who are/should be the targeted public(s) of public diplomacy?

One issue on which there appears to be widespread agreement is that public diplomacy involves foreign, as opposed to domestic publics. An example that illustrates a common view is provided by the Council on Foreign Relations, which defined public diplomacy as "programs and efforts designed to explain and advocate U.S. values

[62] United States Advisory Commission on Public Diplomacy, *Public Diplomacy in a New Europe* (Washington, DC, 1990), 6.

[63] U.S. Department of State, *Dictionary of International Relations Terms* (Washington, D.C., 1987), 85.

[64] Geoffrey Cowan and Nicholas J. Cull, "Public Diplomacy in a Changing World," *The Annals of the American Academy of Political and Social Science* 616 (March 2008): 6.

[65] Michael B. Goodman, "The Role of Business in Public Diplomacy, *Journal of Business Strategy* 27, no. 3 (2006): 5.

[66] "What Is Public Diplomacy?" Edward R. Murrow Center for Public Diplomacy, http://fletcher.tufts.edu/murrow/public-diplomacy.html (accessed January 9, 2009).

and policies directly to foreign publics."[67] Others descriptors falling into the category of "foreign publics" were "foreign audiences," "people in the world," "people of other countries," "foreign publics," "foreign peoples," "foreign citizens," "general public abroad," "societies," "polity," "foreign populations," "the public at large," "individuals and organizations overseas," "publics affiliated with nation states" and "overseas audiences."

At the same time, there is some discussion about whether target publics should be more narrowly defined. For example, John Brown has suggested a more narrow focus, describing public diplomacy as "the art of engaging, informing and influencing key international audiences."[68] Others have made the point that the ultimate public of public diplomacy is not foreign citizens, but foreign leaders and policy makers who are influenced by the citizens of their respective nations. For example, Howard H. Frederick wrote in *Global Communication and International Relations* that public diplomacy "describes activities, directed abroad in the fields of information, education, and culture whose objective is to influence a foreign government, by influencing its citizens."[69]

Whose interests are/should be served by public diplomacy?

There is broad agreement among scholars and practitioners that the interest(s) served by public diplomacy are the interests of the sponsoring government or entity. As an example, Michael Butler, former British permanent representative to the European Union, observed that public diplomacy is intended "to influence opinion in target countries to make it easier for the British government, British companies or other British organizations to achieve their aims."[70]

However, there is also increasing recognition—particularly in discussions concerning the "new" public diplomacy—of the need for public diplomacy to also address the interests of targeted foreign publics. As

[67] "Executive Summary," *Finding America's Voice: A Strategy for Reinvigorating U.S. Public Diplomacy: Report of an Independent Task Force* (New York: Council on Foreign Relations, June 2003): 1.

[68] John Brown, "Public Diplomacy During the Cold War," *Georgetown Journal of International Affairs* 6, no. 1 (Winter/Spring, 2005).

[69] Howard H. Frederick, *Global Communication and International Relations* (Belmont, CA: Wadsworth, 1993), 229.

[70] Sr. Michael Butler, quoted in Mark Leonard, *Public Diplomacy*, 1.

an example, Stephen Johnson and Helle Dale of The Heritage Foundation explained that public diplomacy "encourages mutual understanding and cooperation between a nation and foreign publics by identifying its institutions and activities with those publics' interests."[71]

While the answers to all these questions will help determine future directions in public diplomacy, the most important may be the last—Whose interests are/should be served by public diplomacy? The issue of interests gets at the heart of what public diplomacy is (or should be) all about and reveals the conceptual underpinnings that guide public diplomacy policies and practices.

---

[71] Stephen Johnson and Helle Dale, "How to Reinvigorate U.S. Public Diplomacy," *Backgrounder* (Washington, DC: The Heritage Foundation, April 23, 2003).

CHAPTER FIVE

CONCEPTUAL FOUNDATIONS: FROM WIELDING SOFT POWER TO MANAGING MUTUAL BENEFIT

Public diplomacy is inevitably linked to power.[1]

The importance of public diplomacy is often summed up with two words: "soft power." It is argued that public diplomacy's value lies in helping a nation acquire "soft power," or "the ability to get others to want the outcome you want because of your cultural or ideological appeal."[2] According to Harvard Dean and political scientist Joseph S. Nye, Jr., who coined the phrase, "soft power" is the ability of a nation "to shape the preferences of others" in ways that advance national interests.[3]

The concept of soft power has been widely adopted to explain the rise of public diplomacy in the United States and other nations. The title of a widely quoted book in which prominent international scholars assess the increasing importance of public diplomacy illustrates: *The New Public Diplomacy: Soft Power in International Relations.* Jan Melissen, the editor, wrote that "[p]ublic diplomacy is one of soft power's key instruments."[4] In the same volume, Brian Hocking observed that both the "limitations of hard, or military, power and the advantages that can accrue from the use of 'attractive' power rooted in factors such as culture, ideals and values, which, it is argued, encourages others to want what you want, are *basic assumptions* among advocates of an enhanced role for public diplomacy [*emphasis added*]."[5]

---

[1] Nancy Snow, "Rethinking Public Diplomacy," in *Routledge Handbook of Public Diplomacy*, ed. Nancy Snow and Philip M. Taylor (New York: Routledge, 2009), 3.

[2] Joseph S. Nye, Jr., *Soft Power: The Means to Success in World Politics* (New York: PublicAffairs, 2004), 11.

[3] Ibid., 5.

[4] Jan Melissen, "The New Public Diplomacy: Between Theory and Practice," in *The New Public Diplomacy: Soft Power in International Relations*, ed. Jan Melissen (Houndmills: Palgrave MacMillan, 2005), 4.

[5] Brian Hocking, "Rethinking the 'New' Public Diplomacy," in Melissen, *The New Public Diplomacy*, 33.

In fact, soft power has become broadly accepted as the dominant conceptual paradigm of contemporary public diplomacy. For example, in laying out the fundamental elements of the "new" public diplomacy, Etyan Gilboa proposed that they should include that "it is based on soft power."[6] In commenting on post-9/11 U.S. efforts in public diplomacy, Rhonda Zaharna suggested that "[p]ublic diplomacy is the vehicle nation-states employ to wield soft power resources to influence others in the international arena."[7] Wilson Dizard wrote that in this new era, "soft power" is "the major factor influencing the role of U.S. public diplomacy."[8] Summarizing increasingly popular views, political scientist Jozef Batora observed that public diplomacy "comprises all activities by state and non-state actors that contribute to the maintenance and promotion of a country's soft power."[9]

Soft power does have some critics.[10] For example, in questioning the linkages between soft power and public diplomacy, Hocking suggested a need to "re-examine 'soft power' argumentation with which much of the public diplomacy debate has become entwined."[11] He pointed to the influence of "realist models of public diplomacy as propaganda" on post-9/11 U.S. public diplomacy practices, suggesting that "preoccupations" with public diplomacy after 9/11 may "lead to the danger of misunderstanding the significance of public diplomacy and confusing its role as a mode of exercising power with the changing environments in which power is projected."[12] Hocking noted that "public diplomacy may be more important than we realize, but not always in the ways sometimes assumed."[13]

Others, too, have observed problems with the soft power paradigm. Yin Fan, for example, questioned the perceived link between

---

[6] Etyan Gilboa, "Public Diplomacy: The Missing Component in Israel's Foreign Policy," *Israel Affairs* 12, no. 4 (October 2006): 718.

[7] Rhonda S. Zaharna, "The Network Communication Paradigm: Creating Soft Power in a Global Communication Era," paper presented at the annual conference of the International Studies Association, Chicago, IL, February 29, 2007.

[8] Wilson P. Dizard Jr., *Inventing Public Diplomacy: The Story of the U.S. Information Agency* (Boulder, CO: Lynne Rienner Publishers, Inc., 2004), 227.

[9] Quoted in Gilboa, "Public Diplomacy: The Missing Component in Israel's Foreign Policy," 719.

[10] See, e.g., Barry M. Blechman, "Book Review: Nye's *Soft Power*," *Political Science Quarterly* 119, no. 4 (2005): 680–681; Niall Ferguson, "Power," *Foreign Policy* 134 (2003): 18–24.

[11] Hocking, "Rethinking the 'New' Public Diplomacy," 28.

[12] Ibid.

[13] Ibid.

"attractiveness" and the ability to influence others in the international environment. Fan argued that "the central assumption 'to get others to want what you want' remains untested and it is not clear how this can be achieved in reality," particularly given that soft power is "intangible, uncontrollable and unpredictable."[14] He also observed that two countries in a "power relationship should benefit mutually, otherwise such a relationship will not last."[15]

In describing Nye's conception of soft power as a "blunt instrument," Steven Lukes similarly argued that "'the ability to shape the preferences of others' is a troubling obscure phrase which fails to discriminate between those causal processes which limit and sometimes undermine individuals' capacities to judge and decide for themselves and those which require, facilitate, and expand such capacities."[16] According to Lukes, a key question that must be asked is: "[T]o what extent, in what ways and by what mechanisms do powerful agents influence others' conceptions of their own interests?"[17]

Yet, there has been virtually no serious debate about whether soft power provides a sound conceptual foundation for the practice of public diplomacy. In an effort to spark such discussion, this chapter challenges the fundamental assumptions of public diplomacy policies and practices motivated and directed by the self-interested desire to "get what you want" by co-opting foreign publics "to buy into your values."[18] The chapter reviews the concept of soft power and then addresses the implications of adopting soft power as a conceptual framework for public diplomacy.

The contention is that while political power may be a by-product of successful public diplomacy, it is an inappropriate conceptual basis for the conduct of ethical and effective public diplomacy. For that reason, it is incumbent upon public diplomacy scholars and practitioners to consider other theoretical paradigms. Here, a relational model based on public relations principles and concepts of mutuality is proposed

---

[14] Ying Fan, "Soft Power: Power of Attraction or Confusion?," *Place Branding and Public Diplomacy* 4, no. 2, (2008): 154.

[15] Ibid., 156.

[16] Steven Lukes, "Power and the Battle for Hearts and Minds: On the Bluntness of Soft Power," in *Power in World Politics*, ed., Felix Berenskoettner and M. J. Williams (New York: Routledge, 2007): 95.

[17] Ibid., 97.

[18] Nye, *Soft Power*, 5.

as a theoretical framework for the study and practice of U.S. public diplomacy going forward.

Soft Power

In *Soft Power: The Means to Success in World Politics*, Nye argued that, in the post-Cold War world, U.S. leaders failed to grasp the significance of soft power in achieving the nation's foreign policy objectives. Noting a need for the support and cooperation of other states in dealing with complex matters that cross borders, such as terrorism, trade, financial regulation, climate change, and the spread of infectious disease, Nye contended soft power was critical to advancing the national agenda: "In short, America's success will depend upon our developing a deeper understanding of the role of soft power and developing a better balance of hard and soft power in our foreign policy."[19]

The currency of soft power is different from hard power, i.e., military might and economic muscle, Nye explained, such that soft power "co-opts people rather than coerces them."[20] Co-optive power, he said, rests on "the attractiveness of one's culture, political ideals, and policies, or on one's ability to manipulate other countries' political agendas."[21]

According to Nye, in an environment in which foreign public opinion has become increasingly important and the global flow of information is enhanced by new media, one of a nation's key soft power resources is public diplomacy, which plays a central role in shaping the global climate in which policymaking takes place. When practiced effectively, Nye contended, public diplomacy enhances a nation's ability to wield soft power.

In describing how public diplomacy contributes to the acquisition of "soft power," Nye pointed to three strategies: 1) daily communication to explain the context of foreign policy decisions; 2) strategic communication involving symbolic events and branding activities to advance specific government policies; and 3) relationship-building with key individuals over many years. Combined, Nye said, such efforts "create

---

[19] Joseph S. Nye, Jr., "Soft Power and American Foreign Policy," *Political Science Quarterly* 119 (2004): 270.

[20] Nye, *Soft Power*, 5.

[21] Joseph S. Nye, Jr., "The Velvet Hegemon," *Foreign Policy* 136 (May 2003): 74.

an attractive image of a country and thus can improve its prospects for obtaining its desired outcomes."[22]

Discussions of soft power more recently have evolved to focus on what Nye and others call "smart power," or combining U.S. military and economic might with greater investments in diplomacy.[23] Smart power reflects a more expansive approach to looking at how the United States can best adapt to changes in the international environment. According to communications scholar Ernest J. Wilson III, "smart power" is "the capacity of an actor to combine elements of hard power and soft power in ways that are mutually reinforcing such that the actor's purposes are advanced effectively and efficiently."[24] Noting that soft power institutions historically have been and remain in "subordinate" positions to "hard power" institutions,[25] Wilson called for reforms that would reflect a more balanced approach to the design and conduct of American foreign policy.

As evidence of the intellectual trend toward "smart power," the topic was the focus of a commission comprised of prominent U.S. leaders brought together by the Center for Strategic & International Studies to consider how the United States could "become a smart power," i.e., how the nation could "become the welcomed world leader for a constructive international agenda" and how it could "restore the full spectrum of our national power."[26]

According to the commission's co-chairs Nye and Richard L. Armitage, the report of the commission was "about power and how America wields it in the world."[27] Public diplomacy was one of five areas cited by the commission as critical to the nation's ability to become a smart power. In describing the function of public diplomacy, the commission noted that "governments traditionally use public diplomacy to exercise influence over individuals, groups, institutions, and public opinion abroad in support of their national objectives."[28]

---

[22] Nye, *Soft Power*, 109–110.

[23] Ernest J. Wilson III, "Hard Power, Soft Power, Smart Power," *The Annals of the American Academy of Political and Social Science* 616 (March 2008): 110–124.

[24] Ibid., 111.

[25] Ibid., 117.

[26] Richard L. Armitage and Joseph S. Nye, Jr, *CSIS Commission on Smart Power: A Smarter, More Secure America* (Washington, DC: Center for Strategic & International Studies, 2007).

[27] Ibid., 4–5.

[28] Ibid., 47.

Notably, in her confirmation hearing testimony before the U.S. Senate, Secretary of State Hillary Clinton observed that in restoring America's leadership position in the world, "We must use what has been called smart power, the full range of tools at our disposal—diplomatic, military, political, legal, and cultural—picking the right tool or combination of tools for each situation. With smart power, diplomacy will be the vanguard of our foreign policy."[29]

In many respects, "smart power" is simply a reframing of the debate on the role and value of diplomatic resources. By combining hard and soft power into smart power, diplomacy is elevated to "equal" status with the military and other government resources, refocusing attention from whether one resource is more or less important than another to how resources should be balanced in the national interest.

This is an important debate to have. Public diplomacy's fate largely will be determined by whether state leaders accept that public diplomacy matters to the protection and advancement of national interests and support it accordingly. Also important to public diplomacy's development, however, is a debate about whether the acquisition and wielding of power (of any kind) should be public diplomacy's central purpose.

The problem with soft power

The broad assumption that public diplomacy's value lies in its ability to help a nation wield greater power is reminiscent of historical attempts to justify U.S. public diplomacy's worth on its contribution to wartime objectives. In that regard, one might wonder whether the soft power paradigm has been adopted by public diplomacy scholars and practitioners as a means to the noble end of securing public diplomacy's future in diplomatic affairs.

Perhaps it should not be surprising that public diplomacy has been identified as a soft power resource given historical views of public diplomacy as an instrument of war. After all, many view public diplomacy's greatest historical accomplishment as helping to defeat the Soviet Union, which established America as the sole superpower

[29] Transcript of Hillary Clinton's Confirmation Hearing, January 13, 2009, http://www.cfr.org/publication/18225/transcript_of_hillary_clintons_confirmation_hearing.html (accessed May 1, 2009).

in the world. In fact, the genesis of soft power as a conceptual foundation for U.S. public diplomacy might be found in Cold War attempts to combat communism by making U.S. democratic values and ideals more attractive to the people of Eastern Europe and other states. As Dizard observed in *Inventing Public Diplomacy: The Story of the U.S. Information Agency*, "decisions made under wartime pressures" established the framework for contemporary public diplomacy policies and practices.[30] Clearly, power and public diplomacy have strong historical ties.

Nor should it be surprising that many who value public diplomacy's contribution to the global "war on terror" today view the function through Cold War eyes, seeing public diplomacy as a tool that can help sustain America's strength in the international community. As Shaun Riordan observed in *The New Diplomacy*, a key principle of the "realist" approach to international relations that has dominated traditional diplomacy is that "diplomats should pursue the short-term interests of their country, without regard to other factors."[31] In keeping with such traditions, under the soft power paradigm, public diplomacy has been positioned as a means of helping nations retain or acquire power in a changing world in which power structures have been redefined and states are struggling to adapt.

But equating public diplomacy with power mischaracterizes public diplomacy's central purpose. While effective public diplomacy certainly may help secure a nation's position of strength in the world, the purpose of public diplomacy is not to acquire or retain power. Rather it is—or at least should be—to secure for a nation the autonomy and support needed to pursue its interests and ideals in the world. Public diplomacy's fundamental purpose is *to help a nation establish and maintain mutually beneficial relationships with strategic foreign publics that can affect national interests.*

In fact, Nye advised against seeing public diplomacy "simply in adversarial terms," pointing out that "often there can be gains for both sides."[32] He also advocated actions that reinforce words—"Preaching at foreigners is not the best way to convert them"—and he stressed

[30] Wilson P. Dizard Jr., *Inventing Public Diplomacy: The Story of the U.S. Information Agency* (Boulder: Lynne Rienner Publishers, 2004), 3.

[31] Shaun Riordan, *The New Diplomacy* (Cambridge, UK: Polity, 2003), 2.

[32] Joseph Nye, "Public Diplomacy and Soft Power," *The Annals of the American Academy of Political and Social Science* 616 (March 2008): 106.

the importance of "going beyond conveying information and selling a positive image."[33] According to Nye, "public diplomacy also involves building long-term relationships that create an enabling environment for government policies."[34] By definition, he said, "soft power means getting others to want the same outcomes you want, and that requires an understanding of how they are hearing your messages and adapting them accordingly."[35]

However, the problem with a power-based model of public diplomacy is that it fails to fully recognize the importance of mutuality and dialogue in which *both* parties are conducive to changes in attitudes and behavior and in which the achievement of mutual benefit is the desired outcome. As Riordan has suggested: "[If] tackling the new agenda of security threats [for example] requires the collaboration of other governments and their broader civil societies, a successful public diplomacy must be based not on assertions of values, but on engaging in a genuine dialogue.... This requires a more open, and perhaps humble, approach, which recognizes that no one has a monopoly of truth or virtue, that other ideas may be valid and that the outcome may be different from the initial message being promoted."[36]

Certainly, the practical consequences of adopting a power-based model of public diplomacy were illustrated by misguided U.S. public diplomacy efforts in the post-9/11 environment, in which the "political" mindset dominated. For example, neither the "Shared Values" initiative directed at people in the Middle East nor later efforts to promote U.S. values as "universal" values was well received. These activities demonstrated that foreign publics cannot be viewed simply as "audiences" of public diplomacy efforts. Rather, they must be viewed as participants in an international dialogue about common pursuits and interests. In other words, the old view that "diplomacy is the art of letting other people have *your* way" provides a shaky foundation for the conduct of public diplomacy today.

---

[33] Ibid., 103.
[34] Ibid., 101.
[35] Ibid., 103.
[36] Shaun Riordan, "Dialogue-based Public Diplomacy: A New Foreign Policy Paradigm?," in Melissen, *The New Public Diplomacy*, 189.

Balancing interests

Admittedly, the idea that the U.S. government might adjust its foreign policies in response to foreign public opinion is controversial. One example of the contradictory views on such matters was presented in a *Foreign Policy* article in which former Speaker of the U.S. House of Representatives Newt Gingrich responded to former State Department officials who charged that Gingrich's call for reforms in the State Department reflected a failure to appreciate the "dual mandate" of the State Department to "advocate U.S. foreign policy abroad as well as convey other countries' views to the president."[37] In response, Gingrich said: "The State Department should represent only the United States and our values to the world. Our strategy must be to communicate those values effectively. Where the values of other nations conflict with our own interests and values, we should make the conflict clear so that we are predictable to other countries, so they know where we stand. The State Department should never act on behalf of any other country's interests where they do not coincide with our own."[38]

The problem with such a view, as it applies to public diplomacy, is that a model motivated solely by self-interest—even one based on dialogue and understanding, as Nye has suggested—cannot be effective in an environment in which the United States appears to foreign publics to be more interested in molding their views to mirror those of the United States than in engaging in a true dialogue in which American views and actions might be adjusted to accommodate the interests of foreign parties.

There is considerable evidence that such a negative view of the United States is already prevalent among people throughout the world. According to virtually every study on the subject, anti-Americanism is to a great extent related to perceptions of American *power*. According to the 2005 Pew Global Attitudes Project, for example, "the rest of the world both fears and resents the unrivaled power that the United States has amassed since the Cold War ended."[39]

---

[37] Response, *Foreign Policy* (September/October 2003): 84.

[38] Ibid., 89.

[39] Pew Global Attitudes Project, "Global Opinion: The Spread of Anti-Americanism" (Washington, DC: Pew Research Center, 2005): 106, http://pewglobal.org (accessed January 15, 2006).

Clearly, if one of the goals of public diplomacy is to reduce such fears and resentments and improve the image of America as a responsible steward of its power, then diplomatic strategies designed to increase American power—particularly when they are perceived as such by those public diplomacy is intended to influence—are ill-advised. Rather than counter foreign publics' concerns regarding America's global ambitions, they magnify them.

A later Pew Global Attitudes Project study, which examined global opinion of the United States, found that "anti-Americanism is deeper and broader now than at any time in modern history."[40] Why? According to the study, "At the heart of the decline in world opinion about America is the perception that the United States acts internationally without taking into account the interests of other nations."[41] At the same time, there is a "stark contrast between how the rest of the world views the United States and how the United States views itself."[42]

While many U.S. leaders routinely argue that American values are "universal" values and that people throughout the world "want what we want," people abroad don't necessarily see it that way. In fact, although a majority of people in the world say they like American cultural exports, e.g., music, movies, and television, the study showed that "they view the export of American ideas and customs as a bad thing."[43] With respect to issues of ethics and integrity, the study also showed that foreign publics simply don't trust America. On matters of international security particularly, "The rest of the world has become deeply suspicious of U.S. motives and openly skeptical of its word."[44]

Other studies have produced similar results.[45] For example, Duke University researchers who synthesized polling data on anti-Americanism throughout the world found "widespread erosion of America's image abroad as the United States and its policies are widely viewed with increasing skepticism, even among traditional allies."[46] The 2007

[40] Ibid.
[41] Ibid., 108.
[42] Ibid.
[43] Ibid., 115.
[44] Ibid., 106.
[45] See, e.g., Andrew Kohut and Bruce Stokes, *America Against the World: How We Are Different and Why We Are Disliked* (New York: Henry Holt and Company, 2006).
[46] Ole R. Holsti and Natasha C. Roetter, "How Publics Abroad View the United States," paper presented at the annual meeting of the American Political Science Association, Washington, DC, September 1, 2005.

World Public Opinion study conducted by The Chicago Council on Global Affairs, WorldPublicOpinion.org, and research centers around the world similarly found that "[p]ublics around the world reject the idea that the United States should continue to be the preeminent world leader and prefer that it play a more cooperative role."[47] This group noted that its findings were in line with other global surveys, "which have found that the United States' image abroad is bad and getting worse."[48]

Such results cannot be attributed solely to bad public diplomacy. As the studies showed, there were multiple reasons—including unpopular U.S. policies and an unpopular U.S. president—for the nation's declining image during that time. However, the studies do provide some evidence that post-9/11 American public diplomacy fell short on two fronts: it was not effective in combating negative views of the United States and it did not meet the ethical expectations of the people abroad with whom the nation has—and hoped to improve its—relations. From a practical perspective, an apparent lack of concern for others' interests contributed to feelings of anti-Americanism and hostility toward the United States. As Julia E. Sweig pointed out in *Friendly Fire: Losing Friends and Making Enemies in the Anti-American Century*, a significant element of global antipathy toward the United States is "the near inability of the United States to see its power from the perspective of the powerless."[49]

From an ethical perspective, it suggested a lack of moral awareness, or "awareness of the fact that morality is an integral part of public policy, an element that is present even when it is not consciously included in the calculations of statesmen."[50] Although, as Michael Wesley observed in *Ethics & International Affairs*, "to propose that government should act in accord with general moral interests rather than state interests is to propose an absurdity" to realists, nations by necessity have had to

---

[47] The Chicago Council and WorldPublicOpinion.org, *World Public Opinion 2007* (Chicago, IL, 2007): 28.

[48] Ibid.

[49] Julia E. Sweig, *Friendly Fire: Losing Friends and Making Enemies in the Anti-American Century* (New York: Public Affairs, 2006), 34.

[50] Stanley Hoffman, "The Political Ethics of International Relations" in *Ethics & International Affairs: A Reader*, ed. Joel H. Rosenthal (Washington, DC: Georgetown University Press, 1995), 35.

become "increasingly sensitive to perceptions of the legitimacy of their actions" by those who are affected by them.[51]

Riordan also pointed out that the dramatic changes brought about by globalization and new technology have "severely undermined" the assumptions on which traditional diplomacy has been based and made foreign public opinion an increasingly significant element in foreign policy calculations. Noting specifically the implications of the 24/7 global news environment in which information travels in real time, he said, "While diplomats bemoan this 'CNN effect,' it has strengthened the importance of ethical considerations about the nature of regimes, the absence of which was one of the structural flaws of traditional diplomacy."[52] Increasingly, Riordan observed, governments both at home and abroad are being forced to justify their foreign policy decisions and actions.

A new mindset

So, if soft power falls short, what is the proper conceptual foundation for public diplomacy? In attempting to answer this question, public diplomacy scholars and practitioners might look to the related discipline of public relations, which offers a relational paradigm. As Melissen has observed, "the modus operandi of the new public diplomacy is not entirely different from the public relations approach."[53]

In fact, the conceptual connections between public diplomacy and public relations are significant. Public diplomacy clearly fits within the commonly accepted definition of international public relations as "the planned and organized effort of a company, institution, or government to establish mutually beneficial relations with the publics of other nations."[54] And the evolution of public diplomacy sounds surprisingly familiar to public relations scholars and professionals who have witnessed public relations' evolution from a technical,

[51] Michael Wesley, "Toward a Realist Ethics of Intervention," *Ethics & International Affairs* 19, no. 2 (2005): 57.

[52] Riordan, *The New Diplomacy, 4.*

[53] Jan Melissen, "The New Public Diplomacy," 21.

[54] Dennis Wilcox, Philip Ault, and Warren Agee, *Public Relations: Strategies and Tactics* (Third Edition) (New York: Harper Collins, 1992), 409.

journalistically-inspired communication function to a relationship management function.[55]

Despite such similarities, however, these disciplinary cousins have grown up apart. In fact, public diplomacy professionals have long tried to separate themselves from their "PR" counterparts, who are widely perceived to operate on shakier ethical ground. As an example, in an attempt to explain public diplomacy's worth after the Cold War to members of the Foreign Relations Committee in the U.S. Senate, the last director of the USIA, Joseph Duffy, said: "Let me just say a word about public diplomacy. It is not public relations. It is not flaking for a government agency or even flaking for America. It is trying to relate beyond government-to-government relationships to the private institutions, the individuals, the long-term contact, the accurate understanding, the full range of perceptions of America to the rest of the world."[56]

A more recent example that illustrates the enduring nature of such views is provided by Jim Murphy, Minister for Europe of the UK's Foreign & Commonwealth Office, who in 2008 said that foreign ministries "must stop seeing public diplomacy as a form of public relations, shouting out core messages and top lines, louder and louder, in the false belief that they haven't been heard clearly enough. To succeed in today's world, we need genuine engagement, not clumsy propaganda."[57]

Given that such views of public relations are not uncommon, it may be important to point out that widely held perceptions of "PR" have little in common with either scholarly theories or advanced professional practices in the field. In fact, since the first book was written about public relations (*Crystallizing Public Opinion*) in 1923[58]—the same year the first university course on the subject was taught at Boston University—a sizable literature that examines the theoretical and

---

[55] See Carl Botan and Maureen Taylor, "Public Relations: State of the Field," *Journal of Communication* 54, no. 4 (2004): 652; see also Carl Botan and Vincent Hazleton, "Public Relations in a New Age," in *Public Relations Theory II*, ed. Carl Botan and Vincent Hazleton (Mahwah, NJ: Lawrence Erlbaum Associates, Publishers, 2006), 7.

[56] Quoted in Rosaleen Smythe, "Mapping U.S. Public Diplomacy in the 21st Century," *Australian Journal of International Affairs* 55, no. 3 (2001): 422.

[57] Jim Murphy, "Engagement: Executive Summary," in Foreign & Commonwealth Office Collection of Online Essays and Case Studies, www.fco.gov.uk/en/about-the-fco/publications (accessed December 20, 2008).

[58] Edward Bernays, *Crystallizing Public Opinion* (New York: Boni and Liveright, 1923).

practical aspects of public relations has been developed.[59] Within that body of knowledge lie important insights that may be useful in developing a theoretical paradigm for public diplomacy.

Another common myth about public relations is that it is solely a private sector function associated with corporate marketing or branding efforts. This is not the case. Public relations is not a function or subset of marketing or branding, nor does it encompass only corporate practices. For example, the more than 300 universities in the United States and other nations offering degree programs in public relations prepare students for practice in both the public and private sectors, i.e., in business, non-profit *and* government. Thus, the application of public relations concepts to public diplomacy should not be interpreted as the importation of private sector thinking for government purposes, which—notwithstanding recent calls for the increased "privatization" of public diplomacy[60]—some view as inappropriate for advancing a nation's "public" mission.

Perhaps because of such perceptions, there has been surprisingly little scholarly attention to how the precepts of public relations and public diplomacy, respectively, might inform the other. Certainly, historical tensions may be one reason for the intellectual divide—at least on the side of public diplomacy. Another might be that *government* public relations simply has been of less interest to public relations scholars than private sector public relations functions.

In 1992, for example, public relations scholars Benno Signitzer and Timothy Coombs observed that although governments are recognized as actors in international public relations, "the theoretical and practical public relations literature has been conspicuously silent about this issue."[61] At the same time, these scholars pointed out that they could find only one diplomacy theorist who used the term "public relations" in describing public diplomacy activities—the scholar Hans Jurgen

---

[59] See, e.g., Lynne M. Sallot, Lisa J. Lyon, Carolina Acosta-Alzuru, and Karyn Ogata Jones, "From Aardvark to Zebra: A New Millennium Analysis of Theory Development in Public Relations Academic Journals," *Journal of Public Relations Research* 15, no. 1 (2003): 27–99.

[60] See, e.g., Kathy R. Fitzpatrick, "Privatizing Public Diplomacy," paper presented at the annual conference of the International Studies Association, Chicago, IL, February 28, 2007.

[61] Benno H. Signitzer and Timothy Coombs, "Public Relations and Public Diplomacy: Conceptual Convergences," *Public Relations Review* 18, no. 2 (1992): 138.

Koschwitz, who observed in 1986 that "public relations aspects" were gaining importance in public diplomacy theory and practice.[62]

In exploring what they saw as "conceptual convergences" between public relations and public diplomacy created by modern technology and the needs of modern nation-states, Signitzer and Coombs found commonality between the objectives and tools of the respective disciplines, suggesting that "a relationship between the two areas does exist."[63] Thus, they concluded, "[e]ach area can benefit by learning the strengths of the other area and adapting them to the practice of dealing with foreign publics."[64]

Jacquie L'Etang also examined possible convergences in public relations and public diplomacy, proposing that public relations had much to learn about its historical roots by studying international relations. Observing gaps in the public relations theoretical literature, L'Etang argued that theories related to symmetry, for example, were actually more developed in international relations theory than in public relations theory. She pointed out, for example, that while the former allows for fundamental change in "political architecture," the potential for such change remains unexplored in public relations.[65]

At the same time, L'Etang cited the lack of theoretical study of diplomacy as part of international relations, noting that much of the work in this realm focuses on the strategic dimensions, or "how to do it" aspects, of diplomacy. She contended that diplomacy is "not, therefore, seen as a field of study in itself, but as a technique used to achieve certain ends."[66] Noting that a theoretical study of public relations or public diplomacy must go beyond practical guidance, L'Etang argued that "public relations should properly be considered in tandem with international relations, not simply because it performs a (publicity) function in the process of diplomacy and international relations, but because it is linked to fundamental positions about the

[62] Signitzer and Coombs, "Public Relations and Public Diplomacy," 146, quoting Hans Jurgen Koschwitz, "Diplomatie and Offentlichkeit," *Beitrage zur Konfliktofschung* 16, no. 1, 53–68.

[63] Signitzer and Coombs, "Public Relations and Public Diplomacy," 145.

[64] Ibid.

[65] Jacquie L'Etang, "Public Relations as Diplomacy," in *Critical Perspectives in Public Relations*, ed. Jacquie L'Etang and Magda Pieczka (London: International Thomson Business Press, 1996), 33.

[66] Ibid., 24.

way individuals organize themselves into collectivities."[67] According to L'Etang, "Assumptions about what is considered appropriate in organizational and international discourse and about the rights of organizations and nations to define and fulfill their destinies are as important as the communicative acts that are undertaken in the name of those represented."[68]

Signitizer later worked with public relations scholar Carola Wamser to flesh out the similarities between public relations and public diplomacy. Noting a lack of common culture or community between the disciplines, they questioned whether such a divide "makes sense" given the shift away from the traditional, government-to-government/diplomat-to-diplomat toward government-to-people diplomacy.[69] Signitzer and Wamser, who described public diplomacy as "a specific governmental public relations function,"[70] pointed out that public relations and public diplomacy are both "strategic communication functions of either organizations or nation-states, and typically deal with the reciprocal consequences a sponsor and its publics have upon each other."[71]

Additionally, they noted, personnel in both areas perform a "boundary spanning" role, with "one foot in the organization and one outside."[72] They also cited functional equivalencies in "intelligence gathering (research, environmental scanning), being representational (rhetoric, oratory, advocacy), dialogic (negotiation, peacemaking), and advisory (counseling)."[73] Signitzer and Wamser concluded that in a world that has become increasingly "diverse, complex and intertwined" and that is characterized by the rise of nonstate actors, "the time to attempt a coordination of theoretical concepts, theories, and models [in public relations and public diplomacy] appears to have come."[74]

In one of the few empirical studies to assess links between public relations theory and public diplomacy, public relations scholar Seong-Hun Yun surveyed foreign public diplomats in Washington, DC,

---

[67] Ibid., 34.
[68] Ibid.
[69] Benno Signitzer and Carola Wamser, "Public Diplomacy: A Specific Governmental Public Relations Function," in Botan and Hazelton, *Public Relations Theory II*, 436.
[70] Ibid., 435.
[71] Ibid., 441.
[72] Ibid., 443, citing James E. Grunig and Todd Hunt, *Managing Public Relations* (New York: Holt, Rinehart & Winston, 1994).
[73] Signitzer and Wamser, "Public Diplomacy," 443.
[74] Ibid., 444.

about public diplomacy management and behaviors. In examining the fit of two measurement models identified in the public relations literature, Yun concluded that public relations frameworks are transferable for conceptualizing and measuring behavior and excellence in public diplomacy. According to Yun, such studies demonstrate the potential for theory building in public diplomacy, as well as the ability to get beyond the study of communication effects and to examine "how and why nations practice and manage public diplomacy as they do—comparative public diplomacy."[75]

With respect to the relational dimensions of public relations and public diplomacy, Yun also found significant similarities. In distinguishing a nation's relationships with foreign publics from its national reputation, she observed, "The concept of relationships is associated with publics possessing first-hand experience with the organization or foreign government. In contrast, the concepts of image and reputation are less specific and related to masses with second-hand experience."[76] For that reason, Yun concluded that "a focus of future research should be on the relationships of governments with specific and strategic foreign publics such as congressmen, journalists, and opinion leaders."[77]

Relationship management

The idea that relationships should be the central focus of public relations scholarship and practice was introduced in 1984 by public relations scholar Mary Anne Ferguson, who proposed a conceptual shift away from the communicative aspects of public relations toward the relational aspects. Ferguson's call for relationships to become the core concern of public relations scholarship set the stage for the development of a new theory of public relations that has become the dominant concern of public relations scholarship and practice today: relationship management.

In many respects, the adoption of a relational approach to public relations transformed thinking in the discipline. As public relations

[75] Seong-Hun Yun, "Toward a Public Relations Theory-Based Study of Public Diplomacy: Testing the Applicability of the Excellence Study," *Journal of Public Relations Research* 18, no. 4 (2006): 308.

[76] Ibid., 309.

[77] Ibid.

scholar John Ledingham, who explicated relationship management as a general theory of public relations, suggested, "The relational perspective is said to define the organizational function of public relations."[78] The relational paradigm recognizes that "the purpose and direction of an organization (its mission) is affected by relationships with key constituents (publics) in the organization's environment."[79]

Perhaps the best way to illustrate the significance of this change is to review the four models of public relations developed by public relations scholars James E. Grunig and Todd Hunt in 1984.[80] The models, all of which are still in use today, reflect the historical development of public relations.

Early public relations efforts primarily relied on the *press agentry* model, which is often equated with publicity and describes one-way propagandistic efforts in compliance gaining. Such efforts, in which truth-telling is not necessarily paramount, might include pseudo events and other attention-gaining activities. Historical campaigns that employed these tactics are in large part responsible for the negative images of public relations that persist today.

The next step in public relations' development was toward a *public information* model, which is characterized by one-way efforts to influence audiences through truthful information and education. This model might describe public relations initiatives involving the distribution of materials about an institution to domestic or foreign publics. Both the press-agentry model and public information model rely to a great extent on mediated communication to influence the attitudes and behaviors of targeted publics—but not those of the sponsoring institution.

The *two-way asymmetric* model, which reflects a more sophisticated approach to public relations, is grounded in advocacy and relies on research and audience analysis to frame messages and develop strategic campaigns and programs designed to benefit the sponsoring institution

---

[78] John A. Ledingham, "Explicating Relationship Management as a General Theory of Public Relations," *Journal of Public Relations Research* 15, no. 2 (2003): 182; see also John A. Ledingham and Stephen D. Bruning, "Relationship Management and Public Relations: Dimensions of an Organization-Public Relationship," *Public Relations Review* 24, no. 2 (1998): 55–65.

[79] David M. Dozier, Larissa A. Grunig, and James E. Grunig, *Manager's Guide to Excellence in Public Relations and Communication Management* (Mahwah, NJ: Lawrence Erlbaum Associates, Publisher, 1995), 85.

[80] Grunig and Hunt, *Managing Public Relations.*

but not necessarily the institution's publics. Political campaigns are good examples of the two-way asymmetric model.

Finally, the *two-way symmetric* model, which also relies on sophisticated research and public analysis, is intended to achieve understanding and benefit for *both* the institution and its publics. The two-way symmetric model depicts a relational approach to public relations.

Under the relational paradigm, public relations is defined as "the management function that establishes and maintains mutually beneficial relationships between an organization and the publics on whom its success or failure depends."[81] Public relations contributes to organizational effectiveness "when it helps reconcile the organization's goals with the expectations of its strategic constituents...by building quality, long-term relationships with strategic constituents."[82]

Although "relationship" has been defined in various ways, a common view in public relations is that a relationship is "the state which exists between an organization and its key publics in which the actions of either entity impact the economic, social, political and/or cultural well-being of the other entity."[83] Public relations research suggests that an organization's relationships with its publics might be evaluated by four key indicators: control mutuality, satisfaction, trust, and commitment.[84]

Relationship management theory posits that effective public relations produces supportive public relationships built on trust and accommodation created through genuine dialogue designed to accommodate dual interests. The theory is summarized as follows:

> Effectively managing organizational-public relationships around common interests and shared goals, over time, results in mutual understanding and benefit for interacting organizations and publics.[85]

---

[81] Scott M. Cutlip, Allen H. Center, and Glen M. Broom, *Effective Public Relations* (Englewood Cliffs, NJ: Prentice Hall, 1994), 2.

[82] James E. Grunig, Larissa A. Grunig, and William P. Ehling, "What Is an Effective Organization?," in *Excellence in Public Relations and Communication Management: Contributions to Effective Organizations*, ed. James E. Grunig (Mahwah, NJ: Lawrence Erlbaum Associates, 1992), 86.

[83] Ledingham and Bruning, "Relationship Management and Public Relations: Dimensions of an Organization-Public Relationship," 62.

[84] See James E. Grunig and Linda Hon, *Guidelines for Measuring Relationships in Public Relations* (Gainesville, FL: Institute for Public Relations, 1999), 39.

[85] Ledingham, "Explicating Relationship Management as a General Theory of Public Relations," 190.

Importantly, relational public relations strategies are based on relationship-building, rather than compliance-gaining. Under the relational paradigm, public relations professionals are no longer viewed as communicators. Rather, they are viewed as managers of institutional relationships in which communication is viewed as a tool rather than an objective.[86] In this regard, relationship management theory helps to overcome the assumption that "effectively crafted messages provide solutions to all public relations problems."[87] The theory builds on Grunig's earlier work, in which he stressed the importance of behavioral as well as symbolic relationships between institutions and their publics: "When symbolic (communication-based) relationships are divorced from behavioral relationships (grounded in actions and events), public relations practitioners reduce public relations to the simplistic notion of image building [which] offers little of value to the organization they advise because they suggest that problems in relationships with publics can be solved by using the proper message—disseminated through publicity, or media relations—to change an image of an organization."[88]

In other words, while words matter, deeds that demonstrate an institution's good intentions are required to effectively develop good relationships. As Ledingham and Stephen Bruning noted, "When the organization engages in action and communication that facilitates a sense of openness, trust, commitment, involvement, and investment it builds the symbolic and behavioral relationships with key publics that are critical to accomplishing an organization's mission."[89]

---

[86] See, e.g., Glen M. Broom, and David M. Dozier, *Using Research in Public Relations: Applications to Program Management* (Englewood Cliffs, NJ: Prentice-Hall, 1990).

[87] Stephen D. Bruning and John A. Ledingham, "Perceptions of Relationships and Evaluations of Satisfaction: An Exploration of Interaction," *Public Relations Review* 26, no. 1 (2000): 87.

[88] James E. Grunig, "Image and Substance: From Symbolic to Behavioral Relationship," *Public Relations Review* 19, no. 2 (2003): 136.

[89] John A. Ledingham and Stephen D. Bruning, "Defining the Role of Communications," in *Public Relations as Relationship Management: A Relational Approach to Public Relations*, ed. John A. Ledingham and Stephen D. Bruning (Mahwah, NJ: Lawrence Erlbaum Publishers, Inc., 2000), 65.

Implications of a relational approach to public diplomacy

The adoption of a relational approach to public diplomacy would have significant theoretical and practical implications. As Grunig observed, the presuppositions that define the worldviews of practitioners are "extremely powerful" because they determine both the approaches to and practices of a given function.[90] The assumption here is that the particular worldview of public diplomacy to which a nation subscribes will be predictive of both how public diplomacy is actually practiced and the effectiveness of those practices. In fact, such assumptions are supported by empirical evidence from the public relations literature.[91] For example, practitioners who subscribe to an asymmetric worldview of public relations approach their work differently than practitioners who subscribe to a symmetric worldview.[92]

In this regard, the application of a relational model to public diplomacy would incorporate the foundational principle of mutuality inherent in the "new" public diplomacy, which recognizes that public diplomacy must be more than delivering messages to target audiences. It also would reflect the imperatives of global society for greater collaboration and cooperation among nations and peoples. As Rainer Schlageter has observed, "In order to be successful, today's public diplomacy has to go beyond traditional 'one-way-street' information work: It should be a dialogue and a steady discussion with the goal to establish a long-term relationship with foreign audiences and in particular with the leadership from all fields of society."[93]

To some degree, the adoption of a relational paradigm in U.S. public diplomacy would mean going back to the principles of mutuality and dialogue that helped the USIA succeed during the Cold War—and

---

[90] James E. Grunig, "Communication, Public Relations, and Effective Organizations: An Overview of the Book," in Grunig, ed. *Excellence in Public Relations and Communication Management*, 8; see also Christina P. Deatherage and Vincent Hazleton, "Effects of Organizational Worldviews on the Practice of Public Relations: A Test of the Theory of Public Relations Excellence," *Journal of Public Relations Research* 10, no. 1 (1998): 57–71.

[91] Ibid.

[92] See, e.g., William P. Ehling, "Estimating the Value of Public Relations and Communication to an Organization," in Grunig, *Excellence in Public Relations and Communication Management*, 622.

[93] Rainer Schlageter, "German Public Diplomacy," paper presented at the Madrid Conference on Public Diplomacy, Madrid, Spain, October 10, 2006.

that seemingly were abandoned in the post-9/11 period. As one of the former USIA officers explained, effective public diplomacy "requires sustained relationships of trust and mutual good will."[94]

In other parts of the world, there is some evidence that nations recently becoming more involved in public diplomacy are adopting such thinking. Researchers who conducted a comprehensive review of Australia's public diplomacy, for example, found that in academic research and other studies of public diplomacy, "[a]ll reports have emphasized the importance of building people-to-people links as a means of sustaining a healthy, strong and mutually beneficial relationship."[95] They concluded that "people-to-people links are the lynch pin of Australia's public diplomacy."[96]

If relationship management were adopted as a general theory of public diplomacy, public diplomacy policies and practices would be characterized by symmetry and mutuality and the desired outcome would be mutual understanding and benefit for *both* a nation and its foreign publics. In other words, public diplomacy initiatives would be designed to serve *dual* interests rather than only the government's *self*-interest.

In considering whether relationship management provides a sound conceptual foundation for public diplomacy, a guiding issue should be whether public diplomacy is—or should be—an instrument of power used by a government to benefit itself but not necessarily to benefit the people of other countries *or* whether public diplomacy is—or should be—a means of enhancing human relations between sovereign states and peoples to achieve mutual understanding and benefits. If the latter is the more accurate depiction of public diplomacy, then the idea of a nation using public diplomacy to gain power over the people of another country is inherently contradictory. In that respect, relational theory calls into question the appropriateness of soft power as a conceptual foundation for public diplomacy.

At the same time, it should be noted that a relational approach to public diplomacy would not ignore self-interest. Rather, the motivations guiding public diplomacy policies and practices would be

---

[94] Former USIA officer; see Kathy R. Fitzpatrick, *USIA Alumni Study*, unpublished report, 2007.

[95] Standing Committee on Foreign Affairs, Defence and Trade, *Australia's Public Diplomacy: Building Our Image* (Canberra: Commonwealth of Australia, 2007): 79.

[96] Ibid., 80.

"mixed," meaning that efforts would be intended to balance the self-interest of the nation with the interests of foreign publics.[97] According to Grunig, "a symmetrical model actually serves the self-interest of the organization better than an asymmetrical model because organizations get more of what they want when they give up some of what they want."[98] As Grunig and Hunt pointed out, persuasion occurs under the symmetric model. However, the difference is that "if persuasion occurs, the public should be just as likely to persuade the organization's management to change attitudes and behaviors as the organization is likely to change the public's attitudes or behavior."[99]

Relationship management also would provide an overarching framework for exploring issues within the public diplomacy discipline.[100] Under a relational paradigm, public diplomacy's central function would be relationship management, which would encompass all public diplomacy activities—short-term/long-term, reactive/proactive, information/advocacy/engagement/advisement/etc. All public diplomacy efforts would be designed to contribute to the establishment and maintenance of positive, supportive relationships with strategic foreign publics—and they would be judged accordingly.

This holistic approach would mean that relationship management—now generally viewed as a separate component of public diplomacy called "engagement"—would become the central function of the discipline. Under a relational model of public diplomacy, the management of relationships would encompass all strategic approaches—e.g., monologue, dialogue, collaboration—and all activities involved in establishing and maintaining good relations—e.g., listening, understanding, informing, educating, advocating, engaging, influencing, advising. While specific public diplomacy efforts would have narrowly

---

[97] See Priscilla Murphy, "The Limits of Symmetry: A Game Theory Approach to Symmetric and Asymmetric Public Relations," in *Public Relations Research Annual* 3, ed. James E. Grunig and Larissa A. Grunig (Mahwah, NJ: Lawrence Erlbaum Publishers, 1991), 115–132.

[98] J. E. Grunig, L. A. Grunig, and Dozier, "Models of Public Relations," 312; see also James E. Grunig and Jon White, "The Effect of Worldviews on Public Relations Theory and Practice," in Grunig, ed. *Excellence in Public Relations Management*, 39.

[99] Larissa A. Grunig, James E. Grunig and David Dozier, *Excellent Public Relations and Effective Organizations: A Study of Communication Management in Three Countries* (Mahwah, NJ: Lawrence Erlbaum Publishers, 2002): 312; see also Grunig and Hunt, *Managing Public Relations*, 23.

[100] Ledingham, "Explicating Relationship Management as a General Theory of Public Relations," 192.

defined objectives (i.e., changes in levels of knowledge, attitudes and behaviors), the ultimate objective in every case would be to enhance relationships with people abroad.

Such distinctions could be important in terms of how public diplomacy practitioners approach their work. As an example, in a study of the strategic dimensions of public diplomacy, public diplomacy scholar John Robert Kelley observed marked differences between the relationship-building (engagement) aspects and the informational/advocacy aspects of public diplomacy[101] The communication style of the "influence" model, Kelley contended, is both more propagandistic and more proactive than the information or engagement styles, which he found to be more transparent and involving both reactive and proactive elements. Likewise, the timeframe for engagement is long-term, according to Kelley, while the timeframe for information and influence is both long-term and short-term. Even if one disagrees with Kelley's conclusions regarding the specific features of public diplomacy's dimensions, the compartmentalization of public diplomacy illustrated by his study raises important questions about how the various elements of public diplomacy are reconciled in theory and practice.

A relational paradigm would alleviate the theoretical and practical consequences of viewing and practicing public diplomacy as separate functions with discrete assumptions and objectives. For example, with respect to the issue of time, a relational approach would recognize that good relationships built on credibility and trust take time to form and—for that reason—would emphasize long-term public diplomacy initiatives over short-term quick fixes. At the same time, a relational model would recognize the need for "rapid response" capabilities to address emerging issues that have the ability to affect long-term relationships.

Importantly, a relational approach to public diplomacy also would advance public diplomacy's role in policymaking. The emphasis on communication *and* action under a relational paradigm reflects the importance of public diplomacy's advisory function. As relationship managers who span the boundaries of institutions, public diplomacy professionals clearly are well suited to advise and counsel institutional

[101] John Robert Kelley, "Constructing Relevant Public Diplomacy Strategy in the 21st Century," paper presented at the annual meeting of the International Studies Association, Chicago, IL, February 28, 2007.

leaders on the public implications of decisions and actions and to "reconcile their organizations' ongoing relationships with a range of seemingly amorphous publics that are evolving within a global—yet multicultural and highly diverse—society."[102]

A relational approach to public diplomacy would reflect the importance of aligning institutional policies and actions with communication practices. In this respect, a relational paradigm has implications for organizational behavior as well as public diplomacy theory and practice, suggesting the need for heightened attention to the diplomacy of deeds. Under the relational paradigm, practitioners "contribute to organizational decision making so that the organization behaves in ways that publics are willing to support rather than in ways that publics oppose with their own behaviors."[103]

Additionally, the unit of measurement under a relational approach is relationships, providing a tangible means for evaluating public diplomacy's effectiveness (see Chapter Eight). As Ledingham observed, under a relational paradigm, it is possible to measure outcomes that transcend communication production or outputs by examining the quality of relationships that are formed. In this respect, the relational model offers practitioners a framework for demonstrating the contribution of public diplomacy to the well-being of a nation.[104]

Finally, a relational model of public diplomacy would provide the foundation for the development of ethical principles for public diplomacy practices. In contrast to historical perspectives that public diplomacy conducted in the "national interest" is either indifferent to morality or inherently ethical because it is driven by state interest, a relational approach would recognize the centrality of ethics in how nations manage their relations with the people of other nations.

A return to the four models of public relations practice illustrates this point. As Grunig explained, "The quality of the relationship depends on the model of public relations practiced."[105] Although all four models can be ethical, only "the two-way symmetrical model is inherently

[102] See Dean Kruckeberg, "Public Relations: Toward a Global Professionalism," in Ledingham and Bruning, *Public Relations as Relationship Management*, 146.

[103] James E. Grunig and Larissa A Grunig, "The Relationship Between Public Relations and Marketing in Excellent Organizations: Evidence from the IABC Study," *Journal of Marketing Communication* 4 (1998): 158.

[104] See Ledingham, "Explicating Relationship Management," 191.

[105] James E. Grunig, "Public Relations and International Affairs: Effects, Ethics and Responsibility," *Journal of International Affairs* 47 (1993): 137–162.

ethical," Grunig observed, "because it opens the question of right and wrong to dialogue, collaboration and compromise."[106]

Of course, intent to serve self-interest is not inherently unethical. Indeed, government leaders are expected to protect and advance national interests. But, as Mark R. Amstutz pointed out in a discussion of ethics in politics, "The priority of national interest does not obliterate the moral claims of other actors in the international community."[107] For that reason, the ethical dimensions of *how* a nation manages its relationships with people abroad must be considered.

Although the complexity of ethics in public diplomacy cannot be adequately addressed here, the discussion illustrates the need to recognize the moral—in addition to the theoretical and practical—dimensions of public diplomacy policies and practices. In *Ethics in International Interaction: Perspectives on Diplomacy and Negotiation*, Getinet Belay noted the dearth of historical attention to questions of morality in diplomacy generally, observing the need for a new conceptual paradigm that would reflect the continuing relevance of the nation-state in the global community while transforming "diplomacy from its traditional nation-state-centered moral orientation to an internationalist one."[108] Adopting relationship management as the conceptual foundation of public diplomacy would be a step in that direction.

At the same time, it should be recognized that while this discussion illustrates potential positive implications of adopting a relational approach to public diplomacy, further exploration is needed to deepen understanding of relationship management generally and the application of relational principles to public diplomacy specifically. Issues related to power and culture deserve special attention.

For example, while relationship management theory challenges the assumptions of a power-based approach to public diplomacy, it does not allay all concerns about power imbalances between institutions and publics. Critical public relations scholars point out, for example, that inequalities in the respective resources and negotiating power of institutions and their publics may lead to hegemonic outcomes

---

[106] Ibid.

[107] Mark R. Amstutz, *International Ethics: Concepts, Theories and Cases in Global Politics* (Oxford: Rowman & Littlefield, 1999), 15.

[108] Getinet Belay, "Ethics in International Interaction: Perspectives on Diplomacy and Negotiation," in *Ethics in Intercultural and International Communication* (Mahwah, NJ: Lawrence Erlbaum Publishers, 1997), 261.

achieved through the "manufacturing of consent.'[109] Others question whether relational approaches based on symmetry reflect unachievable "utopian" ideals.[110]

Thus, in addressing issues related to power, it will be important to clarify the concepts of mutuality and dialogue. A better understanding of how (and whether) mutuality can be achieved and the factors that influence perceptions of mutual benefit will be helpful both in conducting effective public diplomacy and in demonstrating the relevance of public diplomacy to nations—and to the world. For example, what does *genuine* dialogue actually entail?[111]

A related issue—and one of the most difficult challenges facing public diplomacy practitioners going forward—will be determining how to balance the interests of nations with the interests of foreign publics and the broader public sphere. In other words, what is the role—and what are the responsibilities—of public diplomacy practitioners in the global marketplace of ideas?

A similar question has sparked considerable debate among public relations scholars and practitioners who have explored the ethical obligations of public relations professionals to balance a primary loyalty to clients or employers with a concomitant obligation to serve the "public interest." Although there is no consensus on the matter, some guideposts emerged from a recent collection of essays by leading scholars who were invited to address the topic of "responsible advocacy" in public relations. A synthesis of the works suggested that critical components of responsible advocacy include: "individual accountability, informed decision-making, multicultural understanding, relationship building, open communication, dialogue, truth and transparency, and integrity."[112]

---

[109] See, e.g., Juliet Roper, "Symmetrical Communication: Excellent Public Relations or a Strategy for Hegemony?," *Journal of Public Relations Research* 17, no. 1 (2005): 69–86.

[110] See, e.g., Jacquie L'Etang, "Corporate Responsibility and Public Relations Ethics" in *Critical Perspectives in Public Relations*, ed. Jacquie L'Etang and Magda Pieczka (London: International Thomson Business Press, 1996), 96–97.

[111] See Michael L. Kent and Maureen Taylor, "Toward a Dialogic Theory of Public Relations," *Public Relations Review* 28, no. 1 (2002): 21–37; see also Mohan J. Dutta-Bergman, "U.S. Public Diplomacy in the Middle East: A Critical Cultural Approach," *Journal of Communication Inquiry* 30, no. 2 (April 2006): 102–124.

[112] Kathy Fitzpatrick and Carolyn Bronstein, *Ethics in Public Relations: Responsible Advocacy* (Thousand Oaks, CA: Sage Publications, 2006): xi.

According to the editors, "Responsible advocacy based on open and honest communications helps businesses, governments, and nonprofits alike meet the ethical expectations of strategic constituents and build the relationships needed to accomplish organizational goals. In this respect, responsible advocacy in public relations might be viewed as strategic advocacy designed to align special interests of organizations with the special interests of stakeholders."[113]

The work also indicated that "a self-interested approach to responsible advocacy in public relations falls short of the professional mandate to serve the public interest. As advocates in the marketplace of ideas, public relations professionals should strive to further the ideals of democratic institutions. Whether in business or government or nonprofit practice, the common good is served only when the 'voices' of special interests present their views in ways that advance informed decision making and contribute to the well-being of greater society."[114]

Does the same hold true for public diplomacy? Sociology scholar Manuel Castells has suggested that it does. The "implicit project behind the idea of public diplomacy," he contended, "is to harness the dialogue between different social collectives and their cultures in the hope of sharing meaning and understanding. The aim of the practice of public diplomacy is not to convince but to communicate, not to declare but to listen. Public diplomacy seeks to build a public sphere in which diverse voices can be heard in spite of their origins, distinct values, and often contradictory interests."[115]

Another issue ripe for future research is whether relational concepts apply in diverse cultures and contexts. Because of the predominance of western influences on the theoretical development of public relations, public relations worldviews reflect a U.S.-centric perspective. To some degree, the same is true in public diplomacy. Thus, the impact of cultural differences on a relational model of public diplomacy must be examined.

As an example, a study by public relations scholar Chun ju Flora Hung, who investigated the impact of Chinese culture on relationship-building, found that cultural characteristics such as family orientation

---

[113] Ibid.

[114] Ibid.

[115] Manuel Castells, "The New Public Sphere: Global Civil Society, Communication Networks, and Global Governance," *The Annals of the American Academy of Political and Social Science* 616 (March 2008): 91.

and relational orientation had an impact on the relationship cultivation strategies of multinational corporations operating in China.[116] Similar studies looking at public diplomacy efforts in various parts of the world would aid understanding of cultural effects on relationship management in public diplomacy.

[116] Chun ju Flora Hung, "Cultural Influence on Relationship Cultivation Strategies: Multinational Companies in China," *Journal of Communication Management* 8, no. 3 (2004): 264–281.

CHAPTER SIX

STRATEGIC DIRECTIONS: THE BRANDING CONTROVERSY

The United States of America is a brand.[1]

Ever since former U.S. Secretary of State Colin Powell introduced the idea of "branding" America, a controversy has raged about whether corporate marketing and branding techniques have a place in public diplomacy's strategic toolbox. The debate over the "commercialization" of public diplomacy has been fueled by provocative comments from those on both sides of the controversy.

For example, soon after advertising executive turned public diplomacy chief Charlotte Beers implemented the "Shared Values" campaign in late 2001, *No Logo* author Naomi Klein denounced the idea of "branding" America. Writing about "the reasons to be wary of mixing the logic of branding with the practice of governance," Klein criticized Beers for seeing the United States' "tattered international image as little more than a communications problem."[2]

According to Klein, "At its core, branding is about rigorously controlled one-way messages, sent out in their glossiest form, then hermetically sealed off from those who would turn that corporate monologue into a social dialogue."[3] Such thinking is inconsistent with democracy, Klein contended. "Unlike strong brands, which are predictable and disciplined, democracy is messy and fractious, if not outright rebellious."[4] She said that America's "strongest 'brand attribute' is its embrace of diversity, a value Ms. Beers is now, ironically, attempting to stamp with cookie-cutter uniformity around the world." According to Klein, "the task is not only futile but dangerous."[5] While

---

[1] Al Ries and Laura Ries, *The Fall of Advertising & The Rise of PR* (New York: HarperCollins, 2002), 280.

[2] Naomi Klein, "America Is Not a Hamburger: President Bush's Attempts to Rebrand the United States Are Doomed," guardian.co.uk, March 14, 2002, http://www.guardian.co.uk/media/2002/mar/14/marketingandpr.comment (accessed January 15, 2009).

[3] Ibid.

[4] Ibid.

[5] Ibid.

"diversity and debate are the lifeblood of liberty," she said, "they are the enemies of branding."[6]

On the other side of the debate, branding and identity consultant Wally Olins argued that because a nation's brand is much like corporate brands, it can be enhanced through commercial marketing strategies. In making a case for nation branding, Olins contended that businesses and nations can use similar techniques to advance their competitive positions. "[P]eople are people whether they work in a company or live in a nation, and that means they can be motivated and inspired and manipulated in the same ways, using the same techniques."[7]

Olins suggested that the "visceral antagonism" with which some view the concept of nation branding, is the result of "snobbery, ignorance and semantics."[8] He explained, "Snobbery because some so-called intellectuals seem to think that business is a contemptible and boring activity with no intellectual, cultural or social content, which is solely dedicated to making profits and has no relevance to society as a whole."[9] With regard to ignorance, "Most business people do not know anything about the history of the nation they were born and live in.... And unfortunately it is also true that most academics know nothing about how business works, so each side assumes that the other lives in another and entirely foreign world."[10]

But it is semantics, Olins said, that is the biggest problem, arguing that it is not the ideas associated with nation branding that others find most objectionable. Rather, he said, it is the fact that "these concepts are associated with those that have been used by clever corporations and their brands."[11] According to Olins, branding opponents see a disconnect between "the words and what they seem to mean—"cheap, transient, crass, commercial trivia which are both superficial and insignificant"—and the nation, which is perceived to be "permanent, deeply significant and has huge emotional and even spiritual connotations."[12]

---

[6] Ibid.

[7] Wally Olins, "Branding the Nation—The Historical Context," *Journal of Brand Management* 9, no. 4/5 (April 2002): 247.

[8] Ibid., 214/246.

[9] Ibid., 246.

[10] Ibid., 247.

[11] Ibid.

[12] Ibid.

Unfortunately, such commentary does little to clarify nation branding's function, purpose or possible value to nations. Nor does it advance the debate on whether nation branding provides a sound strategic direction for public diplomacy.

This chapter sorts out the nation branding controversy by exploring the concept of nation branding in the context of public diplomacy. The aim is to clarify the meaning of nation branding and to consider whether a marriage between nation branding and public diplomacy makes sense. The chapter concludes that, although the two disciplines share some common views regarding the importance of a nation's global reputation to its ability to advance national interests, fundamental differences in worldviews and functions preclude the adoption of nation branding as a viable strategic approach to public diplomacy.

The rise of nation branding

Within the past ten years or so, the concept of nation branding has caught fire in foreign ministries, as evidenced by both the increasing number of state leaders reaching out to "branding consultants" to help enhance their nations' brand images and a growing body of quasi-academic literature dedicated to the subject. At the same time, nation branding has become increasingly linked to public diplomacy. For example, Peter van Ham has suggested that in the United States, "[p]lace branding and public diplomacy are now seen as the keys to making up for a decade of complacency by reinvigorating America's unique and underutilized soft power."[13]

By some accounts, the growth of nation branding, which is generally defined as the application of corporate marketing concepts and techniques to countries, represents the natural progression of branding "from its original application to simple products through to services, companies and organizations and now nations."[14] By other accounts, it represents attempts by marketing professionals to capitalize on an increasing focus on public diplomacy in diplomatic circles. Still others believe the "place branding frenzy" occurring in foreign ministries

[13] Peter van Ham, "Place Branding: The State of the Art," *The Annals of the American Academy of Political and Social Science* 616 (March 2008): 139.

[14] Keith Dinnie, *Nation Branding: Concepts, Issues, Practice* (Boston: Elsevier, 2008), 21.

throughout the world has more to do with forces of change within the global environment than it does with either the evolution of the marketing discipline or with the business development ambitions of marketing practitioners.[15]

According to van Ham, "The practice of nation branding has taken off at a time when the role and power of states (and other territorial actors) are changing. States as well as international organizations (IOs) vie for political authority and loyalty in a dense and highly competitive market, embarking on a quest for the hearts and minds of people both at home and around the world," he said. "The emerging brand state is not a brand new state, but a political player that promotes itself more assertively than before."[16]

The idea that globalization has created more competitive states is a common refrain from nation branding advocates who believe that as national boundaries have become more blurred, the development and/or preservation of national identities has become more important. In explaining the growth of nation branding, Olle Wastberg said, "Globalisation implies of course that all states are in competition with one another. Individual states therefore need both to dress their national brands with the right associations and to combine their product brands with the image of the country of origin."[17]

The thinking is that, as a result of globalization, the world is now one market in which nations must compete for the attention and goodwill of the world's "consumers." In this competitive arena, "the issue is not whether or not to brand, but how to manage and market the [nation] brand."[18] As brand consultant Janine Widler has observed, differentiation between nations "is what competition is all about and it is what branding is all about."[19] The point of nation branding then is to help a nation distinguish itself from other nations in ways that provide a competitive edge that allow it to be successful in the international marketplace.

---

[15] van Ham, "Place Branding," 133.

[16] Ibid., 128.

[17] Olle Wastberg, "Opinion Pieces: How Has Place Branding Developed During the Year that Place Branding Has Been in Publication?" *Place Branding* 2, no. 1 (2006): 17.

[18] Charles Skuba, "Branding America," *Georgetown Journal of International Affairs* 3 (Summer/Fall 2002): 106.

[19] Janine Widler, "Nation Branding: With Pride Against Prejudice," *Place Branding and Public Diplomacy* 3, no. 2 (2007): 147.

According to Simon Anholt, who introduced the concept of "nation branding" in 1996, "the advance of globalization means that every country, city and region must compete with every other for its share of the world's commercial, political, social and cultural transactions. In such an environment, as in any busy marketplace, brand image becomes a critical factor, providing a vital short cut to an informed buying decision."[20]

The idea of nation brands, Anholt said, "is really just a metaphor for how countries can compete more effectively in the modern age."[21] He explained that brand image is equated with national reputation. Nation brands are important, he said, because "[t]he reputation of a country has a direct and measurable impact on just about every aspect of its engagement with other countries, and plays a critical role in its economic, social, political and cultural progress."[22] For this reason, he contended, "all responsible governments, on behalf of their people, their institutions and their companies, need to discover what the world's perception of their country is, and to develop a strategy for managing it."[23]

Schools of nation branding

At the same time nation branding has captured the fascination of foreign ministries, the field is experiencing an internal crisis that threatens to pull it apart. In fact, debate regarding the specific function and parameters of nation branding have led to the emergence of two schools of thought that reflect different views both on precisely what nation branding is and how it should be practiced. The two groups might be described as the "Traditional School of Nation Branding" and the "Anholt School of Competitive Identity," respectively.

The "Traditional School" is represented by traditional marketing and branding specialists, such as Olins, and branding scholars, such as marketing expert Philip Kotler and Keith Dinnie, the author of *Nation*

---

[20] Simon Anholt, "The Importance of National Reputation," in Foreign & Commonwealth Office Online Collection of Essays and Cases, www.fco.gov.uk/en/about-the-fco/publications (accessed December 10, 2008).

[21] Ibid.

[22] Simon Anholt, *Competitive Identity: The New Brand Management for Nations, Cities and Regions* (Houndmills: Palgrave MacMillan, 2007), 9.

[23] Ibid., 2.

Branding: Concepts, Issues and Practices, one of few textbooks focused on nation branding. The "Anholt School" is represented primarily by Anholt, a recognized nation branding authority and founding editor of the journal *Place Branding*. The different views of nation branding represented by these two "schools" must be addressed before the links between nation branding and public diplomacy can be considered.

The "Traditional School of Nation Branding"

The "Traditional School of Nation Branding" represents those who approach the function from a traditional marketing perspective, seeing nations much like products and services that can be branded through commercial marketing activities. Those who fall into this category believe that traditional marketing principles can be applied to "whole" nations.[24] Kotler, for example, observed, "Beyond serving as brand names, countries can be products as well."[25] He pointed out that "countries compete in the market for tourists, factories, business and talented people" and, therefore, "must embark on more conscious country branding."[26]

The "Traditional School" applies a conventional definition of branding, such as "the process by which companies distinguish their product offerings from those of the competition."[27] According to the American Marketing Association, a brand is "a name, term, sign, symbol, or design, or a combination of them intended to identify the goods and services of one seller or group of sellers and to differentiate them from those of competition."[28] "Nation brand" is similarly defined in *Nation Branding* as "the unique, multi-dimensional blend of elements that provide the nation with culturally grounded differentiation and relevance for all of its targeted audiences."[29] According to Dinnie, "In an increasingly globalized economy, the challenge of distinguishing their product offerings from those of the competition has assumed

---

[24] Dinnie, *Nation Branding*, 54.

[25] Philip Kotler and David Gertner, "Country as Brand, Product, and Beyond: A Place Marketing and Brand Management Perspective," *Brand Management* 9, no. 4/5 (April 2002): 258.

[26] Ibid.

[27] Dinnie, *Nation Branding*, 14.

[28] Quoted in Keith Dinnie, *Nation Branding: Concepts, Issues, Practice* (Amsterdam: Elsevier, 2008), 14.

[29] Dinnie, *Nation Branding*, 14.

critical importance for nations competing for both domestic and foreign consumers."[30]

Under the "Traditional School," nation branding has three major objectives: "to attract tourists, to stimulate inward investment and to boost exports."[31] Branding traditionalists also believe that branding techniques can be useful for other purposes related to politics, business, and diplomacy. For example, secondary benefits of effective nation branding might include enhanced political influence, diminished negative stereotypes, improved international relations, and strong credit ratings.[32]

The strategic process of the "Traditional School" focuses on three key questions a nation must ask: Where are we now? Where do we want to go? How do we get there?

In "getting there," the traditionalists stress the importance of "substance" over words. For example, brand strategy consultant Fiona Gilmore emphasized, "The important thing to realize about branding a country is that it must be an amplification of what is already there and not a fabrication."[33] According to Gilmore, "A country or region's positioning can never be an artificial creation imposed from the outside."[34]

Strategic options for implementing the brand image include a range of marketing communication techniques, or "influence tools."[35] For example, in *Marketing Places: Attracting Investment, Industry, and Tourism to Cities, States and Nations*, Kotler, Donald H. Haider and Irving Rein identified a number of options for cities, states and nations "to promote their place to target markets," including advertising, direct marketing, sales promotion, public relations, and personal selling.[36] These authors suggested that "[p]lace image makers can draw on three tools to implement an effective image of a place: (1)

---

[30] Ibid.

[31] Ibid., 17.

[32] See, e.g., Dinnie, *Nation Branding*, 17.

[33] Fiona Gilmore, "A Country—Can It Be Repositioned? Spain—The Success Story of Country Branding," *Brand Management* 9, no. 5 (April 2002): 284.

[34] Ibid.

[35] Philip Kotler, Donald H. Haider, and Irving Rein, *Marketing Places: Attracting Investment, Industry, and Tourism to Cities, States and Nations* (New York: The Free Press, 1993), 166.

[36] Ibid., 162–171.

slogans, themes and positions; (2) visual symbols; and (3) events and deeds."[37]

Advertising is viewed as a "powerful tool" for nation branding.[38] However, the traditionalists emphasize that brand-building is a long-term commitment, and nations need "to adopt a long-term strategic view when building their nation-brand, rather than aiming for a quick fix short-term advertising campaign whose effects may be ephemeral."[39] According to Charles Skuba, although "[a]dvertising has traditionally been the marketing practice that drives branding... branding can also be driven by other instruments from the communications toolbox."[40] In the case of nation branding, Skuba said (without explanation), "public relations is the most obvious primary driver."[41]

Such thinking mirrors that of branding strategists Al Ries and Laura Ries, authors of *The Fall of Advertising & The Rise of PR*, who observed "a dramatic shift from advertising-oriented marketing to public relations-oriented marketing" in branding.[42] The reason, according to Ries and Ries, is that "PR has credibility. Advertising does not. PR provides the positive perceptions that an advertising campaign, if properly directed, can exploit."[43] According to Ries and Ries, "what builds brands are media messages" while advertising maintains brands.[44] "The purpose of advertising is not to build a brand, but to defend a brand once the brand has been built by other means, primarily public relations or third part endorsements."[45] Notably, the view of public relations espoused by Ries and Ries is narrowly focused on the publicity aspects of public relations, rather than on its broader relationship management function.

The "Traditional School of Nation Branding" emphasizes the importance of involving a range of actors from the public and private sectors in brand management and stresses the need to get internal parties on board. Relevant stakeholders include all those who will be affected by

---

[37] Ibid.

[38] Dinnie, *Nation Branding*, 224.

[39] Ibid., 15.

[40] Skuba, "Branding America," 107.

[41] Ibid.

[42] Al Ries and Laura Ries, *The Fall of Advertising & The Rise of PR* (New York: Harper Business, 2002), xi.

[43] Ibid.

[44] Ibid., 99.

[45] Ibid., xiv.

branding activities, i.e., government agencies with a stake in the outcome of branding efforts (e.g., tourism board, consular affairs, public diplomacy, economic development, and aid groups), elected government officials, businesses, NGOs, citizens, and media.

The traditionalists also recognize the importance of culture in nation branding. According to Dinnie, "A deep and authentic nation-brand must include the many elements and expressions of a nation's culture; if it fails to do so, it will rightly be perceived as shallow and superficial and not truly representative of the nation."[46]

The "Anholt School of Competitive Identity"

Anholt offers a different perspective on nation branding. In explaining his views, he recalled that his original observation concerning nation branding "was a simple one: that the reputations of countries are rather like the brand images of companies and products, and equally important."[47] This "simple" observation, Anholt contended, has since been widely misinterpreted—partly, he freely admits, because of his poor choice of words.[48] By way of explanation, Anholt pointed out that nation branding really "is *not* branding."[49] Furthermore, he said, although nations *have* brands, nations cannot *be* branded.

Anholt explained that "there is a big difference between observing that places have brand images (which is simply a useful metaphor) and claiming that places can be branded (which is an excessively ambitious, entirely unproven and ultimately irresponsible claim)."[50] In fact, according to Anholt, "there appears to be no evidence to suggest that using marketing communications to influence international public perceptions of an entire city, region or country is anything other than a vain and foolish waste of taxpayers' money."[51] Therefore, Anholt suggested, "relatively little of what one might learn as a branding or

---

[46] Ibid., 112.

[47] Simon Anholt, *Competitive Identity*, xi.

[48] Lee Hudson Teslik, "Countries Must Earn Better Images Through Smart Policy," interview with Simon Anholt, Editor, *Place Branding and Public Diplomacy*, Council on Foreign Relations, November 6, 2008, www.cfr.prg/publication/14719/ (accessed February 29, 2008).

[49] Simon Anholt, "Place Branding: Is it Marketing, or Isn't It?" *Place Branding and Public Diplomacy* 4, no. 4 (2008): 2.

[50] Ibid.

[51] Ibid., 1.

marketing expert is truly transferable or useful in the fields of policy-making, international relations, public diplomacy, cultural relations and the other components of competitive identity."[52]

At the same time, Anholt recognized that marketing communication techniques are "perfectly justifiable when the task is essentially one of selling a product—and the product can just as well be the holiday resorts or investment opportunities of a country as the products of a corporation."[53] But, according to the "Anholt School of Competitive Identity," such efforts do not make a brand strategy: "Brand management should be treated as a component of national policy, never as a 'campaign' that is separate from planning, governance or economic development.... If brand management is put into the silo of 'communications' or 'public affairs,' there is little it can do. But when it informs policy-making and becomes implicit in the way the country is run, it can dramatically accelerate change."[54]

According to Anholt, a brand is "the context in which messages are received," or "the pre-existing background reputation" that "fundamentally conditions the way in which any message is received and interpreted by the audience."[55] Nation branding, he advised, involves the harmonization of six key "natural" channels of national behavior and communication that form a "hexagon of competitive identity" that includes policy, people, brands, tourism, investment, and culture.[56] "Every act of promotion, exchange or representation needs to be seen not only as an end in itself but as an opportunity to build the country's overall reputation; and all the bodies, agencies and organizations at each point of the hexagon have to work together, meet together, and align their behavior to a common national strategy."[57]

In dismissing the idea that nations can be "sold" like products, Anholt said "it is deeds that principally create public perceptions, not words and pictures."[58] He argued, "Most places get the images they

[52] Ibid., 3.
[53] Ibid., 1.
[54] Simon Anholt, "From Nation Branding to Competitive Identity: The Role of Brand Management as a Component of National Policy," in *Nation Branding: Concepts, Issues, Practice*, ed. Keith Dinnie (Boston: Elsevier, 2008), 23.
[55] Simon Anholt, "Editorial: Nation Brand as Context and Reputation," *Place Branding* 1, no. 3 (2005): 224.
[56] Simon Anholt, "The Importance of National Reputation."
[57] Anholt, *Competitive Identity*, 27.
[58] Simon Anholt, "Place Branding: Is It Marketing, or Isn't It?," 1.

deserve, and imagining they can change the brand of the place without changing the way they behave is the height of delusion."[59] According to Anholt, "People don't change their views about countries—views they may have held for decades—simply because a marketing campaign tells them to."[60]

An important principle of brand management in the "Anholt School" is that it "is first and foremost an *internal* project."[61] In order to be successful, nation branding must unite people—government, business, civil society—with a "common strategic vision" that "can create a powerful dynamic for progress."[62] Key to nation branding's success, according to Anholt, is the "harmonisation of goals, themes, communications and behaviors in the long term."[63]

At the same time, Anholt recognized that it is important for nations to influence public opinion. Rather than adopting marketing communication or "selling" techniques, however, Anholt stressed the importance of "symbolic actions" that enhance a nation's reputation.[64] Examples of "symbolic actions," he said, are "innovations, structures, legislation, reforms, investments, institutions or policies."[65]

The purpose of nation branding, according to Anholt, is to enhance the nation brand in ways that contribute to the competitive identity and reputation of the nation, which in turn influences the nation's ability to compete successfully in the international marketplace. Toward this end, Anholt shares the traditionalists' view that culture is important in nation branding. For example, he noted that cultural representations have "the power to communicate a country's true spirit and essence.... Culture plays an essential role in the process of enriching a country's reputation, in driving public perceptions towards a fuller and more durable understanding of the country and its values."[66]

In an effort to quell the confusion surrounding the concept of "nation branding," Anholt adopted the phrase "competitive identity"

---

[59] Simon Anholt, "Why Brand? Some Practical Considerations for Nation Branding," *Place Branding* 2, no. 2 (2006): 102.

[60] Simon Anholt, "Public Diplomacy and Place Branding: Where's the Link?" *Place Branding* 2, no. 4 (2006): 272.

[61] Simon Anholt, "Why Brand?," 1.

[62] Simon Anholt, "Place Branding: Is It Marketing, or Isn't It?," 3.

[63] Ibid.

[64] Ibid.

[65] Ibid.

[66] Anholt, *Competitive Identity*, 97.

to describe the application of brand management to nations "because it has more to do with national identity and the politics and economics of competitiveness than with branding as it is usually understood."[67] According to Anholt, competitive identity is "essentially a plan for mobilizing the strategies, activities, investments, innovations and communications of as many national sectors as possible, both public and private, in a concerted drive to *prove* to the world that the nation deserves a different, broader and more positive image."[68] The concept of competitive identity, he said, is "based on competition, consumer choice and consumer power."[69]

Nation branding and public diplomacy

In 2006, Anholt announced the "re-branding" of the journal *Place Branding* to *Place Branding and Public Diplomacy* in recognition, he said, of the fact that "no state can hope to achieve its aims in the modern world without a mature and sophisticated fusion of PD and nation branding."[70] In addressing the link between public diplomacy and place branding, Anholt observed that "[i]n the modern age, it…seems natural that governments should turn to the world of commerce for guidance in [the area of public diplomacy], since creating wide-scale changes in opinion and behavior through persuasion rather than coercion, through attraction rather than compulsion, is seen to be the essence of marketing and branding."[71]

Anholt later wrote that his views on the connections between nation branding and public diplomacy had evolved, leading him "to conclude that that they are more distantly related than is often assumed."[72] He explained that public diplomacy has moved from "the initially rather primitive government PR" practiced by the United States after World War II, to "something closer to nation branding (which recognizes the importance played by national image and attempts to influence this, as well as understanding that a one-way sales pitch can't rebrand the nation, and that actions speak louder than words) to the more radical

[67] Simon Anholt, *Competitive Identity*, xi.
[68] Simon Anholt, "The Importance of National Reputation."
[69] Simon Anholt, *Competitive Identity*, 127.
[70] Simon Anholt, "Public Diplomacy and Place Branding: Where's the Link?," 275.
[71] Ibid.
[72] Anholt, "The Importance of National Reputation."

redefinition of public diplomacy" as "an instrument of policy, rather than as a method of communication."[73] As such, he said, "This new approach is fundamentally different from nation branding, since [public diplomacy's] primary purpose is neither to present government policies nor to build, enhance or preserve national reputation. At first sight it might be assumed that it has no connection whatsoever with nation branding, an approach which, no matter how sophisticated and policy-driven it becomes, has reputation as its ultimate concern."[74]

Continuing, however, Anholt pointed out that there is indeed a connection between nation branding and public diplomacy, and that the connection is the "credibility of the perceived source." He explained, "A nation's credibility is virtually synonymous with its 'brand image.'"[75]

Although Anholt's description of public diplomacy's evolution, as well as its purpose, is subject to some debate and the suggestion that public diplomacy has little concern with national reputation runs counter to contemporary thinking in the field, his conclusion that nation branding and public diplomacy share a common concern regarding a nation's credibility is correct. His suggestion that the ties between nation branding and public diplomacy in fact may be more distant than some have imagined is also spot on.

Conceptual connections

Public diplomacy and nation branding viewed broadly share some common beliefs and interests. Both recognize the importance of international reputation to a nation's ability to protect and advance its national interests. Both recognize the need to strategically *manage* a nation's reputational assets. Both recognize the need for a nation to actually be what it desires its image and reputation to be. Both recognize the long-term orientation of establishing a good reputation with people abroad. Both recognize the need for collaboration and cooperation among public and private actors who affect and are affected by a nation's reputation. Both recognize the importance of national culture to a nation's image and reputation. And both recognize that promotional techniques can be effective in accomplishing certain objectives.

---

[73] Ibid.
[74] Ibid.
[75] Ibid.

Additionally, public diplomacy shares the "Anholt School's" view regarding the need for a function to advise policy makers on the public implications of policy decisions and to help align a country's actions with its words.

Those who view public diplomacy as primarily a promotional function—rather than as a relational function—are likely to see other commonalities between public diplomacy and nation branding/competitive identity as well. In fact, one of the difficulties in evaluating the proper relationship between public diplomacy and nation branding is the lack of precise definitions, as well as broad misunderstanding, of both functions. For that reason, it should be noted that public diplomacy is viewed here as a relationship management function (see Chapter Five).

As such, neither the "Traditional School," which focuses on promoting a nation's "products," nor the "Anholt School," which focuses on reconciling the factors that influence a nation's competitive identity, reflects the more expansive worldview of public diplomacy and its deep ties to *international relations*. Nor does either school, both of which concentrate on the projection of a nation's brand or identity, recognize the importance of dialogue and engagement with foreign publics, which are critical to public diplomacy's success.

Conceptual disconnections

For many of the same reasons the four "Ps" of conventional marketing—product, price, place, and promotion—do not apply to public diplomacy, neither do what might be called the four "Cs" of nation branding or competitive identity: country (of origin), competition, commerce, and consumers.

The four "Cs," which represent the fundamental concerns of nation branding, reveal a view of the world in which nations must compete for the attention and affection of world "consumers" who have the ability to influence a nation's prosperity. Marketing and branding specialists see a world in which "differences matter" and nations must distinguish themselves in relevant ways. As Widler observed, "According to nation branders, globalization is reinforcing national boundaries rather than dissolving them."[76]

[76] Janine Widler, "Nation Branding," 146.

Public diplomats see the world differently. They see an increasingly interdependent world in which nations and people are united by common interests and common problems that require common solutions. They see a world in which multilateral collaboration and cooperation matter and in which shared values and interests can overcome tensions and conflicts created by differences.

Where public diplomats seek common ground, marketers seek a competitive edge. As van Ham observed, "Branding is an acknowledgment that territorial actors need to implement competitive global policies and strategies designed to achieve prosperity and influence."[77]

The strategic dimensions of nation branding and public diplomacy, respectively, are also distinct. For example, in both the "Traditional School" and the "Anholt School," the strategic focus is on enhancing a nation's competitive identity and/or image with consumers in the global marketplace. Certainly, public diplomacy is concerned with national image and reputation. But public diplomacy's more expansive portfolio, in principle, includes managing a nation's relationships with *all* foreign publics—not just those potentially interested in engaging in "commercial" transactions with the country.

The issue of national security offers a good example of the different mindsets. Although nation branding practitioners have just begun to explore the security dimensions of a nation's brand, early efforts suggest that the emphasis is not on the potential for nation branding to create a more secure nation and world, which is the focus of public diplomacy. Rather, it is on the potential for a nation's "security brand" to serve as a "Unique Selling Point" for the nation.[78] As guest editors Jon Coaffee and van Ham observed in a special issue of *Place Branding and Public Diplomacy* devoted to "security branding," "The success (or failure) of places, whether they are cities or continents, to brand themselves as safe and secure can have a number of implications for marketing potential."[79]

Efforts to link nation branding and public diplomacy through a nation's "political brand" similarly demonstrate the inappropriateness

[77] Peter van Ham, "Branding Territory: Inside the Wonderful Worlds of PR and IR Theory," *Journal of International Studies* 31, no. 2 (2002), 265.

[78] Jon Coaffee and Peter van Ham, "'Security Branding': The Role of Security in Marketing the City, Region or State," *Place Branding and Public Diplomacy* 4, no. 3 (2008): 191.

[79] Ibid., 193.

of applying a marketing mindset to all matters related to public diplomacy. For example, in examining the possible impact of the United States' "political brand" on the overall brand image of the country, Elizabeth A. Garbacz Rawson suggested that "[a] national political brand theoretically closes the gap between public diplomacy and nation branding."[80] Given the comprehensive nature of nation branding, she said, "[combining] every part of a country that communicates the nation brand to foreign countries and audiences" can strengthen the nation branding field.[81]

These examples illustrate the difficulties of treating all foreign publics as "consumers." Public relations scholars James E. Grunig and Larissa A. Grunig raised a similar concern in contemplating the integration of public relations and marketing. They pointed out that "[m]arkets essentially consist of individuals making individual decisions" while publics include "collectivities" or groups that have the ability to influence both organizational behavior and the social-political environment of organizations.[82] Grunig and Grunig noted, for example, that marketing and advertising strategies aimed at individuals may be of little use when dealing with issues involving groups, such as activists—or, one might add, potential terrorists.

Charles Wolf, Jr. and Brian Wade made a similar point in considering the usefulness of marketing techniques to public diplomacy. Noting that a distinction must be made between "*private goods* and *public (or collective)* goods," they said, "marketing efforts and marketing skills attuned to and grandly successful in promoting the former may be ill-adapted to promote the latter."[83] Wolf and Wade pointed out that the meaning, quality, and benefits associated with public goods—such as "democracy, tolerance, the rule of law and, more generally, American values and the 'American story' "—"largely depend on a high degree of understanding, acceptance, adoption, and practice by others, rather

[80] Elizabeth A. Garbacz Rawson, "Perceptions of the United States of America: Exploring the Political Brand of a Nation," *Place Branding and Public Diplomacy* 3, no. 3 (2007): 218.

[81] Ibid., 220.

[82] James E. Grunig and Larissa A. Grunig, "The Relationship Between Public Relations and Marketing in Excellent Organizations: Evidence from the IABC Study," *Journal of Marketing Communications* 4 (1998): 157–158.

[83] Charles Wolf, Jr. and Brian Rosen, "Public Diplomacy: How to Think About and Improve It," *Occasional Paper* (Santa Monica, CA: RAND Corporation, 2004), 6.

than by an individual acting alone."[84] Additionally, they contended, public goods are "non-rivalrous," meaning that their acceptance and support depends on the collective adoption by a constituent group, whose members collectively share in the benefits of the collective good."[85]

Fundamental differences in nation branding and public diplomacy also are evident in the theories behind the respective functions. Although theory building has not been a focus of those writing about or participating in nation branding initiatives, Anholt explained the basic theory behind competitive identity as:

> [W]hen governments have a good, clear, believable and positive idea of what their country really is, what it stands for and where it's going, and manage to coordinate the actions, investments, policies and communications of all six points of the [competitive identity] hexagon [tourism, brands, policy, investment, culture, people] so that they prove and reinforce this idea, then they stand a good chance of building and maintaining a competitive national identity both internally and externally—to the lasting benefit of exporters, importers, government, the culture sector, tourism, immigration, and pretty much every aspect of international relations.

On the other hand, relationship management theory (as explained in Chapter Five), as applied to nations, is:

> Effectively managing a nation's relationships with foreign publics around common interests and shared goals, over time, results in mutual understanding and benefit for interacting nations and publics.[86]

These statements reveal fundamental differences in both the theoretical underpinnings and central functions of nation branding and public diplomacy—i.e., that nation branders manage brands or identities, and public diplomats manage relationships. As Jan Melissen observed in addressing such differences, "nation branding is crucially about the articulation and projection of identity."[87] On the other hand, "public diplomacy, in its more advanced form, is fundamentally dialogical, an

---

[84] Ibid.

[85] Ibid.

[86] John A. Ledingham, "Explicating Relationship Management as a General Theory of Public Relations," *Journal of Public Relations Research* 15, no. 2 (2003): 190.

[87] Jan Melissen, "Opinion Pieces—How Has Place Branding Developed During the Year that *Place Branding* Has Been in Publication?," *Place Branding* 2, no. 1 (2006): 10–12.

international two-way street and not a one-way messaging system." As Melissen explained, "'PD' is about promoting and maintaining relationships in an international environment that is characterized by multiple links between civil societies and the growing influence of non-governmental actors."[88]

Members of the Public Diplomacy Council (PDC) made a similar point in observing that a branding approach to public diplomacy is inadequate for "engaging international publics on both policy and socio-cultural issues" and for gaining the public support needed for policy and diplomatic initiatives to succeed.[89] According to this group, public diplomacy based on "slogans and brands" should be rejected in favor of "respectful dialog and vigorous engagement at the level of ideas, not images."[90]

The PDC members explained that, if U.S. public diplomacy is to succeed, rather than tell its own story, America should focus on "the human story and how America relates to those outside our borders."[91] Pointing out that a "self-referential focus works against our credibility as moral leaders in an age of globalization," they said, "Understanding what is credible in the context of other societies—with their own history and politics—is the foundation upon which effective public diplomacy is constructed."[92] Therefore, "U.S. public diplomats should focus on how other people make sense of the United States and our shared world and bring that awareness back to the policy discussion."[93] In other words, public diplomacy's "first priority must be observing and listening."[94]

In many respects, the competitive concept of nation branding is similar to the concept of "soft power." In fact, van Ham pointed out that "[p]lace branding can be considered an effort to use strategies developed in the commercial sector to manage, if not necessarily wield, the soft power of a geographical location."[95]

---

[88] Ibid.

[89] Barry Fulton, Bruce Gregory, Donna Marie Oglesby, Walter R. Roberts, and Barry Zorthian, "Public Diplomacy Dissent: Transformation Not Restoration," in *America's Dialogue with the World*, ed, William P. Kiehl (Public Diplomacy Council: Washington, DC, 2006), 189.

[90] Ibid., 190.

[91] Ibid., 191.

[92] Ibid.

[93] Ibid.

[94] Ibid.

[95] Peter van Ham, "Place Branding: The State of the Art," 126–127.

Anholt also indicated that nation branding's market-based worldview is in line with Nye's view of the world. Much like soft power, which Anholt said "is about making people *want* to do what you want them to do," competitive identity "is about making people *want* to pay attention to a country's achievements, and believe in its qualities."[96] According to Anholt, competitive identity "is the quintessential modern exemplar of soft power."[97]

For some of the same reasons that soft power fails to provide an appropriate conceptual foundation for public diplomacy (see Chapter Five), nation branding, or competitive identity, fails to provide a sound strategic foundation for public diplomacy. Clearly, asymmetrical, one-way models of communication that characterize traditional marketing and branding approaches have proven to be ineffective for accomplishing public diplomacy objectives.

Similarly, while symbolic actions designed to showcase a nation's positive aspects, as suggested by Anholt, can be quite useful in enhancing a nation's *reputation*, they may not improve a nation's international *relations*. Establishing and sustaining beneficial relationships with foreign publics require a nation to go beyond marketing communication techniques or symbolic actions and engage in "symbolic *inter*actions" with people abroad.

As an example, veteran USIA officers who participated in the *USIA Alumni Study* (see Appendix One) said that personal contact between U.S. representatives and people abroad was the most important element in effective public diplomacy. When asked to rate the overall effectiveness of various public diplomacy activities, America's public diplomats rated most highly exchange programs, face-to-face interactions with local publics, international visitors programs, and dialogue with political elites.

The *least* effective public diplomacy strategy, according to the USIA veterans, is advertising in national and local media. When asked whether the U.S. government should consider using paid advertising to communicate its messages to people in other countries, only 7 percent of the USIA alumni said yes. A slightly larger number (13 percent) of the former diplomats said that paid media advertising, such as television commercials, could contribute to the future success of U.S. public diplomacy.

---

[96] Anholt, *Competitive Identity*, 127.
[97] Ibid.

Table 6.1 Effectiveness of Public Diplomacy Activities*

Activity	Mean**
Exchange programs	4.85
Educational exchanges, e.g., Fulbright, American Studies	4.85
Face-to-face interactions with local publics	4.84
International visitors programs	4.81
Dialogue with political elites and other opinion leaders	4.67
U.S. government libraries	4.54
Media relations	4.46
Speaker programs	4.35
International broadcasting	4.22
Performing arts	4.18
Interviews with U.S. officials by the foreign media	4.11
Cultural exhibits	3.95
U.S. government publications, i.e., magazines, brochures, etc.	3.88
Wireless file	3.81
Technical and development assistance	3.80
Editorials, op-eds in local media	3.78
Documentaries and films	3.64
Internet sites	3.61
American corners	3.52
Democracy initiatives	3.36
Psychological warfare	2.26
Disinformation campaigns	2.15
Paid advertisements in national/local media	1.19

* The *USIA Alumni Study* (n=213)
** Numeric average of all responses with 1 being "Not Effective" and 5 being "Very Effective."

Such findings raise an important question concerning the links between nation branding and public diplomacy: What is the relationship between reputation and relationships? For example, are good relationships a prerequisite for a good reputation, as Charles Fombrum, editor of *Corporate Reputation Review* has suggested? Fombrum observed that "[t]o acquire a reputation that is positive, enduring, and resilient requires managers to invest heavily in building and maintaining good relationships with their company's constituents."[98] Or is a good reputation a prerequisite for good relationships?

[98] Charles Fombrum, *Reputation: Realizing Value from the Corporate Image* (Cambridge: Harvard Business School Press, 1995), 57.

Although empirical studies that might answer such questions are scant, public relations research provides some evidence that "negative reputations can be improved by building and maintaining good relationships with publics."[99] Future studies that examine the relationship between reputation and relationships, including the respective durability of each, would be worthwhile.

Another important issue that should be considered is whether measures of national reputation, or brand image, provide adequate measures for evaluating the effectiveness of a nation's public diplomacy. For example, in 2005 Anholt developed in conjunction with the research firm GfK Roper the Nation Brands Index (NBI), which provides a ranking of the world's nation brands, or "a barometer of global preference."[100] The Index purports to measure the "power and quality" of the "brand image" of fifty countries by examining and tracking public perceptions of a country's "cultural, political, commercial and human assets, investment potential and tourist appeal."[101]

According to the NBI, countries with the most "powerful" brand values are rich, stable, liberal, democratic Western states that produce well-known branded products and have a strong international presence in the media (created through entertainment and culture or tourist promotions). For example, according to the NBI rankings, even after accounting for the negative "brand equity" attributed to America's unpopular foreign policies, the United States is a brand leader (ranking number 7 in 2008 behind Germany, France, United Kingdom, Canada, Japan, and Italy) and has a financial valuation (contribution to the national economy) of nearly $18 trillion, which exceeds all other countries.[102]

Such findings suggest that "Brand America" is in pretty good shape. Indeed, in *Brand America: The Mother of All Brands*, authors Anholt

---

[99] Sung Un Yang and Jose Mallago, "Exploring Links Between the Concepts of Organization-Public Relationships and Organizational Reputations," paper presented at the annual conference of the International Communications Association, May 23–27, 2003; see also James E. Grunig and C. F. Hung, "The Effect of Relationships on Reputation and Reputation on Relationships: A Cognitive Behavioral Study, " paper presented at the Public Relations Society of America's Educators Academy 5th Annual International, Interdisciplinary Public Relations Research Conference, Miami, Florida, March 8–10, 2002.

[100] Anholt, *Competitive Identity*, 43; see also The Anholt-GfK Roper Nation Brands Index, www.nationbrandsindex.com (accessed January 10, 2009).

[101] Ibid.

[102] Anholt, *Competitive Identity*, 44–45.

and Jeremy Hildreth observed that "Brand America is in a class of its own," comfortably dominating the whole spectrum of brand image.[103]

So, then, how can these results be squared with global attitude surveys that have consistently shown America's image plummeting to an all-time low in recent years? Such discrepancies raise questions about whether such measures are accurate predictors of the state of America's relationships with people abroad or, more importantly, a predictor of foreign publics' predispositions to speak or act in ways that support or harm U.S. interests. It is troubling to think that American public diplomacy might be guided by evaluations related solely to the nation's "brand image."

Beyond branding

This review of nation branding and public diplomacy indicates that although nation branding and public diplomacy share some common principles and practices, fundamental differences in worldviews and functions preclude the adoption of nation branding as a sound strategic approach to public diplomacy. Clearly, the disciplines are not the same thing, as some have argued. Nor is public diplomacy part of nation branding or nation branding part of public diplomacy.[104]

Of course, this does not mean that the ends sought nor the means employed by nation branding and public diplomacy, respectively, are inherently higher or lower value. Nor does it mean that marketing communication techniques are incompatible with certain public diplomacy objectives—because they are not.

Nation branding concepts can be useful in helping underdeveloped countries establish a presence on the world stage that would allow them to develop cultural and economic resources and participate in the global economy. In both developing and developed countries, branding concepts also can be effective in situations involving choices

[103] Simon Anholt and Jeremy Hildreth, *Brand America: The Mother of All Brands* (London: Cyan Books, 2004), 17.

[104] See Gyoygy Szondi, *Discussion Papers in Diplomacy, Public Diplomacy and Nation Branding: Conceptual Similarities and Differences* (The Hague: Netherlands Institute of International Relations "Clingendael," 2008).

by "consumers" that affect the prosperity of nations, e.g., choices of vacation destinations or investments.

Nation brand management also might be useful in ensuring that nations live up to their responsibilities in the global community, or in marketing terms, live up to their "brand promise." As Gilmore observed about company brands, "if defined correctly, a brand represents the core values and ideology of the organization, its raison d'etre and its reputation in the world."[105] As such, "brands are now a counterbalancing force of good against the potential negative use of power of multinationals—companies have to ensure that they meet the public expectations created by their brands." She asked: "Will this be said in the future of governments, too—that they will be pushed to greater accountability by the strength of their countries' brands?"[106]

But the point here is not to list all the possible benefits of nation branding. Rather, it is to suggest that the worldviews and functions of public diplomacy and nation branding are *different.* And, because they are different, nation branding does not provide a sound strategic approach to public diplomacy.

Finally, it also should be noted that semantics really do matter. Public diplomacy has long suffered from its historical association with propaganda. Surely, it would not be wise to advance a new association that would similarly tarnish it going forward. Rightly or wrongly, public diplomacy's future would be diminished by aligning itself too closely with "branding."

---

[105] Fiona Gilmore, "A Country—Can It Be Repositioned?," 285–286.

[106] Ibid., 293.

CHAPTER SEVEN

STRUCTURAL INTEGRITY: COMPETING DESIGNS

The first step toward achieving an adequate diplomacy is conceptualizing it.[1]

The question of how public diplomacy should be structured has probably sparked more controversy than any other among practitioners, policymakers, scholars, and interested observers of U.S. public diplomacy. That may seem odd to those unfamiliar with American public diplomacy. Indeed, the issue is one that easily might be dismissed as a secondary concern that should be sorted out after other more important matters are resolved. But to those who have witnessed or been a part of—or spent time studying—the evolution of American public diplomacy, it is an issue that matters greatly. It is also an issue that seems to defy resolution.[2]

Throughout the past half century, American public diplomacy has been shuffled back and forth between the State Department and the USIA, with other offices charged with public diplomacy responsibilities springing up and then shutting down from time to time. Of course, a defining moment for U.S. public diplomacy came in 1999 with the dissolution of the USIA and integration of public diplomacy functions back into the State Department, and the broadcast units spun off into an independent entity.

Although the marriage between the State Department and the USIA is widely viewed as a flawed arrangement, there is some question about whether divorce makes sense. The issue, of course, is determining what a better structure would look like. On that matter, heated debate continues.

Numerous post-9/11 reports on U.S. public diplomacy have addressed the issue of structure, with most offering recommendations for reform. Proposed options include: 1) reestablishing the USIA; 2) developing a

[1] Smith Simpson, "The Nature and Dimensions of Diplomacy," *The Annals of the American Academy of Political and Social Science* 380 (1968): 144.

[2] See, e.g., David I. Hitchcock, Jr., *U.S. Public Diplomacy Significant Issues Series, X, no. 17* (Washington, DC: The Center for Strategic and International Studies, 1988).

new government body; 3) forming a quasi-private agency; 4) turning over a significant portion of public diplomacy functions to a nonprofit or other private sector entity; 5) restructuring public diplomacy within the State Department; 6) splitting up the public diplomacy functions and developing separate government entities responsible for information/advocacy programs, exchange programs, and policy advisement, respectively; increasing through organizational changes the emphasis on public diplomacy throughout all government agencies (e.g., White House, National Security Council, Defense Department); and 7) maintaining the status quo.[3]

A significant problem in sorting out the various proposals is that there are no specific criteria or benchmarks by which various proposals might be judged. Diverse views regarding public diplomacy's role and function in national strategy, as well as the proper role of the private sector in public diplomacy, have contributed to a lack of progress on the structural front. In an effort to move the discussion forward, this chapter examines structural and organizational factors that contributed to U.S. public diplomacy's effectiveness in the past and considers recent proposals for how public diplomacy resources should be structured in the future.

Structural insights

The *USIA Alumni Study* (see Appendix One), which solicited the anonymous views of former USIA officers on a range of issues related to public diplomacy, provided significant insights into the structural and operational qualities that contributed to the USIA's success—and the qualities that were lost with the integration of public diplomacy into the State Department. According to the study, only 3 percent of America's former public diplomats thought the dissolution of the USIA was a good idea, and more than three-fourths (79 percent) thought the merger with the State Department was a "disaster." Nearly all (91 percent) of the former public diplomats agreed that the integration did *not* enhance public diplomacy policy's role, a key reason for the consolidation.

[3] See, e.g., Congressional Research Service, *Public Diplomacy: A Review of Past Recommendations* (Washington, DC, September 2005).

Table 7.1 USIA Merger with Department of State*

"The dissolution of USIA was a good idea."

Strongly Disagree				Strongly Agree
84%	8%	4%	1%	2%

"The integration of public diplomacy into the State Department was a disaster."

Strongly Disagree				Strongly Agree
2%	7%	11%	24%	55%

"The integration of USIA into the State Department enhanced public diplomacy's policy advisement role."

Strongly Disagree				Strongly Agree
68%	23%	6%	1%	2%

* The *USIA Alumni Study* (rounded percentages of respondents, n=213)

Table 7.2 How Should U.S. Public Diplomacy Be Structured Today?*

Structure	% Respondents
Re-establish USIA	38%
Develop a new government body responsible for U.S. public diplomacy	30%
Restructure public diplomacy units within the State Department	16%
Develop a quasi-private organization	8%
Develop separate government agencies (broadcasting, information/advocacy programs and exchange programs)	4%
Other	3%
Maintain status quo	2%
Outsource U.S. public diplomacy to private parties	0%

* The *USIA Alumni Study* (rounded percentages of respondents; n=213)

In terms of rebuilding U.S. public diplomacy, more than two-thirds of the former public diplomats said that either the reestablishment of the USIA or the development of a new government agency was needed. Thirty-eight percent said, "Re-establish USIA." The second largest group (thirty percent) said, "Develop a new government body responsible for U.S. public diplomacy." Sixteen percent said, "Restructure public diplomacy units within the State Department"; eight percent said, "Develop a quasi-private organization"; four percent said, "Develop separate government agencies responsible for broadcasting, informational/advocacy programs and exchange programs"; and two percent said, "Maintain status quo within State Department and Broadcasting Board of Governors." Less than 1 percent (n=7) of the former diplomats said, "Outsource public diplomacy to private parties."

The USIA alumni were asked to elaborate on their answers to the question of how U.S. public diplomacy should be structured and—in a clear sign of shared concern regarding the current state of U.S. public diplomacy—160 of the public diplomats provided more than 9,000 words of commentary addressing both structural and operational factors that contributed to the USIA's success and the factors they believe have impeded public diplomacy's effectiveness since the merger with the Department of State. The following sections report their collective responses.

Government body

Although the USIA alumni were split on whether the USIA should be reestablished or a brand new government agency should be created, they were in clear agreement on the perceived need for a *government* entity to conduct U.S. public diplomacy. Those recommending that the USIA be reestablished stressed the agency's "proven effectiveness" and "efficiency." As one said, "USIA, over a forty-five-year existence, had become one of the finest of its kind, especially attested to by many of its foreign competitors abroad.... The U.S. has lost a national strategic capability." Voicing the concerns of many, another stressed, "Public diplomacy *worked* under USIA. It's not working now."

Those recommending the establishment of an independent government body—either a rebuilt USIA or a new entity—offered similar reasons for their views. Many of the former public diplomats cited the incompatibility of the cultures of public diplomacy and the State Department. As one put it, "Public diplomacy requires focus and concentration, both of which are nonexistent in the State Department. State Department activities represent a working culture that runs counter to the 'open' culture of public diplomacy."

The USIA alumni also cited the long-term nature of public diplomacy. As one said, "The State Department tends to value activities that support policy objectives of today or this year or this administration...more than those whose payoff might take a generation. We need both, and that requires a separate institution responsive to broader and longer-term objectives than State." Others similarly stressed the importance of long-term relationship-building. One reported, "Real public diplomacy requires a strong commitment to the development of long-term relationships. State Department culture emphasizes short-term activities. In the competition for resources, State's short-term emphasis will always trump long-term programs, both in Washington and in the field. To get the most effective public diplomacy requires that it be removed from State's hierarchy and given its own resources." Another stressed that a separate organization "would free up the creativity and imagination lost with USIA—and which State culture abhors."

Others noted the loss of institutional integrity and status as a result of the merger. One explained that an independent government agency would provide a "[h]igher profile for public diplomacy as an element of foreign policy in the Congress where funding emanates" and reduce the "chance of public diplomacy being relegated within State Department to marginalization." Another stressed that an independent agency with a "comparatively unique profile" would offer greater opportunity to recruit new employees/officers to serve in public diplomacy roles.

At the same time, the former public diplomats cited the need for coordination between the field and State Department, as well as other areas of government. As one said, "There should be a straight line from the top of DC offices to the field and feedback from the field to headquarters. This would allow dialogue both ways and full understanding of programs to and from the field." According to another, "the USIA provided a unique structure that provided both the ability to coordinate various PD programs at home and abroad." On the other hand, this officer said, "The State Department has proven it cannot manage a PD effort."

Still others focused on the need for adequate funding and resources. As one said, "State will never devote the resources required to create and advance an effective PD program." If the USIA were properly reestablished, said one, "the various programs would be an integrated approach to public diplomacy goals. It must be a separate agency with adequate funding and cabinet status, however, to succeed. The funding should be maintained at high levels to address problems in all parts of the world."

Others stressed the need for public diplomacy to be close to the president and to have a defined role in policymaking. As one said, "A separate government body with a permanent charter indicating its importance to national security and having a cabinet seat is needed.

It should be led by a high-level political appointee with direct ties to the White House where his views would be heard seriously." Another said, "A director or secretary of a reestablished USIA or under another name should be an integrated part of the president's cabinet." Another explained that the head of the agency "must have a place at the foreign policy table (NSC [National Security Council] and State) to help influence U.S. foreign policy decisionmaking."

The public diplomats noted the importance of the advisory dimension of public diplomacy to *all* areas of government. For example, one said, "To serve the interests of the executive branch best, an independent organization would best be able to provide the public diplomacy knowledge and capabilities to all of the USG agencies involved in foreign affairs, e.g., Treasury, Commerce, Defense, DEA [Drug Enforcement Administration], Agriculture, EPA [Environmental Protection Agency], Energy, better than the current arrangement in which PD's works are devoted essentially to State Department objectives and practices."

Others cited the need "to represent the U.S. people, culture, and values" abroad rather than the current administration's politics. As one said, public diplomacy is "[n]ot a political mouthpiece for the current administration." Another explained, "Public diplomacy refers not just to backing the U.S. party in power at the moment but is a furtherance of U.S. cultural values—what we stand for—long term."

The importance of public diplomacy's *global* mission was also stressed by the group. As one said, "The main thing is to have a corps of FSOs of adequate size... to maintain an ongoing presence in most countries, with installations (e.g., libraries) and programs to attract both elites and ordinary citizens. This probably is impossible within State." The need for a "singleness of purpose" that could be developed in an independent agency also was noted. As one said, "You need one voice overseas."

The significance of having an active *local* presence was emphasized as well. One of the diplomats explained:

> The United States Information Agency as an entity unto itself was able to generate U.S. presence in foreign media through an aggressive public affairs office with information officers and Foreign Service nationals that is not being accomplished by the current public diplomacy officers in the bowels of our U.S. embassies abroad.... Contemporary PD officers behave more like State Department FSOs [Foreign Service Officers] and not like the FSIOs [Foreign Service Information Officers] of the past who went out on the street, visiting newspaper editors, TV executives, university rectors/professors/student leaders, and working closely with

political and military leaders. Now, PD officers run an embassy website and at times are the ambassador's spokesperson and do not get out to visit news sources nor place the material that the current State PD folks now want to buy commercial space to place. The direct contact with real people over a coffee, a beer, a steak, has disappeared. No one talks directly to editors, publishers, TV directors, university rectors/professors, etc. This personal rapport was what made USIS [United States Information Service] officers in the field different from the State Department stay-behind-embassy walls officers that we have today.

Still others focused on the importance of experienced and expert public diplomacy professionals. To be effective, one said, public diplomacy needed "forward-looking programs" and professionals with "expertise in reaching out to the public." Another observed that the "USIA was a body of creative, proactive professionals that understood the value of pressing the flesh, getting to know counterparts and contacts personally, and always showing respect and understanding of local culture, history, and attitudes. We had good credibility and were not bureaucratically hampered in our ability to react to or anticipate problems of perception and misunderstandings, and disinformation." The importance of professional accountability was also stressed, with one noting that whatever the new entity turns out to be, it must be "manned with professionals with careers on the line and honest evaluations of results."

Others pointed to the lack of respect for public diplomacy in the State Department and the impact on public diplomacy's effectiveness. One of the officers said, "To remain in the State Department is to have no vision, to be permanent second-class citizens, [and to offer] limited careers unattractive to potential information/cultural officers." Echoing such thoughts, another said, "The PD function is completely undervalued in the State Department. This has led to a complete breakdown of the professional PD cadre and an influx of officers from other cones into PD jobs. While some 'cross-fertilization' is healthy, there is a terrible loss of professional expertise."

The need for flexibility and operational autonomy was cited as extremely important to public diplomacy's success. As one advised:

A public diplomacy agency should be able to develop and pursue goals in a flexible, agile way to advance U.S. foreign policy objectives while also taking advantage of opportunities that arise and should be exploited quickly. It should not be overly bureaucratic but rather be more responsive to the president and also to the goal of informing foreign publics about a broad range of U.S. policy issues and about American values and

> social, cultural, and educational traditions. It should work with other U.S. government agencies and also with private institutions to achieve its goals. It should employ the leading information technologies in many different languages to reach foreign audiences. The new agency should have an open, less hierarchical structure that permits the rapid development and exchange of information and ideas between bureaus and offices.

The importance of strong leadership was also noted. In recommending a "fresh start" with the establishment of a new agency, one of the former diplomats said, "Very important would be solid, competent, and respected political leadership. The old USIA suffered from poor leadership at the top—folks with little foreign policy credibility inside the Beltway, and little potential clout." Echoing such thinking, another said, "USIA was weak and lacking in influence."

The significance of having a domestic constituency was also emphasized. As one of the former officers advised, "An effort needs to be made to convince the American people that a 'decent respect for the opinions of mankind' needs to be a significant independent element of American foreign policy."

Those recommending the development of a new agency recognized that the new entity had to reflect the requirements of a new age. For example, one pointed out that "going back to USIA is to possibly overlook a chance to see what was good and not so good about USIA and to take the best and leave the worst in forming the new organization." Others said the development of a "new" agency would provide the opportunity for "fresh" thinking and a "new beginning" that could take advantage of the best of the USIA, while correcting problems experienced in the past. In this respect, several pointed to the need to incorporate new technologies into public diplomacy programming. As one said, "We need to make a new start considering the technological changes in communicating with other people." Another said, "Times and tools (i.e., Internet) have changed, so reestablishment of USIA is not a guarantee of success."

The public diplomats also observed that a new agency would provide the opportunity to "[r]edefine goals of U.S. public diplomacy." As one said, "USIA is now history, so probably a new agency makes sense—would give forward-looking emphasis, not reinventing the past." Another observed that the USIA "can probably not be successfully 'resuscitated.' A new government agency can define its structure and set goals that are relevant for today's world."

Restructuring within the State Department

Most of the USIA alumni who recommended restructuring public diplomacy within the State Department indicated that their choice was based in part on skepticism that a new independent agency was possible. For example, one reported, "It's too late to reinvent, create USIA; involvement of USIA-type activities within State is probably the only pragmatic (and feasible) course." Another who chose restructuring within the State Department said that a new government body was "better but unlikely." This officer said restructuring was selected "in part because it is practical—the units of PD are likely to reside in State for the foreseeable future."

Still another said, "I do not believe we have the resources and political will to recreate USIA. Therefore, the next best thing would be to reorganize in State, in a manner that would make operations more efficient and effective. We are stuck with what we have and what is really needed is a total reform of State, not just PD!" Another similarly pointed out the perceived futility of any option but restructuring: "Restructuring within State is not optimum course to follow but most realistic one. Current status is, of course, failure. Recreating USIA or a new (quasi-public or not) agency is not in the cards, and the other options offered...are not to be considered seriously surely. Ergo, [restructuring is] the least 'evil' course."

At the same time, several of the officers who chose restructuring within the State Department cited the need to encourage collaboration and unity among the public diplomacy units. As one put it, being part of State could "[e]ngender collaboration across divisions and belief in a common goal." Another said that public diplomacy "parts must be integrated to fully complement each other and achieve a sum much larger than the parts." Another cited links between the policy role of public diplomacy and the State Department, noting, "Good public diplomacy should be close to and a part of policy formulation—what better place than in the State Department, but public diplomacy *should be a full-fledged career cone.*"

Nearly all of those who chose restructuring advised that substantial reforms were needed in order for restructuring to be effective. As one said, "The official connection is essential [but] State must be transformed." Another said that State Department reforms should be accompanied by the establishment of a new public diplomacy position, i.e., a "counselor to the president in the White House." According to another, "Public diplomacy (USIA) within State makes sense *only* if PD is accorded *separate and equal* status. That is, PD at present appears to be almost an afterthought without as much influence as administrative or consular operations; it is buried within the bureaucracy with barely a voice." Focusing on the heightened status of being associated with the State Department, another advised that although "USIA activities have more clout within the State Department, many more resources need to be directed to PD."

Separation (or integration?)

One matter on which the USIA alumni were split is whether the information, advocacy, engagement, and policy advisement functions of public diplomacy, as well as international broadcasting, should be separate or integrated. Half (50 percent) of the former public diplomats said the public diplomacy units should not be separated; 35 percent said they should be separate entities; and 14 percent expressed a neutral view on this issue, with 1 percent offering no response. At the same time, two-thirds (69 percent) of the former public diplomats said that international broadcasting should be integrated with the other functions of U.S. public diplomacy.

Those recommending integration of the public diplomacy units pointed to the perceived efficiencies and effectiveness of having them all under the same umbrella. As one put it, "Under USIA, information, cultural, and exchange programs were mutually reinforcing."

Those choosing separation expressed diverse views on both why separation makes sense and how the units should be structured. For example, one of the former diplomats said to separate "with press/policy information remaining in the State Department." Another suggested, "Exchanges have little meaningful connection to short-term advocacy, especially with today's visa delays. Information programs would work best on their own—*not* linked to policy units."

Another said: "I think press/information programs should stay in the State Department and [these programs] should be merged. I would spin off education, cultural, and exchange programming into a new entity akin to the British Council, Alliance Foundation, Goethe Institute, etc." Another expressed similar sentiments, "Other western countries (UK, Germany notably) appear to have gained greater credibility and impact by separating international broadcasting, cultural and education exchanges, and foreign information programs."

Those suggesting that broadcasting should be separate from the other units pointed to the need for broadcasting to preserve its independence. As one explained, "Broadcasting needs to stay separate to have credibility."

Quasi-private organization

Fifteen (8 percent) of the USIA officers chose the development of a "quasi-private organization" as the best structural option for rebuilding U.S. public diplomacy. Those choosing this option cited the government's perceived lack of credibility with foreign publics as the top reason for turning to the private sector.

One of the public diplomats suggested that public diplomacy's "situation is so utterly, utterly disastrous today that an organization more loosely affiliated with the USG might have a slightly better chance of restoring some credibility to the USG and its policies." Another advised, "A major effort to rebuild friends and alliances around the world could be more efficiently accomplished outside State. Government no longer carries the credibility that it used to."

Other reasons cited for seeking private sector support were the need for fresh ideas ("New thinking, independent of the State Department, is required."), the need to build a domestic constituency for public diplomacy ("Lack of grassroots constituency was basic USIA weakness."); the need to inform the American public of public diplomacy's purpose and mission ("Let the American public contribute."); and the need for public diplomacy to be free of bureaucratic constraints and politics.

Status quo

One of three USIA alumni who chose the option of maintaining the status quo explained that it is "[i]mpossible to change now; need to work towards improving present structure at State." Another said, "It's better to make your current system more effective than to establish a new one." The third suggested, "The current structure per se is O.K. However, leadership of the PD function needs to be improved, with appointees chosen who are willing to listen to the career staff."

Outsourcing

The outsourcing of public diplomacy was dismissed out of hand by the USIA alumni. One of the former diplomats explained, "Outsourcing to private entities hasn't worked in past... and probably won't in future." Another officer said, "Outsource—no way!" This option elicited similar responses from others, with one saying, simply, "Egad!"

Characteristics of success

These responses offer important insights regarding the qualities, or distinctive characteristics, USIA alumni believe are required for a public diplomacy entity to be successful in carrying out the U.S. public diplomacy mission. Although there was no consensus among America's public diplomats on what an "ideal" structure of U.S. public diplomacy would look like, there was strong agreement that an independent government agency is needed. Even the majority of those who chose restructuring within the State Department indicated that the "best" option was either rebuilding the USIA or creating a new government agency. They simply didn't believe these options were within the realm of possibility.

There also was considerable agreement on the structural and operational qualities required for public diplomacy to be effective. According to USIA alumni, the public diplomacy structure must provide autonomy and freedom from bureaucratic constraints that undermine the public diplomacy mission and interfere with public diplomats' ability to respond quickly and effectively to unfolding events on the ground. Public diplomacy must have a permanent global mandate, a permanent role in policymaking, and the respect and support of the president, the Congress, and the State Department, as well as the backing of an informed domestic constituency.

Effective public diplomacy requires interagency coordination and cooperation, strong field support with a feedback loop from the field to policymakers, and accountability to taxpayers. In order to succeed, public diplomacy must have strong, sustained leadership and a corps of committed, qualified, experienced professionals with a defined career path.

The public diplomacy operating culture should be open and transparent and encourage proactive, forward-looking, and innovative thinking. Public diplomacy practices should be guided by national interests and values (rather than the specific interests and values of successive administrations).

The focus of public diplomacy operations should be on long-term relationship-building with foreign publics, which requires a local presence and active engagement at the local level on a sustained basis. In order to be effective, public diplomacy requires sophisticated and technologically-advanced programs and activities that emphasize the human dimensions of international relations.

Most importantly, effective public diplomacy requires adequate funding and the resources needed to accomplish the public diplomacy mission.

Competing designs

Nearly all the task forces, commissions, and other groups that have studied U.S. public diplomacy since 9/11 have made structure a central component of their recommendations for improving U.S. public diplomacy. This section reviews a sampling of structural recommendations from selected proposals, providing a picture of the continuing debate on such matters.

Report of the U.S. Advisory Commission on Public Diplomacy

Soon after 9/11, the U.S. Advisory Commission on Public Diplomacy issued a report calling for the reform of U.S. public diplomacy's structure.[4] Observing that "U.S. foreign policy has been precariously weakened by a failure to systematically include public diplomacy in the formulation and implementation of policy," the Commission proposed that five steps be taken:[5] 1) Issue a presidential mandate that makes clear "public diplomacy is a strategic component of American foreign policy and that significant reform is needed";[6] 2) fully implement the White House Office of Global Communications to ensure a "sustained and flexible coordinating structure that links Presidential leadership with

---

[4] U.S. Advisory Commission on Public Diplomacy, Building America's Public Diplomacy Through a Reformed Structure and Additional Resources (Washington, DC, 2002): 4.

[5] Ibid., 5.

[6] Ibid.

the departments and agencies that carry out public diplomacy, along with our coalition allies and private sector partners";[7] 3) Review the consolidation of USIA into the State Department to ensure that public diplomacy is "brought into all aspects of foreign policy making";[8] 4) Integrate Congress into public diplomacy efforts to ensure both that when members of Congress communicate directly or indirectly with foreign audiences that they reinforce—rather than undermine—public diplomacy messages—and that Congress supports public diplomacy with adequate resources and appropriate oversight;[9] and 5) Involve the private sector to gain the "support, insight and critical judgment" essential to U.S. public diplomacy.[10]

Report of an Independent Task Force Sponsored by the Council on Foreign Relations

The following year, the Council on Foreign Relations formed a task force comprised of "leading thinkers and practitioners from academia, government, public relations, journalism, and broadcasting" to prepare recommendations intended to "reinvigorate public diplomacy" and "devise fresh and creative responses to a problem that has too often received short shrift by the U.S. government."[11] In addition to offering recommendations geared toward making the formulation of foreign policy more sensitive to public diplomacy concerns and for improving public diplomacy strategic practices, the task force issued specific recommendations for "restructuring the foreign policy bureaucracy to manage the overall process more effectively."[12]

Key structural recommendations included strengthening the internal public diplomacy coordinating structure and bridging the gap between public and private sector initiatives by creating an independent, not-for-profit "Corporation for Public Diplomacy" much like the Corporation for Public Broadcasting.[13] According to the task force, such an organization would address the lack of trust in the U.S. government

[7] Ibid.
[8] Ibid., 6.
[9] Ibid., 7.
[10] Ibid.
[11] Independent Task Force Sponsored by the Council on Foreign Relations, Peter G. Petersen, Chair, *Finding America's Voice: A Strategy for Reinvigorating U.S. Public Diplomacy* (New York, NY, 2003): vi/v.
[12] Ibid., vi.
[13] Ibid., 37.

and among people abroad and improve cross-cultural relations, as well as provide support for indigenous new media channels or joint think tanks on issues important in various regions of the world.

The task force also recommended the establishment of an "Independent Public Diplomacy Training Institute" to "attract and train modern Foreign Service professionals who would understand the critical role of public diplomacy."[14] According to the task force, such an entity could "attract the best talent and techniques from U.S. corporations and universities involved in research, marketing, campaign management, and other relevant fields," allowing the government to "apply private sector 'best practices' in communication and public diplomacy.[15] The group also recommended the establishment of a "Public Diplomacy Reserve Corps" (patterned on the Federal Emergency Management Agency's disaster relief model) to augment U.S. and overseas operations with the experience and expertise of private sector experts.[16]

Report of the Defense Science Board Task Force on Strategic Communication

In 2004, the Defense Science Board, a Federal Advisory Committee established to provide independent advice to the Secretary of Defense, issued an extensive report calling for the transformation of U.S. strategic communication: "We need to move beyond outdated concepts, stale structural models, and institutionally-based labels."[17] With regard to structure specifically, the Board said that "new structures grounded in legislation that address 21st century realities" are required.[18]

Specifically, the Board recommended the establishment of "a permanent strategic communication structure within the NSC" that would work with Congress to create legislation and funding for a Deputy National Security Advisor for Strategic Communication; a Strategic Communication Committee within the NSC, and an independent, non-profit, non-partisan Center for Strategic Communication.[19] The

[14] Ibid., 39.
[15] Ibid.
[16] Ibid.
[17] Office of the Under Secretary of Defense For Acquisition, Technology, and Logistics, *Report f the Defense Science Board Task Force on Strategic Communication* (Washington, DC, September 2004): 3.
[18] Ibid.
[19] Ibid., 65.

new Center would be a tax-exempt "hybrid organization modeled on federally funded research and development centers, such as the Rand Corporation and National Endowment for Democracy," and receive an annual appropriation approved by Congress as part of the Department of State budget.[20] Its purpose would be to 1) "provide information and analysis on a regular basis to civilian and military decision-makers on issues vital to U.S. national security" 2) "develop mandated and self-initiated plans, themes, products and programs for the creation and implementation of U.S. communications strategies that embrace diplomatic opportunities and respond to national security threats"; and 3) "support government strategic communications through services provided on a cost-recovery basis that mobilize non-governmental initiatives; foster cross-cultural exchanges of ideas, people, and information; maintain knowledge management systems, language and skills inventories, and procedures to recruit private sector experts for short term assignments, deploy temporary communications teams; augment planning, recruitment, and training; and continually monitor and evaluate effectiveness."[21]

According to the plan, the Deputy National Security Advisor for Strategic Communication would provide program and project direction to the Center, which would be governed by an independent, non-partisan Board of Directors that would include "distinguished Americans drawn from relevant professions and members of Congress appointed on a bipartisan basis."[22] The Board also recommended that the secretary of state redefine the role and responsibility of the under secretary of state for public diplomacy and public affairs to be both policy advisor and manager for public diplomacy and the State Department's principal representative on the NSC's Strategic Communication Committee.[23] Similarly, the Board suggested that the under secretary of defense for policy would serve as the Department's "focal point for strategic communication" and the Department's principal on the NSC Committee.[24]

[20] Ibid., 66.
[21] Ibid., 66–67.
[22] Ibid., 69.
[23] Ibid., 77.
[24] Ibid., 83.

Report of the Public Diplomacy Council

In 2005, the Public Diplomacy Council, a non-partisan group of professionals with extensive experience in public diplomacy, issued a call for U.S. government leaders to "revitalize public diplomacy."[25] Three of the Council's five recommendations addressed structural concerns.

The Council recommended the establishment of "an agency within the Department of State and the National Security Council process, the U.S. Agency for Public Diplomacy (USAPD), to manage the U.S. government's civilian information and exchanges functions and to coordinate all U.S. government public diplomacy efforts"; the establishment "by Presidential Directive an Interagency Committee on Public Diplomacy at the Cabinet Level to coordinate and direct the national public diplomacy strategy, with a permanent secretariat and associated working groups, co-chaired by the Deputy National Security Advisor for Communication and the Director of the new USAPD agency; and the creation of a "public-private partnership 'Foundation for the Global Future' to provide permanent off-budget funding for international exchanges conducted by civilian and military federal agencies."

Notably, some of the Councils own members issued a dissent from these recommendations, which they criticized for drawing too heavily on the past and proposing an organization (that resembled the USIA within the State Department) that "would weaken public diplomacy by separating it from policy formulation and implementation," "undercut needed efforts to change the Department's organizational culture," and be "unlikely to gain political traction within the Department and in Congress."[26] Rather than propose an alternative structure, the dissenting group emphasized the need for public diplomacy to be focused on "personal engagement within foreign cultures" and to be responsible for influencing the development of foreign policy.

[25] Public Diplomacy Council, *A Call for Action on Public Diplomacy* (Washington, DC, 2005): 3.

[26] Barry Fulton, Bruce Gregory, Donna Marie Oglesby, Walter R. Roberts, Barry Zorthian, "Public Diplomacy A Dissent: Transformation Not Restoration," in *America's Dialogue with the World*, William P. Kiehl (ed.) (Washington, DC: Public Diplomacy Council, 2005): 187.

Report of the Brookings Institution

More recently in 2009, the Brookings Institution, a private nonprofit organization devoted to research, education, and publication on issues related to domestic and foreign policy, issued a report by Kristin Lord that called for "a new organization that fills a gap in our national public diplomacy strategy."[27] The Brookings proposal called for the creation of a new nonprofit organization called the USA World Trust "to complement and support U.S. government efforts" in public diplomacy.[28]

This proposal specifically rejected the idea for "a new cabinet-level government agency to conduct public diplomacy"[29] contending that "[t]hough some now regret the demise of the United States Information Agency (USIA) and we might be pleased with that organization if it existed today, we should not simply recreate it now. Creating a large new bureaucracy would absorb energy and resources, diverting them from the crucial mission of engaging foreign publics."[30]

At the same time, the plan called for "relatively little organizational changes within existing government structures." Rather than restructure internally, the report recommended "bolstering existing government agencies and giving them the chance to work." The rationale for such thinking was that "[o]ur country knows from experience how much energy organizational restructuring can take, how long it takes for organizational cultures to evolve, and how much attention they can sap." For those reasons, "the costs are too high" to engage in organizational restructuring.[31]

The objectives of the proposed organization would be to 1) "present a more accurate and nuanced vision of America to counterbalance the one-side views sometimes promulgated by popular culture and foreign media"; 2) "contribute to an environment of mutual trust, respect, and understanding in which cooperation is more feasible; promote shared values and their champions"; 3) and inform and support our government's public diplomacy efforts thorough the sharing

---

[27] Kristin Lord, *Voices of America: U.S. Public Diplomacy for the 21st Century* (Washington, DC: The Foreign Policy Program at Brookings and the Brookings Project on U.S. Relations with the Islamic World, November 2008).

[28] Ibid., 1.

[29] Ibid., 4.

[30] Ibid.

[31] Ibid.

of knowledge regarding communication, public opinion, foreign cultures, and technology."[32] These objectives would be met by engaging in five activities—conducting research and analysis; working on new initiatives with the private sector; providing grants and venture capital to endeavors that would advance the organization's objectives; identifying, cultivating and experimenting with new technologies and media products; and bringing together practitioners and scholars to address public diplomacy challenges.

Collectively, these and other proposals, along with the *USIA Alumni Study*, illustrate strong views on all sides of the debate about how U.S. public diplomacy should be structured. The Congressional Research Service, which reviewed 29 articles and studies identified by the State Department as "being credible reports with valuable suggestions" for improving public diplomacy, found some areas of agreement—and some areas of disagreement—on specific matters related to structure.[33] For example, ten of the proposals identified a need for the White House to take a more proactive role in public diplomacy. Eight of the proposals recommended the establishment of a new government agency. Six of the reports recommended that public diplomacy be reorganized at the State Department. Ten of the plans suggested increasing private sector involvement in public diplomacy. Sixteen recommended increases in cultural and educational exchanges and/or American libraries overseas.

The structural challenge

The development of an effective public diplomacy entity will require U.S. leaders to marry time-proven structural and operational requirements with the requirements of a new time. In contemplating structural options, two issues related to the "privatization" of public diplomacy deserve special attention. The first is whether public diplomacy is an inherently government enterprise. The *USIA Alumni Study* indicated that America's public diplomats clearly believe that it is. Yet, the public diplomacy literature, including some of the recent proposals for

---

[32] Ibid.

[33] Congressional Research Service, *Public Diplomacy: A Review of Past Recommendations* (Washington, DC, September 2005): Summary.

restructuring, indicates growing support for the notion that "public diplomacy" encompasses the activities of nongovernmental actors.

The resolution of this issue has tremendous implications for all aspects of public diplomacy. If public diplomacy is expanded to include "diplomatic" work performed both by and for nongovernmental institutions, e.g., businesses, nonprofit institutions, and NGOs, then serious consideration must be given to the impact on public diplomacy principles, policies, practices, training—and structure.

For example, how would a "corporate public diplomacy" operation be different from a "government public diplomacy" operation or a "nonprofit public diplomacy" operation or a quasi-government public diplomacy operation? How should the respective functions be structured? How should a "network" of public and private public diplomacy entities be structured? What entity should (could) provide oversight of all the participants and activities that form a nation's public diplomacy? How might training programs for public/private public diplomats be affected?

Additionally, if public diplomacy is expanded to include the activities of nonstate actors unaffiliated with government, then where is the line between the official diplomatic actions of a nation and the unofficial "diplomatic" acts of private parties to be drawn? Certainly, the list of private parties whose words and actions shape a nation's relations and reputation with people abroad is long—e.g., private citizens (tourists, participants in exchange programs), news media, NGOs, businesses, educational institutions, nonprofits and individuals (artists, celebrities, entertainers, sports figures). If all such parties are deemed to be engaging in "public diplomacy" when they interact with foreign publics, then public diplomacy's identity as a unique function of statecraft may be lost.

For this reason, distinctions should be made between the official public diplomacy of nations and the unofficial international public relations/communications activities of private parties. Unless private actors are acting at the behest of and in cooperation with the government, their efforts should not be characterized as "public diplomacy."

The second issue is whether—and, if so, to what extent—public diplomacy should be "privatized." While the USIA alumni roundly rejected the idea of "outsourcing" public diplomacy, America's public diplomats agreed that collaborations with the private sector contribute to public diplomacy's effectiveness. A few of the former public diplomats also indicated a desire to see U.S. public diplomacy operations restructured as a "quasi-private" entity that might have more credibility with people abroad than the U.S. government.

Of course, America's public diplomats have long worked with private sector partners to accomplish public diplomacy objectives. For example, America's early wartime public diplomacy initiatives had the support of American businesses and professionals, and the USIA had public-private committees that provided advice and counsel to USIA officials on various matters. Louise Wheeler, a former director of the USIA's Office of Private Sector Committees, described the arrangement as providing "a direct link to [business] leaders in the U.S. who support the USIA's public diplomacy mission overseas."[34]

This tradition was continued after the dissolution of the USIA. In 2007, for example, Karen Hughes hosted "The Private Sector Summit on Public Diplomacy" at which 150 top public relations professionals and U.S. State Department leaders discussed opportunities for greater private sector participation in U.S. public diplomacy.[35] Upon her retirement, Hughes cited as one of her signature accomplishments the establishment of an office charged with overseeing public/private partnerships,[36] which were deemed "key to meeting international challenges."[37]

Such examples indicate that U.S. officials recognize the potential for private actors to contribute to public diplomacy's success. Indeed, the objectivity and expertise rendered by outside observers—described by public diplomacy scholars Geoffrey Pigman and Anthony Deos as "fresh eyes" and "fresh brains"—is often invaluable.[38]

But there is a big difference in "partnering" with the private sector on special initiatives and "outsourcing" public diplomacy functions to private parties, which appears to be gaining traction in diplomatic

---

[34] Albert G. Holzinger, "The Changing Voice of America," *Nation's Business*, April 1, 1992, http://findarticles.com/p/search?qt=changing+voice%20of%20america%20and%20holzinger&qf=all&qta=1&tb=art&x=0&y=0 (accessed January 9, 2009).

[35] "Business Leaders Make Major Commitment to Support American Public Diplomacy," News Release, U.S. Department of State Office of the Spokesman, January 11, 2007.

[36] "Changing the Nature and Scope of Public Diplomacy," News Release, Office of the Under Secretary for Public Diplomacy and Public Affairs, November 1, 2007.

[37] "Public-Private Partnerships Key to Meeting International Challenges," U.S. Department of State, Bureau of Public Affairs, February 15, 2007, www.state.gov (accessed October 3, 2008).

[38] Geoffrey Allen Pigman and Anthony Deos, "Consults for Hire: Private Actors, Public Diplomacy," *Place Branding and Public Diplomacy* 4, no. 1 (2008): 87.

circles both in the United States and other parts of the world.[39] As Hocking observed, "The proposition that states, confronted by challenges to their legitimacy and capacity to act, are assigning more and more functions to the private sector, whose authority rests in part on its expertise in specific policy areas, has become a recognized phenomenon."[40]

Although none of the serious proposals for restructuring U.S. public diplomacy have called for the complete privatization of public diplomacy, i.e., turning over all functions to private parties, recommendations for the establishment of quasi-private entities and/or private nonprofit entities suggests a movement toward the outsourcing of many public diplomacy functions traditionally handled by the government.

Certainly, many good results might be achieved by the strengthening of public/private public diplomacy partnerships. For example, the Brookings proposal placed significant emphasis on learning and innovations, as well as on the development and sharing of resources and ideas, all of which are needed to improve U.S. public diplomacy's effectiveness. The Defense Science Board's plan rightly stressed the importance of research and analysis in strategic communication planning and evaluation. The Public Diplomacy Council's proposal recognized the value of expanding exchange programs. The Council on Foreign Relations' recommendations addressed the need to enhance the training of public diplomacy officers. All these ideas, many of which have been recommended by others as well, deserve serious consideration—along with the many good ideas from task forces and commissions and other groups that seemingly have been largely ignored by U.S. public diplomacy officials to date.

At the same time, calls to increase the participation of private entities in the conduct of U.S. public diplomacy should be approached with some caution. An important question that must be considered is: Could the formation of *private* entities to perform public diplomacy functions actually undermine public diplomacy's *public* mission? As John Hemery, founder and director of the Centre for Political and

---

[39] See, e.g., Crocker Snow, Jr., "The Privatization of U.S. Public Diplomacy," *The Fletcher Forum of World Affairs* 32, no. 1 (Winter 2008): 189–199.

[40] Brian Hocking, "Privatizing Public Diplomacy?" *International Studies Perspectives* 5 (2004): 148.

Diplomatic Studies in the United Kingdom, has observed, "There is a fine but important line between facilitating the creation of worthwhile new organs and linkages within civil society, and establishing what in effect would be 'front' organizations."[41]

A RAND Corporation study directed at improving public diplomacy—and actually attempting to make a case *for* the outsourcing of "major elements of the public diplomacy mission"—made a similar point in offering the caveat that "[w]hile outsourcing may put some distance between a potentially favorable message (pluralism, freedom, and democracy) and an unfavorable messenger (the United States government), inevitably the two will be linked."[42]

In considering the potential for U.S. public diplomacy to gain greater credibility through associations with private parties, it also should be noted that businesses in particular have a credibility problem of their own. For example, the 2009 Edelman Trust Barometer study, now in its tenth year, found that trust in business plunged dramatically since last year with 62 percent of "informed publics" saying they trust business less now than they did a year ago.[43] Indeed, according to this research, in order to regain the public's trust, "Business must partner with *governments* and NGOs to address key policy issues and the world's most pressing problems, not merely the ones that impact their bottom line [*emphasis added*]."[44]

Funding is another concern. For example, in addressing a recommendation by the Public Diplomacy Council (PDC) to provide for "permanent off-budget funding" by the private sector to support international exchanges, the group of dissenting PDC members argued that such direction is "impractical." As they pointed out, "History does not inspire confidence in the willingness of the private sector to provide sustained public diplomacy funding."[45]

---

[41] John Hemery, "Training for Public Diplomacy: An Evolutionary Perspective," in *The New Public Diplomacy: Soft Power in International Relations*, ed. Jan Melissen (Houndmills: Palgrave Macmillan, 2005), 202.

[42] Charles Wolf, Jr. and Brian Rosen, "Public Diplomacy: How to Think About and Improve It," *Occasional Paper* (Santa Monica, CA: RAND Corporation, 2004): 23.

[43] Edelman Public Relations, *Edelman Trust Barometer Executive Summary* (New York, January 27, 2009): 1.

[44] Ibid., 6.

[45] Barry Fulton, Bruce Gregory, Donna Marie Ogleby, Walter R. Roberts, and Barry Zorthian, "Public Diplomacy A Dissent: Transformation Not Restoration," 187.

Most importantly, as has been argued elsewhere, while private entities can play an important role in supporting U.S. government efforts, privatization should not "provide an excuse for U.S. officials to avoid making the critical changes—and providing the resources—needed to improve public diplomacy's long-term success."[46] The nation would be ill-served if government leaders look *outside* for the innovations needed to rebuild U.S. public diplomacy while neglecting the need to rebuild public diplomacy capabilities *inside* government.[47]

As Paul R. Verkuil observed in *Outsourcing Sovereignty*, when sovereign powers to govern "are delegated to outsiders, the capacity to govern is undermined."[48]

An "outside in" approach

A notable distinction in the recommendations of former USIA officers and many of the post-Cold War/post-9/11 proposals for the restructuring of U.S. public diplomacy is that the former public diplomats focus on what's happening *there*, i.e., abroad, while others generally focus on what's happening *here*, i.e., in Washington. For example, the USIA alumni emphasized the importance of public diplomacy officials in the field having the autonomy and freedom from bureaucratic constraints to respond to local conditions and issues without having to seek clearance from Washington before acting. They recognized the need for strong field support to ensure that those in the field had the human and other resources and capabilities needed to carry out the public diplomacy mission. They cited the significance of incorporating field perspectives and insights in policy making, as well as in policy promotion. They stressed the need to have a global mission and the importance of having a field, or local, presence throughout the world that would allow U.S. representatives to actively engage with people abroad.

These views are not surprising coming from those who witnessed first hand both the effectiveness of the USIA's work during the Cold

[46] See Kathy R. Fitzpatrick, "Privatized Public Diplomacy," in *Toward a New Public Diplomacy*, ed. Philip Seib (Houndmills: Palgrave MacMillan, 2009), 168.

[47] Ibid.

[48] Paul R. Verkuil, *Outsourcing Sovereignty* (New York: Cambridge University Press, 2007), 1.

War and the damaging consequences of post-Cold War changes in U.S. public diplomacy—the closing of American libraries, cultural centers, and other facilities; the demise of U.S.-sponsored publications, exhibits, and speaker programs; reductions in overseas public diplomacy operations and staff, including foreign nationals who had been part of U.S. communities abroad for many years; discontinued language and arts programs; reduced educational and cultural exchanges; diminished opportunities for dialogue and discussion among U.S. representatives and local opinion leaders in local venues; cuts in international broadcast offerings; and the decreased participation of U.S. representatives in local media and other affairs.

Although the damaging impacts of such actions are now widely recognized, few of the restructuring proposals have incorporated a broad field perspective focused on how U.S. public diplomacy might best address the needs, interests, and ambitions of people abroad—rather than the needs, interests and ambitions of people in Washington. One exception is the Public Diplomacy Council's proposal for a new U.S. Agency for Public Diplomacy that was described as "field-driven" not "Washington-driven." According to this plan, "field offices would not merely receive instructions from Washington headquarters to carry out specific programs but rather provide input into Washington decision making."[49]

Unfortunately, there is a dearth of field-based research that would help to identify structures, resources, and processes needed to adequately address contemporary public diplomacy challenges. One recent study that took a small step in that direction concluded that it was time for America "to get back in the game" of public diplomacy. A report to members of the Committee on Foreign Relations, presented by Paul Foldi of Senator Richard Lugar's staff, included the findings of a recent study designed "to examine U.S. Public Diplomacy facilities as platforms for engagement with foreign audiences, including the role of English language instruction as a vehicle to facilitate greater access to information about the United States and interaction with core American values."[50] The study, which was based on site visits and discussions with embassy and local officials in the Middle East and

[49] Public Diplomacy Council, *A Call for Action on Public Diplomacy*, 12.

[50] Paul Foldi, *U.S. Public Diplomacy—Time to Get Back in the Game*, A Report to Members of the Committee on Foreign Relations, United States Senate (Washington, D.C., 2009): 6.

Latin America, focused "on the need for greater direct U.S. engagement with average citizens overseas who now have virtually no contact with Americans."[51]

In presenting the results, Lugar pointed out that the public diplomacy efforts of other nations—including Britain, France, and Germany—were on a much broader scope and scale than those of the United States. "Where once we were seen as the world's leader in intellectual discourse and debate, we are now viewed as withdrawn and unconcerned with views other than our own," he said. Although "the re-creation of the USIA is not realistic," Lugar indicated, the nation should establish programs, such as "the American Centers that use the teaching of English to offset costs," that would "demonstrate that we are committed to re-engaging in a dialogue with the world."[52]

Although this report was narrowly focused, it provided insights into circumstances "on the ground," which are critical in analyzing the structural and operational requirements of U.S. public diplomacy. It also illustrated the importance of including a field-based perspective in efforts to develop an effective public diplomacy structure going forward. As veteran public diplomacy officer Don Streeby observed, "America's goals in the world may originate in Washington, but it is up to the Foreign Service in the field to directly advocate U.S. policies and goals and to represent U.S. society and culture in other nations."[53]

---

[51] Ibid., 4.

[52] Ibid., 5.

[53] Dan Sreebny, "Public Diplomacy: The Field Perspective," in Kiehl, *America's Dialogue with the World*, 91.

CHAPTER EIGHT

MOVING THE NEEDLE: MEASURES OF SUCCESS

It is not only the future of public diplomacy that depends upon the question of its evaluation—so does the very theoretical conception of power and influence in international relations.[1]

Does public diplomacy work? This question has plagued public diplomacy practitioners and scholars and is the subject of ongoing debate. A central issue, of course, is whether public diplomacy is worth government officials' time or the people's money. Unfortunately, despite the renewed attention to public diplomacy in the post-9/11 period, there is little hard evidence to prove that it is. As Pierre C. Pahlavi observed in *The Hague Journal of Diplomacy*, although "public diplomacy is no longer a mere sideshow in foreign policy efforts, there are still no definitive means to attest irrefutably to its strategic role, or its utility in political, economic or security terms."[2]

Given public diplomacy's unstable history in the United States, it is particularly surprising that measures of success have received so little attention by public diplomacy scholars and practitioners.[3] Clearly, documentation of public diplomacy's effectiveness would go a long way toward securing a place for public diplomacy in the national diplomatic hierarchy. Indeed, proof that public diplomacy can "move the needle" of foreign publics' knowledge, attitudes, and behaviors may be the one thing most important to public diplomacy's future.

Yet, with few exceptions,[4] public diplomacy scholars have not seriously explored the topic of evaluation, and practitioners have not

---

[1] Pierre C. Pahlavi, "Evaluating Public Diplomacy Programmes," *The Hague Journal of Diplomacy* 2 (2007): 280.

[2] Ibid., 278.

[3] Etyan Gilboa, "Searching for a Theory of Public Relations," *The Annals of the American Academy of Political and Social Science* 616 (March 2008): 74.

[4] See, e.g., Edward P. Djerejian, Chairman, *Changing Minds, Winning Peace: A New Strategic Direction for U.S. Public Diplomacy in the Arab and Muslim World* (Washington, DC: The Advisory Group on Public Diplomacy for the Arab and Muslim World, 2003); see also Joe Johnson, "How Does Public Diplomacy Measure Up?," *Foreign Service Journal*, October 2006, 44–52.

made evaluation a priority in practice. In fact, evaluation sometimes appears to be an afterthought—i.e., a good idea but perhaps not critical to accomplishing the public diplomacy mission. For example, when Karen Hughes laid out her plans for U.S. public diplomacy, she identified the four "Es" of success: education, exchanges, empowerment, and engagement. Only later did she note that she should have added a fourth "E"—evaluation—to the list.[5] Similarly, in the U.S. national strategy for public diplomacy (more on this below), evaluation is addressed only in an attachment to the plan.[6]

This chapter addresses the evaluation gap in public diplomacy. It first examines why evaluation has been neglected. It next explores the meaning of "success" in public diplomacy. It then considers the state of evaluation in U.S. public diplomacy, as reflected in government assessments and the national public diplomacy strategy. Finally, the chapter identifies the need for new approaches to evaluation that focus on what public diplomacy is about: relationships.

Reasons for neglect

There are a number of reasons that explain why public diplomacy practitioners and scholars have shied away from evaluation. First, from a practical perspective, a measurement mindset raises expectations for success—and thereby increases the pressure to produce beneficial results. Indeed, *no* proof of outcomes may be perceived to be better than proof of negative outcomes—particularly if such results could affect one's prospects for re-election or re-appointment.

Second, the long-term nature of public diplomacy means that the true impact of public diplomacy may not be evident for years, if not decades. Although intermediate assessments can be useful in guiding the development of new and continuing programs, such measures do not provide proof of long-term success.

Third is the difficulty of determining what constitutes "success" in public diplomacy and how it should be measured. For example, do

---

[5] Remarks by Karen Hughes, Shell Distinguished Lecture Series, Baker Institute for Public Policy, Houston, TX, March 29, 2006, http://www.state.gov/r/us/64106.htm (accessed on January 6, 2009).

[6] U.S. National Strategy for Public Diplomacy and Strategic Communication, 33, http://www.state.gov/documents/organization/87427.pdf (accessed on January 2, 2009).

public opinion polls of foreign publics' attitudes toward the United States provide a good measure of U.S. public diplomacy's success? If not, what other methods provide better measures of public diplomacy's effectiveness?

Fourth is the perceived futility of developing a credible measurement scheme. For example, public diplomacy often succeeds when *nothing* happens. As Edward R. Murrow said, "It is very difficult to measure success in our business. No computer clicks, no cash register rings when a man changes his mind."[7] How can it be proven that nonstate actors predisposed to act against U.S. interests were moved to *in*action by public diplomacy as opposed to other influences? If demonstrations against U.S. embassies are prevented or negative media reports about the United States are not written—as a direct result of public diplomacy efforts—then how are these achievements documented?

Fifth, the resources and funding needed to conduct public diplomacy research and evaluation may not be available—or at least not earmarked for such purposes. In deciding where to spend their budgets, public diplomacy officials may decide that implementation of programs is more important than evaluating results—particularly if Congress fails to provide funding specifically targeted at measuring results.

Sixth, limited official oversight gives public diplomacy officials the discretion to *not* make evaluation a priority. For example, a recent study found that although U.S. policymakers have questioned the effectiveness of post-9/11 American public diplomacy efforts, "congressional committee members today seem undisturbed with the lack of concrete explanations and have not threatened to reduce program funding."[8]

In fact, notwithstanding a few notable exceptions, which are discussed below, there have been few demands from policymakers or others to make evaluation a priority for public diplomacy going forward. As an example, a 2005 review of recommendations for improving public diplomacy conducted by the U.S. Congressional Research Service,

---

[7] Quoted in William A. Rugh, *American Encounters with Arabs: The "Soft Power" of U.S. Public Diplomacy in the Middle East* (Westport, CT: Praeger Security Studies, 2006), 50; see also Thomas C. Sorenson, *The Word War* (New York: Harper and Row, 1968), 144–145.

[8] Foad Izadi, "'Culture of Measurement' in U.S. Public Diplomacy: Recent Congressional Hearings for a Contested Strategy," paper presented at the annual meeting of the International Studies Association, Chicago, IL, February 28, 2007, 29.

which looked at twenty-nine studies and articles on U.S. public diplomacy identified as "being credible reports with valuable suggestions," identified fourteen "key recommendations for public diplomacy reform."[9] Evaluation was not on the list.

Defining "success"

One of the most important questions that must be considered in developing an adequate evaluation scheme for public diplomacy is: What constitutes "success"? On this matter, there is no consensus. In fact, in examining whether U.S. public diplomacy during the Cold War could be deemed a "success," John Robert Kelley found that "a normative approach to defining success works well, because a brief glimpse into [U.S. public diplomacy's] history reflects constantly changing standards of success in relation to social conventions and the accepted conduct of statecraft by way of certain practices."[10]

In examining the objectives associated with different dimensions of public diplomacy—i.e., information, advocacy and engagement—Kelley noted that the "success" of U.S. public diplomacy during the Cold War might be defined as creating "qualitatively and visibly positive changes towards the end of fostering understanding and support for US foreign policy initiatives."[11] By these measures, Kelley concluded, "the answer is not straightforward."[12] While there is some evidence to suggest that public diplomacy was successful, he said, the lack of available data, and reliance on insufficient anecdotal evidence, preclude certainty.

Of course, definitions of "success" in public diplomacy are tied to expectations of what public diplomacy was supposed to accomplish in the first place. For example, if public diplomacy's objective is perceived to be defeating terrorism, then only when terrorism is eliminated—or perhaps when acts of terrorism decline—will public diplomacy be deemed successful.

---

[9] Susan B. Epstein and Lisa Mages, *Public Diplomacy: A Review of Past Recommendations* (Washington, DC: Congressional Research Service, The Library of Congress, 2005).

[10] John Robert Kelley, "US Public Diplomacy: A Cold War Success Story?" *The Hague Journal of Diplomacy* 2 (2007): 63.

[11] Ibid., 65.

[12] Ibid., 77–78.

Similarly, if during the Cold War, U.S. public diplomacy's purpose was perceived to be defeating communism, then once the Berlin Wall fell, public diplomacy was perceived to have succeeded. In fact, such reasoning was, to a great degree, the cause of U.S. public diplomacy's demise in the post-Cold War period. Many of those in a position to decide public diplomacy's fate thought that since the USIA had accomplished its mission, the agency was no longer needed.

It is interesting to note that USIA officers who spent their careers in American public diplomacy held a very different view of public diplomacy's mission. For example, when asked about the importance of specific strategic objectives to public diplomacy's success in accomplishing its mission during the Cold War, USIA alumni listed ten other objectives before "to defeat communism."[13] Similarly, when asked about the importance of specific strategic objectives to public diplomacy's mission today, they, once again, listed ten other objectives before "to defeat terrorism."[14]

In fact, according to the *USIA Alumni Study*, the top six strategic objectives considered by American public diplomacy experts to have been most important during the Cold War are the same as the top six strategic objectives they consider to be most important today. Both then and now, the top objectives pertain to the advancement of U.S. foreign policy, the development of a positive image for the United States, the development of understanding of American life and institutions among people in other countries, and the establishment and maintenance of good relationships with people abroad.

Other strategic objectives USIA alumni identified as important to the public diplomacy mission were to identify and address the host country's problems and goals; to counter negative images of the United States created by the U.S. media; to foster democracy; and to build international linkages between American and counterpart institutions abroad.

---

[13] Kathy R. Fitzpatrick, "The Collapse of American Public Diplomacy: What Diplomatic Experts Say About Rebuilding America's Image Around the World—A View from the Trenches, paper presented at the annual meeting of the International Studies Association, San Francisco, CA, March 27, 2008, 8–9.

[14] Ibid.

Table 8.1 USIA Alumni Views on the Importance of Strategic Objectives to the Public Diplomacy Mission*

Objective	Mean** Cold War	Mean** Today
To create understanding of and support for U.S. and its policies	4.80	4.51
To present clear statements of U.S. government policies to people abroad	4.72	4.41
To advance U.S. foreign policy	4.62	4.45
To create a positive image for the U.S. with people in other countries	4.62	4.34
To create an understanding of American life and institutions among people abroad	4.57	4.23
To establish and maintain good relationships with people abroad	4.56	4.27
To build confidence and trust in U.S. world leadership	4.32	4.05
To defend U.S. ideals abroad	4.27	4.05
To demonstrate respect for other cultures and values	4.20	4.12
To combat anti-Americanism	4.14	4.01
To defeat communism	4.12	N/A
To defeat terrorism	N/A	4.17
To advance peace in the world	4.06	3.83
To counter disinformation campaigns by others	4.04	3.81
To establish and maintain U.S. leadership position in the world	3.98	3.81
To shape a global environment where democracy can flourish	3.86	3.68
To improve life for all people around the world	3.47	3.05
To advance U.S. economic interests	3.46	3.47
To establish and maintain U.S. power in the world	3.30	3.42
To convert people abroad to U.S. beliefs and values	2.88	2.91

* The *USIA Alumni Study* (n=213)
** Numeric average of all responses, with 1 being "Not Important" and 5 being "Very Important."

Notwithstanding their rankings of specific objectives, a significant majority (72 percent) of the USIA alumni agreed that the USIA played a critical role in causing attitude changes that contributed to the defeat of communism and the fall of the Soviet Union. Similarly, a large majority (76 percent) agreed that U.S. public diplomacy has a critical role to play in the war on terror today.

Table 8.2 USIA Alumni Views on Public Diplomacy's Role in Defeating Communism and Terrorism*

"USIA played a critical role in causing attitude changes that contributed to the defeat of communism and the fall of the Soviet Union."				
Strongly Disagree				Strongly Agree
0%	4%	23%	37%	35%
"U.S. public diplomacy has a critical role to play in the war on terror."				
Strongly Disagree				Strongly Agree
1%	5%	17%	26%	50%

* The *USIA Alumni Study* (n=213); rounded percentages of all respondents

The *USIA Alumni Study* clearly illustrated that the agency's work was not defined—at least not by those responsible for carrying out the public diplomacy mandate—by one objective alone. And, despite both the historic and contemporary emphasis on public diplomacy's role in advancing foreign policy, the study also showed that America's public diplomats viewed their broad charge as encompassing a range of strategic objectives intended to improve the nation's relations with people abroad. In other words, public diplomacy was not viewed as *solely* an instrument of foreign policy.

Bruce Gregory made a similar point in observing, "Countries use public diplomacy to strengthen economic performance, support long-term foreign policy goals, enhance visibility, project identity, prevent and manage crises as well as counter adverse stereotypical images."[15] Less-developed "small and middle powers," Gregory noted, also use public diplomacy "to achieve their desire to be noticed."[16]

The point here is that because public diplomacy is a resource for accomplishing a range of strategic objectives, public diplomacy's success cannot be defined—nor should it be measured—by one yardstick alone. Evaluation of both short-term programmatic outcomes and long-term relational outcomes—as well as the connections between the two—are needed.

---

[15] Bruce Gregory, "Public Diplomacy and Governance: Challenges for Scholars and Practitioners," in *Global Governance and Diplomacy: Worlds Apart?*, ed. Andrew F. Cooper, Brian Hocking, and William Maley (Houndmills: Palgrave MacMillan, 2008), 243.

[16] Ibid.

Evaluation in U.S. public diplomacy

By most accounts, the overall state of evaluation in American public diplomacy is weak. In fact, according to veteran U.S. public diplomacy official Joe Johnson, "Washington cannot quantify even the most basic outputs of its embassies."[17] Writing for the *Foreign Service Journal*, Johnson said, "The most critical challenge for State's PD leadership is not to get more appropriations for new programs. It is to develop a well-trained field component and to impose baseline standards and processes to measure results. These are the keys to building confidence in our nation's public diplomacy."[18]

A 2007 study by Foad Izadi that assessed the current state of the evaluation phase of U.S. public diplomacy campaigns similarly concluded that a "culture of measurement is not yet established."[19] According to Izadi, "the measurement of effectiveness of public diplomacy has not been a priority of public diplomacy officials and…the State Department and other relevant agencies do not have a concrete strategy for systematic quantitative analysis of public diplomacy programs' impact on target populations."[20]

Earlier studies had reached similar conclusions. For example, the 2003 report of a Congressionally-appointed advisory group charged with evaluating U.S. public diplomacy efforts in the Middle East called for a "new culture of measurement" in all public diplomacy structures, finding that "sophisticated and meaningful measurement has simply not been given proper emphasis in public diplomacy."[21] A GAO report published the same year concluded that U.S. "public diplomacy is not systematically and comprehensively measuring progress toward its public diplomacy goals. Its overseas performance measurement efforts focus on anecdotal evidence…rather than gauging progress toward changing foreign publics' understanding and attitudes about the United States."[22]

---

[17] Joe Johnson, "How Does Public Diplomacy Measure Up?," 49.

[18] Ibid., 51.

[19] Foad Izadi, "'Culture of Measurement' in U.S. Public Diplomacy," 37.

[20] Ibid.

[21] Edward P. Djerejian, Chairman, *Changing Minds, Winning Peace: A New Strategic Direction for U.S. Public Diplomacy in the Arab and Muslim World* (Washington, DC: The Advisory Group on Public Diplomacy for the Arab and Muslim World, 2003), 9.

[22] Government Accountability Office, *State Department Expands Efforts but Faces Significant Challenges*, GAO-03-951 (Washington, DC: 2003): 65.

In 2005, the U.S. Advisory Commission on U.S. Public Diplomacy included measurement as one of ten suggested improvements in U.S. public diplomacy for the future. The report advised, "Polling needs to play a larger role in outreach efforts. Public diplomacy is not just about getting audiences to know you; it also is about getting to know your audiences. We need to know more about public diplomacy's effects on attitudes and behavior. Moreover, we need to avoid standardized approaches, and instead encourage country-specific research strategies."[23]

In 2006, the GAO again cited weaknesses in the evaluation component of U.S. public diplomacy: "Among the missing elements are core messages and themes, target audience segmentation and analysis, details on program strategies and tactics, in-depth research and evaluation to inform strategic communication decisions, and a fully developed communication plan to tie everything together."[24] At the same time, the GAO noted that the State Department had "begun to institute a 'culture of measurement,' which should significantly impact the rigor and sophistication of its strategic planning and evaluation efforts."[25]

The report noted that in response to the GAO's earlier assessments, the department had created an Office of Policy, Planning, and Resources within the office of the under secretary of state for public diplomacy and public affairs, as well as a Public Diplomacy Evaluation Council to share best practices with officers in the field. According to the report, the department had also developed an evaluation schedule, "which places a new emphasis on assessing the department's strategic information programs."[26]

In June 2007, a task force report of the Foreign Affairs Council, which provided an "independent" assessment of the management of the State Department under Condoleezza Rice, also identified progress in the area of public diplomacy. At the same time, noting that those responsible for U.S. public diplomacy were "standing tall in a deep

---

[23] U.S. Advisory Commission on Public Diplomacy, *2005 Report* (Washington, DC, 2005): 27.

[24] Government Accountability Office, *U.S. Public Diplomacy: State Department Efforts to Engage Muslim Audiences Lack Certain Communication Elements and Face Significant Challenges*, GAO-06–535 (Washington, DC: 2006): 22.

[25] Ibid., 28.

[26] Ibid.

hole,"[27] the report identified on a list of things "yet to be done" the need for "systematic evaluation of PD program effectiveness, including evaluation over extended time periods."[28]

A national strategy for public diplomacy

During the same month the Foreign Affairs Council report was published, Hughes announced the completion of the "U.S. National Strategy for Public Diplomacy and Strategic Communication," described as the first comprehensive national strategy for public diplomacy ever developed (a curious claim given the existence of earlier plans produced by the USIA) and the result of more than a year's work.[29] (The full document appears in Appendix Two.) This plan, which many expected would "tie everything together" in U.S. public diplomacy, was designed to provide strategic direction "to govern America's public diplomacy and strategic communication with foreign audiences" going forward.[30]

For those hoping to see an increased emphasis on evaluation, however, the plan was disappointing. Four specific weaknesses related to the assessment of American public diplomacy are noteworthy.

First, the document is not a strategic plan *per se*, which, by definition, should include measurable objectives and means of evaluation. Rather, it is a broad statement of philosophy and operating principles. The document begins by outlining a mission that includes four points:

- Underscore our commitment to freedom, human rights and the dignity and equality of every human being;
- Reach out to those who share our ideals;
- Support those who struggle for freedom and democracy; and
- Counter those who espouse ideologies of hate and oppression.[31]

---

[27] Foreign Affairs Council, *Task Force Report: Managing Secretary Rice's State Department: An Independent Assessment*, (Washington, DC, June 2007): 20.

[28] Ibid., 22.

[29] U.S. National Strategy for Public Diplomacy and Strategic Communication, http://www.state.gov/documents/organization/87427.pdf (accessed January 2, 2009).

[30] Ibid., 2.

[31] Ibid.

It next reviews three "strategic objectives": 1) "Offer positive vision of hope and opportunity that is rooted in our most basic values"; 2) "Isolate and marginalize violent extremists who threaten the freedom and peace sought by civilized people of every nation, culture and faith"; and 3) "Nurture common interests and values between Americans and peoples of different countries, cultures and faiths across the world."[32]

The plan also identifies three "priorities" for programs and activities to "achieve our mission": 1) "Expand education and exchange programs"; 2) "Modernize communications"; and 3) "Promote the "diplomacy of deeds."[33]

These collective statements provide strategic guidance to public diplomacy officials charged with carrying out the public diplomacy mission. However, there is no indication of how public diplomacy efforts will or should be evaluated. The lack of specificity in terms of precisely what is to be accomplished, combined with the lack of measurement criteria and timeframes, limits the document's usefulness in terms of evaluation.

Second, the plan reflects a view of public diplomacy as primarily a communication/promotional function. This view is evident in the focus on the communication and promotional aspects of public diplomacy throughout the document and the neglect of public diplomacy's policy role. The choice of the term "audiences" in reference to foreign publics, combined with an emphasis on "core messages" and the use of "mass media" techniques to reach targeted audiences, also suggests a communication mindset. Additionally, the statement that "our public diplomacy and communication programs" should to be tailored "to specific audiences, using the most appropriate and effective media available" suggests a reliance on mediated communication, rather than on relational techniques.

A promotional perspective of public diplomacy is also reflected in the section on "Diplomacy of Deeds," which emphasizes the need to "promote" and "communicate" with people abroad about U.S. aid initiatives. The plan states, "All agencies and embassies should make a major commitment to more aggressively tell the story of how [aid] programs are helping people improve their lives and opportunities."[34]

---

[32] Ibid., 3.
[33] Ibid., 6–7.
[34] Ibid., 7.

The significance of such perspective for evaluation is that when public diplomacy is viewed as a communication and/or promotional function, evaluation techniques are generally limited to "audience" measures (such as message reach and/or media impressions) and/or communication output. Post-9/11 examples illustrate this point. The "Shared Values" initiative implemented soon after 9/11 by former U.S. Under secretary for Public Diplomacy Charlotte Beers—who viewed public diplomacy as primarily a promotional function—focused on whether messages "reached" targeted audiences in the Middle East. Later efforts by Hughes—who frequently referred to public diplomacy as a communication function and to herself as a "communicator"—were evaluated on the basis of communication "outputs," or tasks accomplished during her tenure.[35]

Third, the plan includes no specific measurement criteria or guidance for evaluating public diplomacy's effectiveness. In fact, evaluation is not part of the plan at all; rather, evaluation is addressed in Attachment E, which indicates that evaluation and accountability are the responsibility of the Policy Coordinating Committee (PCC), which is expected to "conduct periodic agency-specific reviews of public diplomacy and strategic communication efforts to validate successful programs, recommend the continuation of activities, and direct resources."[36]

According to the attachment, the PCC is charged with establishing a culture of measurement, establishing common core performance indicators, establishing mechanisms for data collection, and conducting reviews of public diplomacy and strategic communication efforts. A bit ironically, the attachment states that "all United States government agencies must build evaluation and measurement into strategic and public diplomacy program design"—something that is missing in the plan itself.

Fourth, the plan focuses inordinate attention on public diplomacy's role in combating terrorism at the expense of public diplomacy's broader mission. For example, the plan includes eight "core messages" described as "general"—arguably more than are needed for a "national" strategy.[37] However, it includes twice as many—sixteen—"core mes-

---

[35] See "Changing the Nature and Scope of Public Diplomacy," News Release, Office of the Under Secretary for Public Diplomacy and Public Affairs, November 1, 2007.

[36] Ibid., 33.

[37] Ibid., 27.

sages" described as "specific to the war on terrorism."[38] It would be hard to make a compelling case that such lack of specificity meets that 9/11 Commission's challenge to the U.S. government to "define what [America's] message is, what it stands for."[39]

Additionally, the plan offers nothing in the way of explanation for how the *impact* of such messages will be evaluated, or in the commission's words, how U.S. officials will "measure success."[40] As the commission stated, the American people "are entitled to see some standards of performance so they can judge, with the help of their elected representatives, whether the objectives are being met."[41]

Notwithstanding the fact that evaluation is relegated to an attachment to the actual plan and that the plan itself includes no specific criteria for evaluating public diplomacy's success, there is some indication that U.S. public diplomacy officials recognize the need for improvements in evaluation techniques. For example, Attachment E cites the importance of measurement and evaluation to both the development of effective public diplomacy programs and their long-term success: "Evaluation should measure progress toward the achievement of goals, allowing managers to adjust methods and means, and make informed decisions about resources. Performance measurement and evaluation ensure accountability and transparency so that stakeholders, including the American public, can justify program expenditures as a prudent use of taxpayer funds."[42]

It also should be noted that the public diplomacy plan does not address evaluation efforts related to U.S. international broadcasting, an area in which measurement historically has received more attention. For example, the Broadcasting Board of Governors recently asked the University of Southern California Center on Public Diplomacy to assess the quality and effectiveness of Alhurra Television, which was established by the U.S. government shortly after 9/11 to improve broadcast efforts in the Middle East. A team of researchers led by USC journalism and media professors conducted a content analysis of more than seventy-five hours of news programming broadcast by Alhurra

---

[38] Ibid., 28–30.

[39] *The 9/11 Commission Report: Final Report of the National Commission on Terrorist Attacks Upon the United States* (New York: W. W. Norton & Company, 2002), 376.

[40] Ibid., 364.

[41] Ibid., 365.

[42] U.S. National Strategy for Public Diplomacy and Strategic Communication, 33.

and held extensive discussions with opinion leaders throughout the Middle East to assess the perceived impact of the programming. Alhurra's broadcasts were evaluated on the basis of the Middle East Broadcasting Network's Journalistic Code of Ethics, which outlines Alhurra's journalistic mission.[43]

The results of the study were not encouraging. The researchers found:

> Alhurra provided a lack of news and topical programming tailored to the interests of the Arab audience, that the quality of Alhurra's journalism was substandard, that Alhurra's association with the Bush administration and American policy in general resulted in widespread perceptions of bias that tainted its ability to be seen as "credible" in the eyes of most of its audiences, that Alhurra's reporting was often biased in favor of the American or western perspective at the expense of the Arab perspective, that Alhurra too often relied on unsubstantiated information in its reporting, and that the broadcaster lacked a fundamental connection to the "Arab street," a prerequisite for significant viewership in today's saturated news-media environment.[44]

Recommending "significant overhaul in Alhurra's operations," the researchers concluded that "the status quo would result in a failed effort at improving understanding of American policies and culture in the region."[45]

This type of systematic, objective evaluation is exactly what is needed for U.S. public diplomacy to improve. Although the negative findings clearly illustrate why U.S. officials might be reluctant to open their work to such scrutiny, the process illustrates the value of such evaluation.

Unfortunately, even if U.S. public diplomacy officials made evaluation a priority, the resources to build an adequate system of evaluation have not been provided. For example, the 2006 GAO review of public diplomacy found that "research and evaluation efforts to inform all facets of strategic communication are limited by the relatively small

---

[43] *An Evaluation of Alhurra Television Programming* (Washington, DC: U.S. Broadcasting Board of Governors, 2008), http://uscpublicdiplomacy.org/media/AlHurraReport.pdf (accessed January 6, 2008).

[44] "An Evaluation of Alhurra Television Programming," *CPD Announcements*, USC Center on Public Diplomacy, December 16, 2008, http://uscpublicdiplomacy.com/index.php/newsroom/announcements_detail/an_evaluation_of_alhurra_television_programming/ (accessed January 6, 2009)

[45] Ibid.

budget in Washington, D.C., allocated to such efforts and a general lack of expertise in the field with regard to commissioning and conducting such studies."[46]

Polling

In the absence of other data, public opinion poll results have received considerable attention as indicators of U.S. public diplomacy's effectiveness. In fact, most of the reports that have examined public diplomacy in the post-9/11 period have cited increasing anti-Americanism, as reported in global attitude surveys, as evidence of public diplomacy's perceived failure. Clearly, such measures are important gauges of America's image and reputation among citizens of other nations. What is less clear, however, is the extent to which public opinion polls are valid or reliable measures of public diplomacy's success.

The relationships among public opinion polling, public diplomacy, and foreign policy was explored in a 2006 forum that brought together prominent public opinion professionals and academics who strongly agreed that "polling is integral to developing a better understanding of the barriers to and the opportunities for effective public diplomacy campaigns."[47] Specific benefits of polling, as cited by participants in the forum, were to "identify trends in public opinion, specify public concerns, and perhaps most importantly, provide information about how changes in policy affect the attitudes and behaviors of particular audiences."[48]

At the same time, participants recognized the limitations of public opinion polling. "Simply put, polling cannot provide the tools required to sway mass opinion."[49] They cited the difficulty in anticipating changes in attitudes and opinions at the local level for which, they said, "field research" is better suited[50] and cautioned against overemphasizing

---

[46] Government Accountability Office, *U.S. Public Diplomacy: State Department Efforts to Engage Muslim Audiences Lack Certain Communication Elements and Face Significant Challenges*, GAO-06-535, 20 (Washington, DC: 2006).

[47] "Executive Summary: Public Diplomacy and World Public Opinion Forum," *Public Diplomacy: Practitioners, Policy Makers, and Public Opinion, A Report of the Public Diplomacy and World Public Opinion Forum* (Los Angeles: USC Center on Public Diplomacy and Washington, DC: Pew Research Center, 2006), 10.

[48] Ibid., 9.

[49] Ibid.

[50] Ibid.

media effects: "Causal correlations between media usage and public opinion change are almost impossible to establish. Thus, it remains unclear whether simply modifying messages carried via the media can ever be, in and of itself, an effective public diplomacy strategy."[51]

Marc Lynch, who participated in the forum, explained, "The fashionable fixation with "moving the needle" [of foreign public opinion] with public diplomacy is badly misplaced; so many different factors go into the formation of public opinion that it will be rare that the effects of a public diplomacy campaign would register in public opinion surveys."[52] Thus, Lynch said, the usefulness of public opinion polls for designing policy initiatives is limited. "[T]hey paint too broad a brush and tell policy makers little about how publics will respond to changes in the status quo."[53]

Rather, Lynch advised, "Survey research is better at identifying constants—enduring themes, recurrent patterns—than at anticipating the response to dramatic new initiatives."[54] For that reason, he said, "A better way to think of the policy use of survey research is as a diagnostic—checking the effects of policies, and providing warning signs of policy failure."[55]

Perhaps most important, the participants recognized the need to use public opinion polling more strategically in efforts to measure foreign public opinion. Recommendations included the use of more longitudinal polling to reveal long-term trends; identifying degrees as well as directions of opinion; disaggregating objects of opinion, i.e., governments vs. populations; sharing polling information among government departments and coordinating polling goals; and utilizing polling data in the launch of new policies as well as in developing communication strategies.[56]

---

[51] Ibid., 10.

[52] Marc Lynch, "Public Opinion Survey Research and Public Diplomacy, in *Public Diplomacy: Practitioners, Policy Makers, and Public Opinion, A Report of the Public Diplomacy and World Public Opinion Forum* (Los Angeles: USC Center on Public Diplomacy and Washington, DC: Pew Research Center, 2006), 42.

[53] Ibid., 43.

[54] Ibid.

[55] Ibid.

[56] "Executive Summary: Public Diplomacy and World Public Opinion Forum," 17–18.

Notwithstanding the value of such efforts, the limitations of public opinion polling illustrate the need for other methods to measure the achievement of public diplomacy objectives and to better understand the effectiveness of various types of public diplomacy strategies and tactics. In that regard, other techniques, such as media content analysis and network analysis, have received some attention. As an example, network analysis was used in a recent study of the British Council's "Network Effect," a three-year program designed to "nurture networks between the next generation of [European] leaders."[57] The program, which was aimed at young professionals between the ages of 25 and 35, brought participants from throughout Europe together to address and learn about long term challenges facing their societies, such as "placing their economies on a sustainable low carbon footing, managing the democratic transition of an ageing population, building cohesive communities in the face of growing social diversity."[58]

The evaluation was based on a network analysis that included a survey of participants designed to evaluate network development and effects.[59] Among the key findings of the study was the development of an expanding network with more than 300 links, which had resulted in more than 120 collaborations or intentions to collaborate among participants at the time of the study. These and other results allowed researchers to make recommendations regarding the achievement of specific objectives, the potential value of the program to the UK, and steps that could be taken to enhance future development of the program.

New directions in public diplomacy evaluation

Notably absent from the public diplomacy literature is any serious discussion of public diplomacy's success in helping nations establish and maintain good *relationships* with people abroad. Although the value of public diplomacy is assumed by many to lie in the creation of positive relationships that encourage supportive attitudes and behaviors and

[57] Ali Fisher and Sarah Curnow, *Evaluation of British Council Project: The Network Effect* (Mappa Mundi Consulting, March 2009, http://www.britishcouncil.org/networkeffect-about-the-project.htm (accessed May 21, 2009).

[58] Ibid.

[59] Ibid.

discourage harmful attitudes and behaviors among foreign publics, there is scant empirical evidence to show that good relationships actually lead to supportive actions or that they deter harmful actions.

Certainly, the "new" public diplomacy, which emphasizes dialogue over monologue, publics over audiences, and engagement over information, would seem to require that practitioners move away from communication-centered and media-based models of measurement that examine one-way short-term effects on targeted audiences toward more sophisticated two-way evaluation methods that examine long-term effects on the state and quality of relationships between nations and their strategic publics and the implications of such relationships.

A similar shift occurred in the field of public relations when scholars and practitioners began to conceptualize public relations' primary mission as establishing and maintaining relationships, rather than influencing public opinion.[60] Recognizing the inadequacy of public opinion surveys for describing organization-public relationships, public relations scholars refocused their attention on the need to better understand both the phenomenon of relationships and how to measure them.

The adoption of a relational mindset in public diplomacy would be significant for evaluation. In addition to providing concrete data concerning the true impact of public diplomacy in diplomatic affairs, relationship measures could enhance the credibility of public diplomacy as a critical component of a nation's international relations. In fact, one of the potential benefits of adopting a relational model of evaluation is that it would help practitioners demonstrate their value as both policy advisors and communication management specialists.

For example, public relations scholars who examined how public relations makes organizations more effective found that organizations are able to achieve their goals by choosing goals that are "valued both by management and by strategic constituencies both inside and outside the organization. When organizations choose such goals, they

[60] See, e.g., William P. Ehling, "Estimating the Value of Public Relations and Communication to an Organization," in *Excellence in Public Relations and Communications Management*, ed. James E. Grunig, David M. Dozier, William P. Ehling, Larissa A. Grunig, Fred C. Repper, and Jon White (Hillsdale, NJ: Lawrence Erlbaum Associates, Inc., 1992), 617–638.

minimize efforts of publics to interfere with organizational decisions and maximize support from publics."[61]

In the context of public diplomacy, this means that if nations choose goals and policies that are congruent with foreign publics' expectations, they reduce public opposition to their policies and actions. According to James Grunig and Linda Hon, "effective organizations choose and achieve appropriate goals because they develop relationships with their constituencies.… Ineffective organizations cannot achieve their goals, at least in part, because their publics do not support and typically oppose management efforts to achieve what publics consider illegitimate goals."[62] In the latter case, Grunig and Hon pointed out, publics sometimes oppose institutional policies and decisions in ways that often result in "issues" or "crises."[63]

These researchers noted that, notwithstanding the fact that "most management decision-makers believe that they choose goals and make decisions that are best for the organization and that they, rather than publics, know what decisions are best…organizations generally make better decisions when they listen to and collaborate with stakeholders before they make final decisions rather than simply trying to persuade them to accept organizational goals after decisions are made."[64]

In applying this thinking to public diplomacy, public diplomats help nations choose policies and actions that are congruent with foreign publics' expectations, thereby both improving the chance that people abroad will support such policies and actions and reducing the potential for conflicts. Grunig and Hon explained: "Public relations makes an organization more effective…when it identifies the most strategic publics as part of strategic management processes and conducts communication programs to develop and maintain effective long-term relationships between management and those publics."[65]

---

[61] James E. Grunig and Linda Hon, *Guidelines for Measuring Relationships in Public Relations* (Gainesville, FL: The Institute for Public Relations Commission on PR Measurement and Evaluation, 1999), 8.

[62] Ibid.

[63] Ibid.

[64] Ibid.; see also Michael Porter, "Toward a Dynamic Theory of Strategy," in R. P. Rumelt, D. E. Schendel, and D. J. Teece, ed. *Fundamental Issues in Strategy: A Research Agenda* (Boston: Harvard Business School Press, 1994).

[65] Grunig and Hon, *Guidelines for Measuring Relationships in Public Relations*, 9.

The value of public relations to an organization, then, can be determined by measuring "the quality of relationships with strategic publics" and, by extension, measuring "the effects of [communication programs] and correlating them with relationship indicators."[66] Noting that such correlations have been shown in public relations research,[67] Grunig and Hon advised, "Organizations that communicate effectively with publics develop better relationships because [organizational decision makers] and publics understand one another and because both are less likely to behave in ways that have negative consequences on the interests of the other."[68]

Measuring relationships

If the goal of public diplomacy is to establish and sustain beneficial relations between a nation and people abroad, then measures of public diplomacy's effectiveness should include relationships. Three areas of research that have been explored by public relations scholars could be particularly useful in defining an evaluation research agenda for public diplomacy: 1) antecedents of relationships; 2) relationship maintenance strategies; and 3) outcomes of relationships.[69]

Relationship antecedents have been defined as the reasons parties enter into relationships: "social and cultural norms, collective perceptions and expectations, needs for resources, perceptions of uncertain environment, and legal/voluntary necessity."[70] Relationship maintenance strategies include communication and other efforts to maintain relationships between parties, e.g., accommodation, compromise, cooperation, including negotiation and conflict resolution strategies.[71]

---

[66] Ibid.

[67] See, e.g., David M. Dozier, Larissa A. Grunig, and James E. Grunig, *Manager's Guide to Excellence in Public Relations and Communications Management* (Mahwah, NJ: Lawrence Erlbaum Publishers, 1995).

[68] Grunig and Hon, *Guidelines for Measuring Relationships in Public Relations*, 10.

[69] See, e.g., Glen M. Broom, Shawna Casey, and James Ritchey, "Concept and Theory of Organization-Public Relationships," in *Public Relations as Relationship Management*, ed. John A. Ledingham and Stephen D. Bruning (Mahwah, NJ: Lawrence Erlbaum Publishers, 2000), 3–22.

[70] Glen M. Broom, Shawna Casey, and James Ritchey, "Toward a Concept and Theory of Organization-Public Relationships, *Journal of Public Relations Research* 9 (1997): 94.

[71] See James E. Grunig and Yi-Hui Huang, "From Organizational Effectiveness to Relationship Indicators: Antecedents of Relationships, Public Relations Strategies, and

Relationship outcomes are key features or dimensions of relationships, e.g., trust, satisfaction, commitment, and resulting actions.[72]

A great deal of evaluation research in public relations has focused on measuring targeted publics' perceptions of their relationships with organizations and the impact of those perceptions on the targeted publics' attitudes and behaviors. A number of relationship measurement scales have been developed, with significant attention to a model developed by Grunig and Hon in 1999 and since validated by other studies.[73] It provides a good example of the potential usefulness of such measures in public diplomacy.

The Grunig and Hon model focuses on four dimensions of relationships that can be used to measure perceptions of organizational-public relationships through such methods as surveys, interviews, and focus groups. The dimensions are described as follows: 1) control mutuality—"the degree to which parties agree on who has the rightful power to influence one another"; 2) trust—"the level of confidence in and willingness to open oneself to the other party"; satisfaction—"the extent to which each party feels favorably toward the other because positive expectations about the relationship are reinforced"; and commitment—"the extent to which each party believes and feels that the relationship is worth spending energy to maintain and promote."[74]

Grunig and Hon also identified two types of relationships that affect both participants' perceptions and desired outcomes: "exchange relationships" and "communal relationships." An exchange relationship is a relationship in which "one party gives benefits to the other only because the other has provided benefits in the past or it expected to do so in the future."[75] A communal relationship is a relationship in which "both parties provide benefits to the other because they are concerned

Relationship Outcomes," in Ledingham and Bruning, *Public Relations as Relationship Management*, 23–54.

[72] Eyun-Jung Ki and Linda Childers Hon, "Reliability and Validity of Organization-Public Relationship Measurement and Linkages among Relationship Indicators in a Membership Organization," *Journalism & Mass Communication Quarterly* 84, no. 3 (Autumn 2007): 419–438; see also Samsup Jo, "Measurement of Organization-Public Relations: Validation of Measurement Using a Manufacturer-Retailer Relationship," *Journal of Public Relations Research* 18 (2006): 225–248.

[73] Grunig and Hon, *Guidelines for Measuring Relationships in Public Relations.*

[74] Walter K. Lindenman, "Overview," in *Guidelines for Measuring Relationships in Public Relations*, ed. James E. Grunig and Linda Hon (Gainesville, FL: The Institute for Public Relations Commission on PR Measurement and Evaluation, 1999), 2–3.

[75] Ibid.

for the welfare of the other—even when they get nothing in return."[76] For most public relations activities, these researchers suggested, "developing communal relationships with key constituencies is much more important than would be developing exchange relationships.[77]

Under a relational paradigm, in addition to evaluating publics' perceptions of their relationships with institutions, institutional perceptions of their relationships with publics also should be measured. Such two-way studies allow researchers to determine incongruencies in how institutions and their strategic publics, respectively, perceive their relationships. According to public relations researcher Walter K. Lindenmann, "Such a gap analysis will suggest strategies for maintaining or repairing relationships."[78]

As an example, in a study of relationships between public health organizations and their strategic publics, public relations scholar Kurt Wise found that public health organizations would be most effective if they strategically managed their relationships with their constituents, giving these publics a voice in organizational decisions that affect them. Wise concluded, "If public relations is practiced symmetrically, strategic constituents are not just 'heard.' Their expectations are taken into consideration during the organization's goal-setting process and the organization's goals may change as a result of the process."[79] Wise advised, "Symmetrical communication can take many forms...but key to all is the fact that information gathered from strategic constituents is *considered* and communication with constituents is important from a *results* standpoint and not merely a process perspective."[80]

Public relations researchers also have begun to explore linkages among targeted publics' perceptions of their relationships with organizations and the attitudes and behavioral intentions of those publics toward an institution. This research should be of particular interest to public diplomacy practitioners keen to better understand why people act in ways that support or harm national interests. For example, Eyun-Jung Ki and Hon found that among the six relationship indicators noted above, "perceptions of satisfaction and control mutuality were

[76] Ibid.
[77] Ibid.
[78] Ibid., 5.
[79] Kurt Wise, "Linking Public Relations Processes and Organizational Effectiveness at a State Health Department," *Journal of Health and Human Services Administration* 25, no. 4 (Spring 2003): 503.
[80] Ibid.

the best predictors of a positive attitude toward the organization"[81] and that a "positive attitude was a precursor to supportive behavioral intentions toward the organizations."[82]

Public relations scholars also have recognized the need to go beyond measures of relationship participants' perceptions of their relationships. As Glen Broom, Shawna Casey, and James Ritchey observed, relationships should be studied "as phenomena distinct from the perceptions held by parties in the relationships."[83] According to these researchers, "relationships have unique and measurable properties that are not shared with the participants in the relationships and that define relationships as being something separate from the participants."[84] They defined the organization-public relationship as "represented by patterns of interaction, transaction, exchange, and linkage between an organization and its publics. These relationships have properties that are distinct from the identities, attributes, and perceptions of the individuals and social collectivities in the relationships. Though dynamic in nature, organization-public relationships can be described at a single point in time and measured over time."[85]

Although public relations researchers are just beginning to scratch the surface of evaluation in the study of organization-public relationships, this discussion illustrates the potential for such studies to contribute to the development of a viable and credible measurement scheme focused on relational outcomes in public diplomacy. Thus, in addition to pursuing traditional methods of evaluation involving polling and other techniques, public diplomacy scholars and practitioners should explore the potential for relational measures both to improve the effectiveness of public diplomacy programs and to demonstrate public diplomacy's success.

---

[81] Eyun-Jung Ki and Linda Childers Hon, "Testing the Linkages Among the Organization-Public Relationship and Attitude and Behavioral Intentions," *Journal of Public Relations Research* 19, no. 1 (2007): 1.

[82] Ibid.

[83] Broom, Casey, and Ritchey, "Concept and Theory of Organization-Public Relationships," 17.

[84] Ibid.

[85] Ibid., 18.

CHAPTER NINE

THE NEW PUBLIC DIPLOMAT: CONSTRUCTING A PROFILE

People are what make PD effective.[1]

Not long before the USIA was dissolved, the agency's last director, Joseph Duffy, appeared before the U.S. House Appropriations Committee to discuss the mission and work of the agency. Duffy began by saying he would like to set forth "why I think the mission of USIA is vital to the national security and the national interest of the United States."[2] He went on to list a number of examples in which USIA officers had played key roles in opening channels of communication useful to U.S. policy interests in areas where America's relations with foreign publics were strained or where the United States had no diplomatic relations at all. "No other nation has an organization like USIA," Duffy said, emphasizing that the agency was "unique in the field of foreign relations."[3]

The people responsible for the USIA's enduring success, Duffy said, were the men and women who had served on the frontlines of American public diplomacy. In fact, he noted, the blended specialties represented within the USIA had "given the world a new profession—the public diplomat." That new diplomat, he added, was "a tough-minded advocate of U.S. media and information technology and an agile promoter of American national interests through the exchange of people, the articulation of our values, and the promotion of ideas."[4]

More than a decade later, the "new profession" to which Duffy referred continues to evolve. The need for public diplomacy professionals has never been greater. Both in the United States and around

[1] Former USIA officer; see Kathy R. Fitzpatrick, *USIA Alumni Study*, unpublished report, 2007.

[2] "Prepared Testimony of Joseph Duffy, Director, United States Information Agency before the U.S. House Appropriations Committee, Commerce, Justice, State and the Judiciary Subcommittee," *Federal News Service*, February 26, 1998, http://www.fnsg.com/transcripta.htm (accessed July 10, 2006).

[3] Ibid.

[4] Ibid.

the world, new diplomatic challenges call for highly-qualified specialists who can lead their nations' efforts to develop and sustain beneficial relations with foreign publics. Clearly, a key to rebuilding U.S. public diplomacy is the government's ability to attract and retain qualified public diplomacy professionals who can effectively manage the nation's relations with people abroad.

In all the debate surrounding public diplomacy, however, little attention has been paid to the people who are responsible for carrying out the public diplomacy mission. In 2008, the American Academy of Diplomacy published a special report, which presented recommendations for enhanced staffing of U.S. diplomacy, citing a need for increases in public diplomacy personnel.[5] According to the Academy, public diplomacy is "under-staffed and under-funded" with a FY 2008 budget of $859 million and a staff of 1,332 Americans, which, the report noted, was 24 percent less than in 1986, when the number was 1,742.[6] The report said: "To have a reasonable chance of accomplishing its goals, PD needs to cover an employment shortfall, establish additional positions, obtain greater program funding and significantly expand training."[7]

This report followed a 2007 report in which the GAO reported that 22 percent of public diplomacy positions worldwide were vacant, up from 15 percent in May 2006.[8] The same report revealed that 30 percent of language-designated public diplomacy positions were filled by officers without the required levels of proficiency.

In 2008, the U.S. Advisory Commission on Public Diplomacy, which is charged by Congress to provide oversight of and recommendations for improving U.S. public diplomacy, addressed the need for more attention to those charged with carrying out the public diplomacy mandate by focusing its annual report on the "people part" of U.S. public diplomacy (more on this report below).[9] Beyond these efforts,

[5] The American Academy of Diplomacy, *A Foreign Affairs Budget for the Future: Fixing the Crisis in Diplomatic Readiness* (Washington, DC, October 2008).

[6] Ibid., 14.

[7] Ibid.

[8] Government Accountability Office, *U.S. Public Diplomacy: Strategic Planning Efforts Have Improved but Agencies Face Significant Implementation Challenges* (Washington, DC, 2007).

[9] The United States Advisory Commission on U.S. Public Diplomacy, *Getting the People Part Right: A Report on the Human Resources Dimension of U.S. Public Diplomacy* (Washington, DC, 2008).

however, little serious attention has been directed to the twenty-first century public diplomat. Canadian diplomat Daryl Copeland identified this gap in the literature, noting that "the essence of the public diplomat as a person and as a professional has attracted almost no notice."[10] For that reason, he suggested, the "portrait" of the modern public diplomat must be filled in.

This chapter begins to construct a profile of the contemporary public diplomat by considering the fundamental knowledge, skills, and traits required for success in the field and exploring new challenges ahead that will require new capabilities.

The "people part"

The 2008 report of the U.S. Advisory Commission on Public Diplomacy revealed that the "brain drain" in public diplomacy that occurred just before and after the USIA was dismantled, followed by a decade in which public diplomacy has been neglected by national leaders, has taken a very serious toll on the nation's public diplomacy capabilities. In fact, the report made clear that the United States faces a staffing crisis in public diplomacy that leaves the nation at risk and will take years, if not decades, to fix.

Perhaps the most startling finding in the report was that "the Department of State makes no special effort to recruit individuals into the PD career track who would bring into the Foreign Service experience or skills specifically relevant to the work of communicating with and influencing foreign publics."[11] At the same time, neither the Foreign Service Officer Test nor Oral Assessment of candidates specifically tests for public diplomacy instincts or communication skills.[12]

In fact, according to the report, "there is no evident connection between current Department recruiting activities and current or future Department policy or programmatic priorities."[13] For example, the State

---

[10] Daryl Copeland, "No Dangling Conversation: Portrait of the Public Diplomat," in *Engagement: Public Diplomacy in a Globalized World: A Collection of Essays and Case Studies* (London: UK Foreign & Commonwealth Office, 2008), http://www.fco.gov.uk/en/about-the-fco/publications/publications/pd-publication/21c-foreign-policy (accessed August 28, 2008).

[11] The United States Advisory Commission on U.S. Public Diplomacy, *Getting the People Part Right*, 4.

[12] Ibid.

[13] Ibid., 9.

Department does not recruit public diplomacy specialists from schools of communication or other "feeder" institutions, nor does it recruit for "PD-salient skills and competencies, such as foreign language fluency (and relatedly, 'cultural fluency'), marketing, coalition-building, and the like."[14] Rather, it hires "generalists" with the assumption that they can learn public diplomacy skills through training and/or on-the-job experience.

These "generalists" have the option of choosing public diplomacy from among five career tracks in the U.S. Foreign Service, including political, economic, consular, public diplomacy, and management. Thus, the commissioners pointed out, "The only certain connection to the public diplomacy field State's incoming officers have is having checked the PD box while registering to take the Foreign Service Written Examination."[15]

This problem is exacerbated, the commission found, by the fact that on-the-job training in public diplomacy is inadequate. The commission reported that, although training in public diplomacy has improved substantially since 9/11, the "relatively spare public diplomacy training budget, while significantly larger than that of recent years, is a constraint."[16] The commission identified "a number of conspicuous, and serious, blind-spots in the Department's public diplomacy training," including the lack of area-specific courses.[17] Only five courses, it determined, "totaling perhaps three or four weeks of training," actually "deal at all with what might be termed the substance of the communication field."[18] Somewhat incredulously, the commissioners reported, "In the nation that practically invented the study of persuasive communication, in a training program designed specifically for those tasked with communicating purposefully and effectively with key audiences on behalf of our nation, not a single course on the science of communication is offered."[19]

Thus, the commission concluded, "The State Department deliberately recruits generalists, does not rigorously test these officers for PD expertise or skills in the examination process, and then largely fails to

---

[14] Ibid.
[15] Ibid., 14.
[16] Ibid., 9.
[17] Ibid., 15.
[18] Ibid., 16.
[19] Ibid.

train them in such basics as how to influence, persuade and counter misinformation overseas. The Commission believes this state of affairs must be rectified."[20]

The training situation is quite different in the State Department's other tracks, the commission noted, citing a nine-month course that provides economic officers a "rigorous, master's level experience in the discipline of economics."[21] Political and consular officers receive similar training in their respective areas. Thus, the commission observed, "[T]he absence of an intensive, months-long training program for PD officers seems very conspicuous."[22]

The commissioners also found that State Department employee evaluations lacked specific requirements regarding "outreach" and that "[p]ublic diplomacy officers are being asked to spend the overwhelming majority of their time on administration and management, not outreach."[23] According to their research, "at least 90 percent of the tasks assigned to public diplomacy officers stationed overseas—those presumably in the business of communicating purposefully with foreign publics—were essentially administrative in nature."[24] The report stated, "This was true for officers at all levels and of all positions, from first-tour junior officer assistant cultural affairs officers (ACAOs) and assistant information officers (AIOs), to senior-level PAOs [public diplomacy officers] at major posts."[25]

The report went on to note that the official responsibilities of most public diplomacy officers in the field do not require either communications with host-country publics or the use of foreign language skills. Additionally, the commissioners found, the performance evaluations of public diplomacy officers are not necessarily based on their contributions to public diplomacy objectives. These discoveries led the commissioners to conclude (with some astonishment) that "public diplomacy officers are simply not being utilized in direct pursuit of key USG communication objectives. And if they aren't, who is?"[26]

That is an important question. The answer, it seems, is "everyone"—in theory at least if not in practice. According to a deputy assistant

---

[20] Ibid.
[21] Ibid.
[22] Ibid., 17.
[23] Ibid., 4.
[24] Ibid., 22.
[25] Ibid.
[26] Ibid.

secretary of state responsible for human resources policy who met with the commissioners, "PD is part of the job" for all Foreign Service officers, including ambassadors, and "everyone is expected to do some outreach as part of his or her job."[27] This mandate came directly from Secretary of State Condoleezza Rice, whose strategic plan for "transformational diplomacy" emphasized that "public diplomacy is an important part of every diplomat's job description."[28] In a 2007 assessment of Rice's efforts, the Foreign Relations Council reported, "The message is out that public diplomacy is everyone's responsibility overseas."[29]

The problem with this approach to public diplomacy is three-fold. First, if public diplomacy is everyone's job, it may turn out to be no one's job. The commission's report made clear that public diplomacy specialists in the field have little to do with advancing the public diplomacy mission. Additionally, according to the commission's findings, "everyone" has no incentive to engage in outreach efforts because their performance is not judged by whether or not they have done so.

Second, public diplomacy is not something that anyone—or "everyone"—can do. As the commissioners pointed out in their report, "Public diplomacy is, in our judgment, the least 'generalist' of the five [State Department] career tracks."[30] While it is very important for Foreign Service officers in all areas of government to understand the impact of their words and actions on U.S. relations with people abroad—as well as how they might contribute to public diplomacy's success—public diplomacy should be directed and conducted by trained professionals.

Third, "outreach" does not equal "impact." Thus, even if the department were to incorporate specific "outreach" requirements in every Foreign Service officer's job description and performance evaluation, it could have little impact on the achievement of specific public diplomacy objectives. In order to be effective, public diplomacy must be a *strategic*, planned effort. Simply asking officers in the field to engage in "outreach" could very well prove to be a pointless exercise.

---

[27] Ibid., 19.

[28] Fact Sheet, "Transformational Diplomacy," Office of the Spokesman, U.S. State Department, January 18, 2006.

[29] Foreign Affairs Council, *Task Force Report: Managing Secretary Rice's State Department: An Independent Assessment* (Washington, DC, June 2007): 22.

[30] The United States Advisory Commission on U.S. Public Diplomacy, *Getting the People Part Right*, 10.

At the same time, notwithstanding the flawed execution of State Department "outreach" efforts, the "whole of government" approach to public diplomacy that has won favor among some U.S. officials, as well as in other foreign ministries, rightly recognizes the importance of *inter*-governmental collaboration in what has become a multi-actor, multi-stakeholder public diplomacy enterprise. At a time when an increasing number of government agencies and representatives (e.g., White House, Congress, Defense, Commerce, Treasury, USAID) interact directly with foreign publics, internal coordination is needed to both mobilize and manage the nation's public diplomacy resources.

But the increased involvement of an expanded range of government actors in public diplomacy does not alleviate the need for trained professionals to direct and coordinate the many activities that comprise the nation's public diplomacy. In fact, just the opposite. It means that public diplomacy's charge has *expanded* to include the oversight and management of a much larger network of groups and individuals and agencies that have the ability to either contribute to or interfere with public diplomacy's success in improving U.S. international relations.

The same is true outside government. As more nongovernmental actors become involved in "diplomatic" initiatives, the responsibilities of public diplomacy specialists will further expand. As a result, the United States will need many more public diplomacy specialists to advise U.S. officials throughout government on the public implications of their decisions and actions; to develop and implement a global public diplomacy strategy; to conduct public diplomacy in the field; to direct and coordinate the activities of multiple government agencies and individuals involved in public diplomacy—and to train those who participate in such efforts; and to oversee public/private sector public diplomacy initiatives. This will require both a separate public diplomacy career track within the State Department and intensive recruitment and training of public diplomacy specialists.

The new public diplomat

If the United States is to successfully rebuild the nation's public diplomacy capabilities, it must address the loss of talent and expertise that occurred as a result of the marginalization of public diplomacy after the Cold War and the dissolution of the USIA. If public diplomacy is to advance its status as an emerging "profession," practitioners and scholars also must delineate the qualifications of the successful public diplomat.

Perhaps it is not surprising that the required credentials of the public diplomat have received little attention given the diverse challenges and broad range of capabilities required for success in this field. Admittedly, it is difficult to precisely define the background and training required to become a public diplomacy professional. As Andrew F. Cooper, Brian Hocking, and William Maley observed, diplomatic skills are sometimes viewed as "a type of knowledge possessed by a particular set of professionals and handed down via a long apprenticeship."[31] In fact, former USIA officers similarly noted that a significant reason the agency was effective was not because everyone came from the "same mold" or background, but rather, because they were from diverse backgrounds—"lawyers, teachers, artists, journalists, among other fields"—whose collective expertise contributed to the broad public diplomacy mission.[32]

Nevertheless, it is possible to identify knowledge, skills, and values, as well as traits and characteristics—and possibly the "instincts"[33]—that would be helpful to someone hoping to establish a successful career in public diplomacy. Certainly, the men and women who spent their careers on the frontlines of American public diplomacy can identify the special qualifications that helped them succeed. Their counsel and insights will be particularly helpful to the next generation of public diplomats.

Of course, all diplomats operate in a dynamic political and communications environment and must constantly adapt to meet new conditions and new challenges. Certainly, this is true for public diplomats operating in a transformed global society characterized by new media and a new global governance structure. Thus, the new public diplomat must supplement foundational knowledge, skills, and values that have served public diplomacy specialists well in the past with new capabilities.

---

[31] Andrew F. Cooper, Brian Hocking, and William Maley, "Introduction: Diplomacy and Global Governance: Locating Patterns of (Dis)Connection," in *Global Governance and Diplomacy: Worlds Apart?*, ed. Andrew F. Cooper, Brian Hocking, and William Maley (Houndmills: Palgrave MacMillan, 2008), 1.

[32] Kathy R. Fitzpatrick, *USIA Alumni Study*, 2007, unpublished report.

[33] The United States Advisory Commission on U.S. Public Diplomacy, *Getting the People Part Right*, 9.

Knowledge, skills, and values

The more than 200 American public diplomats who participated in the *USIA Alumni Study* were among the highest ranking officers in the agency with an average of twenty-five years experience in all parts of the world. These public diplomacy specialists were asked what credentials were most important to the success of a public diplomacy professional.[34] In response, they cited cross-cultural understanding, interpersonal and oral communication skills, writing skills, and foreign language capabilities. Also deemed important were U.S. Foreign Service experience abroad, problem-solving skills, experience in public diplomacy, managerial skills, and knowledge of U.S. history.

Less important, according to the USIA alumni, are research skills, training/experience in journalism, travel or study abroad, training/experience in public relations, and training/experience in advertising.

Additional qualities and skills cited by the USIA alumni as important to a public diplomat's success include an ability to listen and observe. In fact, "listening" was the number one response in the "other category" on the survey, which invited comments. As one former officer put it, public diplomats need an "ability to look quietly, understand what you are seeing and translate that into policy/action."[35] Other representative responses were "listening skills"—"willingness to listen"—"ability and willingness to listen and understand the other person"—"being a responsive listener."[36]

The former diplomats also emphasized the importance of being knowledgeable about and having respect for foreign cultures. Representative responses were: "knowledge of the foreign society where you are working"—"curiosity about foreign cultures/societies"—"knowledge of the local culture, including value system"—"understanding and appreciation for how host country nationals perceive the United States and its government's policies."[37]

---

[34] Kathy R. Fitzpatrick, *USIA Alumni Study*, 2007; see also Kathy R. Fitzpatrick, "The Collapse of American Public Diplomacy: What Diplomat Experts Say About Rebuilding America's Image Around the World—A View from the Trenches," paper presented at the annual meeting of the International Studies Association, Chicago, IL, March 27, 2008.

[35] Kathy R. Fitzpatrick, *USIA Alumni Study*.

[36] Ibid.

[37] Ibid.

Table 9.1 Importance of Credentials to Success of a Public Diplomacy Professional*

Credentials	Mean**
Cross-cultural understanding	4.90
Interpersonal skills	4.86
Oral communication skills	4.84
Foreign languages	4.70
Writing skills	4.65
U.S. Foreign Service experience abroad	4.62
Problem-solving skills	4.53
Public diplomacy experience	4.48
Managerial skills	4.34
Knowledge of U.S. history	4.30
Research skills	3.55
Training/experience in journalism	3.51
Travel or study abroad	3.42
Training/experience in public relations	3.07
Training/experience in advertising	1.79
Other: Ability to listen and observe	
Knowledge about/respect for foreign cultures	
Collaborative, networking and creative skills	
Patience, flexibility and adaptability	
Tolerance and empathy	
Sense of humor	

* The *USIA Alumni Study* (n=213)
** Numeric average of all responses with 1 being "Not Important" and 5 being "Very Important"

The USIA alumni also noted the importance of more intangible qualities, including the ability to collaborate, network, and apply creative solutions to problems; flexibility and adaptability; patience, tolerance, and empathy; and a sense of humor. (Perhaps in a nod to historic views of diplomats as "striped-pants cookie pushers," one also cited "an ability to hold liquor.")[38]

In addition to the qualifications required for success in public diplomacy, the USIA officers were asked about the values most important to public diplomacy professionals in working with people abroad. When provided a list of values and asked to choose the five most

[38] Ibid.

important, the USIA alumni rated the following values highest: credibility (87 percent), respect (75 percent), truthfulness (65 percent), dialogue (61 percent), and openness (47 percent).[39]

The profile of the successful public diplomat that emerged from the *USIA Alumni Study* is this: The successful public diplomat is someone who is curious about and understands other cultures, communicates well in writing and in person—and in foreign languages—and has some Foreign Service experience, including public diplomacy experience, abroad. The successful public diplomat possesses the ability to solve problems, manage people and resources, collaborate with others, and conduct research. The successful public diplomat possesses flexibility, adaptability, patience, tolerance, empathy, and a sense of humor. The successful public diplomat respects other peoples and cultures and engages in open and truthful dialogue with people abroad.

Table 9.2 Values Important to Public Diplomacy Professionals*

Value	Percentage**
Credibility	87%
Respect	75%
Truthfulness	65%
Dialogue	61%
Openness	47%
Expertise	40%
Trust	38%
Objectivity	28%
Mutuality	24%
Fairness	16%
Advocacy	7%
Diversity	7%
Loyalty	1%
Other	1%

* The *USIA Alumni Study* (n=213)
** Rounded percentages reflect respondents choosing a particular value as among the five most important.

39 Ibid.; see also Kathy R. Fitzpatrick, "The Collapse of American Public Diplomacy."

A more public diplomacy

Diplomacy is often referred to as the "management of change."[40] Perhaps at no time in history has that descriptor been more apt. As Shaun Riordan observed, the scale and speed of changes in the world of international relations are such that "*all* diplomatic services need radical overhaul if they are to meet the global challenges of the twenty-first century."[41] Most important to diplomacy's future success, Riordan suggested, will be an increased focus on the public aspects of diplomacy.

Citing the need for a "broader and deeper" diplomatic paradigm that "alters the whole approach to diplomacy," Riordan said the merging of foreign and domestic policy, the growing importance of the media, and an increasingly complex network of new governmental and non-governmental actors in international affairs "mean that publics matter more than before."[42] As a result, the new diplomacy requires a more collaborative effort by "all aspects of civil society, state and nonstate actors alike, and all levels of government" to promote exchanges on cultural and political ideas and values.[43] According to Riordan, "The use of public diplomacy to promote civil society should become a central (if not the central) element of Western diplomacy."[44]

At the same time, Riordan emphasized that "public diplomacy is not simply about the willingness to engage in debate."[45] Rather, public diplomacy has a big role to play in policy formulation as well. "The traditional style of formulating policy within a hermetically sealed foreign ministry and then presenting it as a *fait accompli*, to be amended at the edges, but basically to be forced through, will not wash with either modern publics or the new players in international relations, whether governmental, non-governmental, or corporate."[46] The bottom line, according to Riordan, is that "[a] new paradigm of policy formulation must be devised which is genuinely collaborative, in which other

[40] See, e.g., Jan Melissen, "The New Public Diplomacy: Between Theory and Practice," in *The New Public Diplomacy: Soft Power in International Relations*, ed. Jan Melissen (Houndmills: Palgrave Macmillan, 2005), 23.
[41] Shaun Riordan, "Reforming Foreign Service for the Twenty-First Century," *The Hague Journal of Diplomacy* 2 (2007): 173.
[42] Shaun Riordan, *The New Diplomacy*, 123.
[43] Ibid., 133.
[44] Ibid., 125.
[45] Ibid., 123.
[46] Ibid.

players are involved and consulted during the policy-formulation process."[47]

Others, too, have predicted a more "public" diplomacy in the future. For example, in contemplating diplomacy's possible futures, Alan Henrikson identified five possible "projective visions":[48] 1) distintermediation, in which diplomatic "middle-men" are no longer needed and private sector entities engage directly with foreign publics;[49] 2) Europeanization, in which national diplomatic services are subordinated or replaced by integrated international or joint diplomatic services;[50] 3) democratization, or "democracy at the international level," in which diplomats are more involved in multilateral work and global issues management;[51] 4) thematization, in which diplomats engage in a more reactionary, event-based type of diplomacy that requires "crisis management" skills and involvement at the local level;[52] and 5) Americanization, or an "American politics as world politics" model in which "informal" influences on global affairs and foreign policies are more prevalent and more powerful.[53]

In all of these possible futures for diplomacy, Henrikson said, "[t]he need to win public support, if not necessarily to involve people directly in diplomacy, is evident."[54] For example, the possibility of disintermediation "will mean that all diplomacy must be much more attentive to the people, both as consumers and as citizens, rather than just as abstract 'public opinion.'"[55] Similarly, Henrikson observed, democratization "is also sensitive to others' points of view, which can be the perspectives of sovereign states," as well as "those of different social groups in various regional and subregional settings."[56] Additionally, "the thematization of foreign policy, and of the diplomacy that accompanies it, is also people-sensitive."[57]

---

[47] Ibid., 123–124.
[48] Alan Henrikson, "Diplomacy's Possible Futures," *The Hague Journal of Diplomacy* 1, no. 1, 2006: 7.
[49] Ibid., 7–10.
[50] Ibid., 10–14.
[51] Ibid., 15–18.
[52] Ibid., 18–20.
[53] Ibid., 20–26.
[54] Ibid., 3.
[55] Ibid., 26.
[56] Ibid., 27.
[57] Ibid.

In examining the diplomatic corps ["accredited foreigners representing states and international organizations"] as an institution of international society, Paul Sharp and Geoffrey Wiseman expressed similar views regarding the increasingly public nature of diplomacy.[58] They pointed out that "the institution of the diplomatic corps, like so much else, has been profoundly affected by the great changes international relations have been undergoing over at least the half century"—notably "what international relations are about, who participates in them, and how they are conducted."[59] Noting the growing participation in global affairs of "new actors of increasingly greater diplomatic significance," Sharp and Wiseman identified two possibilities for diplomacy's future.[60] First, the corps either "fades into increasing irrelevance" or, more optimistically, "the corps might increasingly take on the functions of a lobbying group, professional association, or even trade union for its members" thus growing "from bodies connected with collective representations toward their hosts, into bodies also concerned with collective representatives towards these new diplomatic actors."[61] Second, [r]ather than fading from sight or shrinking into defensive organizations for the representatives of states within diplomatic communities broadly defined, diplomatic corps may find themselves at the forefront of a campaign to extend the formal membership categories of international society."[62]

In examining these possibilities for diplomacy's future (while noting that other alternatives were also possible), Sharp and Wiseman concluded that the diplomatic corps will continue to be important. Once the contours of a new world society are constituted, the identities of its new participants become stabilized, and the terms of engagement are established, they suggested, the "idea of a diplomatic corps, or something like it, will become very useful once again."[63]

On this last point, Henrikson reached a similar conclusion, suggesting that the dynamics of globalization offer opportunities for diplo-

---

[58] Paul Sharp and Geoffrey Wiseman, "Conclusion: The Diplomatic Corps' Role in Constituting International Society," in Paul Sharp and Geoffrey Wiseman (eds.), *The Diplomatic Corps as an Institution of International Society* (Houndmills: Palgrave Macmillan, 2007): 267.

[59] Ibid., 274.

[60] Ibid.

[61] Ibid.

[62] Ibid., 275.

[63] Ibid., 277.

mats, rather than signal their demise. "More than leaders or officials at home ever can, diplomats experience directly the upheavals that globalization and related turbulences can produce,"[64] he said. "Diplomats should be in a position, if they are prepared and politically authorized and popularly supported, to *lead* a 'dialogue of civilizations.'"[65]

Echoing Riordan, Henrikson also pointed out that diplomats will have an important role to play in policy making. "Diplomats are uniquely well placed to swim in... historical and cultural crosscurrents" and, therefore, "should be able to interpret the essential messages, and relay these to their government and also to their publics."[66] According to Henrikson, "No group is better situated to filter out the feedback effects of globalized communication."[67]

And no group of diplomats is better situated to take on the increased responsibilities of an increasingly public diplomacy than the public diplomats who serve at the intersections between nations and peoples. In fact, in this new environment, public diplomacy capabilities that were shunned in an earlier era have become "indispensable" for the more collaborative models of diplomacy called for today.[68] As Jan Melissen observed, "[t]he world in which public diplomacy was considered as one of the leftovers of diplomatic dialogue is rapidly disappearing."[69]

But, while the blurring of distinctions between traditional diplomacy and public diplomacy may be good news for public diplomats, it doesn't mean the road ahead will be easy. Many of the same changes that have increased the requirements for a more public diplomacy have created new challenges for public diplomats.

New challenges; new credentials

Specific trends affecting diplomatic policies and practices include:

- Globalization of economies, markets, communities, and ideas
- Growing interdependence and interconnectedness among nations and peoples

64 Henrikson, "Diplomacy's Possible Futures," 5.
65 Ibid.
66 Ibid., 6.
67 Ibid.
68 Melissen, *The New Public Diplomacy*, 5.
69 Ibid., 11.

- New global security threats
- Growing religious-based conflicts
- Diffusion of power among state and nonstate entities
- Shared global governance
- Increasing involvement of nonstate actors in world affairs
- Privatization of government functions
- Technological innovations
- Expanded public access to information and places
- 24/7 global news
- Greater transparency and openness
- Demands for increased accountability

These changes in global society have created both a new operating environment and new strategic challenges for public diplomats. For example, in a more interdependent world, the public diplomacy specialist is likely to spend more time on "issues management" in dealing with matters related to terrorism, the environment and climate change, trade, finance, law enforcement, health and disease, drug and people trafficking, economic development, and a list of other matters that require collaboration and coordination among nations and their citizens.

Terrorism tops the list of concerns for U.S. leaders. And, notwithstanding the overemphasis on the "war on terror" by public diplomacy officials in the post 9/11 environment, public diplomats have a critical role to play in combating terrorism. That role will be focused on understanding and influencing the predispositions that cause people to engage in terrorist acts, helping to alleviate the underlying sources of hostile attitudes, and cultivating peaceable worldviews that reject violence as a means of resolving differences. One significant challenge in this regard, will be better understanding the religious dimensions of international conflicts.[70]

As an example of the increasing importance of interfaith dialogue in diplomacy, Samina Yasmeen pointed to the "cartoon controversy" surrounding the publication of the Prophet Mohammad in a Danish newspaper that sparked a protest among Danish Muslims, who

[70] See, e.g., Lee Hamilton, foreword to Douglas Johnston, ed. *Faith-Based Diplomacy: Trumping Realpolitik* (New York: Oxford University Press, 2003), x; see also Madeleine Albright, *The Mighty & the Almighty: Reflections on America, God, and World Affairs* (New York: HarperCollins Publishers, 2006).

demanded an apology from the newspaper that published the cartoons. This incident led to further incidents when other newspapers reprinted the cartoons, sparking "heated debates on the place of Islam in today's world and the inherent incompatibility between Western and Muslim civilizations."[71]

According to Yasmeen, "The growing relevance of religion in world politics, magnified through the cartoon controversy, suggests that both diplomatic and governance institutions will increasingly have to deal with future controversy centering around different notions of sacred as well as debates on secularism vs. religious beliefs. Diplomats need to be trained in religious and cultural diversity, as well as the nuanced differences within religious traditions.... Such understanding would attune them to emerging fault lines linked to religious or cultural beliefs *before* they result in conflicts."[72]

In *Faith-Based Diplomacy: Trumping Realpolitik*, editor Douglas Johnston also addressed issues linking religion and diplomacy, writing that "the cultural and religious dynamics of conflicts...are exceeding the bounds of the rational-actor model of decisionmaking to which traditional diplomacy has long been tied."[73] Johnston argued that "what is needed is a form of diplomacy that can uncover and deal with the deeper sources of conflict by rebuilding relationships and making concessionary adjustments whenever possible."[74] According to Johnston, "The price of freedom is cultural engagement—taking the time to learn how others see the world, to understand what is important to them, and to determine what can realistically be done to help them realize their legitimate aspirations."[75]

Veteran USIA officer Barry Fulton similarly suggested that public diplomacy's primary role going forward "should be to stimulate the imagination of those who make a difference within their own cultures—to give them the means and motivation to address the global requirements of the 21st century, herein enhancing security for the

[71] Samina Yasmeen, "Interfaith Dialogue, Diplomacy, and the Cartoon Controversy," in *Global Governance and Diplomacy: Worlds Apart?*, ed. Andrew F. Cooper, Brian Hocking, and William Maley (Houndmills: Palgrave MacMillan, 2008), 229.

[72] Ibid., 239.

[73] Douglas Johnston, ed., *Faith-Based Diplomacy: Trumping Realpolitik* (New York: Oxford University Press, 2003), 7.

[74] Ibid.

[75] Ibid.

sponsoring nation."[76] According to Fulton, the need "is no longer overtly and narrowly to represent the short-term parochial interests of our countries, but to provide knowledge to the curious, the innovative and the restless whose imagination can be nurtured."[77] The new public diplomat, according to Fulton, should serve as "cultural interpreter" and "identify those in society who may make a difference and to feed their appetite for positive change—through the arts and sciences. The public diplomat must enable connectivity."[78]

In addressing the implications of shared global governance among state and nonstate actors, Mark Leonard explained the new public diplomacy as requiring "a new type of multilateral public diplomacy—retooling embassies to become lobbying and policy-exchange organisations; creating an infrastructure to link up political parties and NGOs across borders to create a common policy space; and planning proactive communication campaigns."[79] According to Leonard, "Public diplomacy is about building relationships; understanding the needs of other countries, cultures and peoples; communicating our points of view; correcting misperceptions; looking for areas where we can find common cause."[80]

From a practical standpoint, this means that in addition to managing communication efforts, public diplomacy professionals must spend more time managing complex relationships among state and nonstate actors who influence the ability of nations to effectively address the world's concerns. In this respect, the new public diplomats must be "players in or facilitators of the amorphous transnational networks" between people and institutions coexisting with governments.[81]

As John Hemery observed, "So much of international interaction is now non-governmental that the diplomat simply has to inhabit both dimensions in order to seek to represent effectively the national interest (however widely that may now be defined) in the complex web of governmental and non-governmental relationships that comprise the

[76] Barry Fulton, "Geo-Social Mapping of the International Communications Environment or Why Abdul Isn't Listening," *The Hague Journal of Diplomacy* 2 (2007): 307.
[77] Ibid.
[78] Ibid.
[79] Mark Leonard, *Public Diplomacy* (London: The Foreign Policy Center, 2002), 7.
[80] Ibid., 8.
[81] John Hemery, "Training for Public Diplomacy: An Evolutionary Perspective," in Jan Melissen, *The New Public Diplomacy*, 196.

contemporary international system."[82] In this era of shared global governance, in which "cooperative problem-solving arrangements on a global plane"[83] are required, the public diplomat must help to develop a nation's partnerships with a web of internal and external agents who share responsibility for managing the world's collective affairs.

In fact, the need for "networking" capabilities has been cited as one of the most important capabilities modern diplomats must possess. In addressing changes that affect the structures of traditional state-based diplomacy, for example, Cooper, Hocking, and Maley cited "the redefinition of the stakeholders, both domestic and international, with whom Ministries of Foreign Affairs (MFAs) need to engage, and the development of structures for such engagement."[84] In discussing the shift from the "club" to "network" model of diplomacy Jorge Heine similarly suggested that, "[m]ore and more, diplomacy is becoming "complexity management."[85]

A related trend that will affect public diplomats is the increasing privatization of government functions. As Paul Verkuil suggested, the implications of greater involvement of private sector entities in government functions represent a regime change for government agencies. He said, "In a privatized world, the government official must manage and direct a smaller bureaucracy but a larger contractor community in which oversight and accountability are key factors."[86] Although the specific contributions of the private sector to public diplomacy in the United States and other nations is yet to be determined, private actors are likely to be more involved in the years ahead, adding to the complexity of the public diplomacy network.

The policy advisory role of public diplomats has also become more important as increased public access to information and 24/7 global

---

[82] Ibid., 203.

[83] Ramesh Thakur, "Conclusion: National Diplomacy and Global Governance," in *Global Governance and Diplomacy: Worlds Apart?*, ed., Andrew F. Cooper, Brian Hocking, and William Maley, 289.

[84] Andrew F. Cooper, Brian Hocking, and William Maley, "Introduction: Diplomacy and Global Governance: Locating Patterns of (Dis)connection," in *Global Governance and Diplomacy: Worlds Apart?*, ed., Andrew F. Cooper, Brian Hocking, and William Maley, 4.

[85] Jorge Heine, "On the Matter of Practicing the New Diplomacy," in *Global Governance and Diplomacy: Worlds Apart?*, ed., Andrew F. Cooper, Brian Hocking, and William Maley, 273.

[86] Paul R. Verkuil, *Outsourcing Sovereignty* (New York: Cambridge University Press, 2007), 159.

media have redefined the communications environment and increased demands for public accountability. Indeed, the ability of public diplomats to help nations interpret and respond to the international environment of opinion—and to a growing number of constituencies—may well earn them their keep. It will be the job of the public diplomat to ensure that national goals and actions are congruent with public expectations. In this respect, attention to issues of ethics and values will be important.

As suggested by Alex Evans and David Steven, the new public diplomat must "be genuinely at ease with discussion of values (rather than mere interests), understanding that without clearly stated principles—and consistent adherence to them—it will be impossible to animate coalitions of state and nonstate actors, and even harder for members of that coalition to work together to deliver a common good."[87] According to Evans and Steven, "The new public diplomat brings to the task a willingness to pull together all the tools of international relations and mix them together to create a coherent whole. The aim is to blend analysis, policy-making and communications; the focus is more on what the country does than on what it says."[88]

Innovations in new technology require changes in public diplomacy practices as well. Messages delivered around the clock to all corners of the world require greater vigilance on the part of governments to both monitor and to respond to media and other reports. New media also present new means for interacting with foreign publics and for establishing long-distance relationships. Although technology cannot replace face-to-face dialogue in terms of effectiveness, it does enhance opportunities for connecting with new publics.

The compression of time and space means that the new public diplomat must be media-educated and media-savvy, someone who understands both old and new media concepts and practices, as well as the potential for and limitations of new technologies to be useful in accomplishing public diplomacy objectives. As Joshua Fouts observed in contemplating the potential for "virtual worlds" to serve as a "tool of engagement" for public diplomacy, "In a world in which technology

[87] Ibid.

[88] Alex Evans and David Steven, "Towards a Theory of Influence for Twenty-First Century Foreign Policy: Public Diplomat in a Globalised World," UK Foreign & Commonwealth Office, http://www.fco.gov.uk/en/about-the-fco/publications/publications/pd-publication/21c-foreign-policy (accessed December 4, 2008).

changes, enhances and modifies the way generations of people interact, it behooves the public diplomacy foreign policy establishment to keep current."[89]

Finally, increased demands for accountability in all areas of government will require the new public diplomat to focus considerably more attention on the measurement and evaluation of public diplomacy efforts. In this regard, public diplomacy specialists will be called upon to answer two questions: 1) Is it possible to devise a true measure of public diplomacy's effectiveness in enhancing international relations? and 2) If so, what would it be? Public diplomacy's future may well depend on their answers.

The public mandate

This discussion of the changing contours and contexts of global society and the impact on diplomacy generally and public diplomacy specifically illustrates both the evolving nature of international relations and the need for contemporary public diplomacy policies and practices to keep pace. Three points raised by the discussion warrant further emphasis.

First is the need for public diplomacy going forward to be more about "them" than about "us." The new rules of engagement in global affairs require that the United States specifically (because of the nation's power, status and wealth) create a more even playing field in which those who are influenced by—and, importantly, who have an increased ability to influence—U.S. policies and actions get to play, too. As Fulton and his colleagues observed, the nation's ability "to become credible in this world" will turn not on how effectively the nation's interests are served, but rather "the extent that we are seen to be working to solve global problems that affect their lives... to the extent that we recognize their hopes and ambitions... to the extent we satisfy their desire for equal recognition."[90]

---

[89] Joshua Fouts, "Rethinking Public Diplomacy for the 21st Century: A Toolbox for Engaging the Hearts and Minds of the Open Source Generation," paper presented at the APSA Political Communication Conference on International Communication and Conflict," Washington, DC, August 31, 2005.

[90] Barry Fulton, Bruce Gregory, Donna Marie Oglesby, Walter R. Roberts, Barry Zorthian, "Public Diplomacy A Dissent: Transformation Not Restoration," in William

Second is that there is no place in contemporary public diplomacy for "yes" men and women afraid to speak truth to power and to provide critical—sometimes unwelcome—input on policy matters. Public diplomats should be judged on their abilities to interpret foreign societies—to analyze the attitudes, behaviors and expectations of foreign publics—and to counsel government leaders on the public implications of their decisions and actions. Indeed, this is what a more *public* diplomacy requires—that the needs, wants, issues, interests, values, and ideas of those who have the ability to influence a nation's destiny be considered in the development and implementation of its foreign policies.

Third is that, while communication skills and other traditional capabilities will be important to the modern public diplomat's success, the ability to *manage*, i.e., to conceptualize and direct, a complex web of relationships—both at home and abroad—will be required. In this respect, concepts of relationship management (see Chapter Five) will be useful. As Kurt Wise pointed out, "Practitioners using a relational perspective see themselves as managers of relationships, not [managers of] communication."[91]

Of course, the successful implementation of a relational model of public diplomacy will require more than either recognition of the potential for such a model to improve public diplomacy's effectiveness or a desire on the part of institutional leaders to change current public diplomacy policies and practices. Formal training in forming, maintaining, and evaluating relationships will be important to the ability of public diplomats to become effective relationship managers.

Professional advancement

As an emerging profession, public diplomacy clearly has made some strides in developing the accoutrements associated with professional status. The body of knowledge is expanding. Academic training in the field is available, although it is limited. Master's degree programs in public diplomacy are offered at USC and Syracuse University. Pro-

P. Kiehl (ed.) *America's Dialogue with the World* (Washington, DC: Public Diplomacy Council, 2006): 191.

[91] Kurt Wise, "The Organization and Implementation of Relationship Management," *Health Marketing Quarterly* 24, no. 3/4, 2007: 155.

grams and courses in public diplomacy are offered at others, including Tufts University, Georgetown University, and George Washington University.

At the same time, there is no professional credential required to practice public diplomacy—nor perhaps is one desirable. An argument could be—and has been—made that public diplomats are not "professionals"—that neither diplomacy generally nor public diplomacy specifically can be classified as a distinct profession that provides a unique and special service to society. Debate regarding the professional status of diplomats is likely to continue.[92] But such discussions should not stand in the way of the continued development of education and training programs for public diplomacy specialists.

According to a study of twenty countries on all continents, Hemery found "an evolutionary path in training for public diplomacy that is defined partly in terms of resources and partly of intellectual and professional approach."[93] He observed that "there appears to be no direct correlation between the sophistication of the approach to public diplomacy and scale of resources devoted to it, and the specific training—if any—of diplomats for the task."[94]

Limitations in public diplomacy training, according to Hemery's study, are due to lack of resources, limited communications infrastructure, and resistance to engaging in public interactions. Hemery noted, "Governments themselves consequently have to decide whether the opportunity cost of invisibility is greater than the cost of developing an effective public diplomacy."[95]

Interestingly (in light of the U.S. Advisory Commission on Public Diplomacy's 2008 report discussed above), Hemery pointed to the United States as the "pre-eminent exemplar, with enviable resources" of public diplomacy training. He noted, however, that training in the United States is practically based and "concentrates almost exclusively on the transmission of policy, on 'managing the message.'"[96] In comparison, Hemery found that "[a]t the top of the evolutionary tree in training for public diplomacy... is the Republic of Korea [that] deals in

---

[92] See Glen H. Fisher, "The Foreign Service Officer," *The Annals of the American Academy of Political and Social Science* 368 (1966): 77–82.

[93] John Hemery, "Training for Public Diplomacy," 197.

[94] Ibid.

[95] Ibid., 198.

[96] Ibid., 201.

communication and media skills and promoting the national interest," as well as provides "a programme for mid-career and senior diplomats that seeks to understand how the practice of diplomacy itself is being affected by changes in the international system, how the concept of national interest is changing, and how civil society and international NGOs contribute to transnational relations."[97]

Hemery concluded that the Korean approach "seems an appropriate way forward for training in public diplomacy."[98] Such an approach, he suggested, would address gaps in the majority of training programs, which focus on "the national priorities of the states they serve," while neglecting the need for "comprehensive and conscious engagement with the expanding and changing nature of the international environment in which the professional diplomat operates."[99] According to Hemery, "No one has developed a core syllabus that confronts the young diplomat with his or her two universes—the state-centered and the network—and that provides them with the twin toolboxes necessary to engage with both universes at the same time and in coherent synergy."[100]

An international commission on education and training in public diplomacy could be very useful in defining both training requirements and a career path for the next generation of public diplomats. One issue that such a commission could address is whether the new public diplomat should be prepared for service in both the public and private sectors, as USC, which established the first graduate degree program in public diplomacy in the United States, suggests. USC's course catalog states, for example, that students studying public diplomacy "may decide to emphasize public diplomacy training most appropriate for a career in public service, the corporate world or in a nongovernmental organization (NGO) working in the ever expanding global society."[101] This expansive view of public diplomacy suggests a fundamental change from the role of the traditional public diplomat serving as a representative of a nation and, as such, warrants some attention as the educational requirements for the new public diplomat are refined.

---

[97] Ibid., 204.
[98] Ibid., 205.
[99] Ibid.
[100] Ibid.
[101] "Courses," Master's Programs, USC Annenberg School for Communication, http://annenberg.usc.edu/Prospective/Masters/PubD/Courses.aspx (accessed December 10, 2008).

Another area requiring attention is the lack of professional principles and values to guide public diplomacy professionals in their work. Toward that end, the time may be right for the formation of a new international association—perhaps the International Public Diplomacy Association—to support the development of the public diplomacy field and the professional advancement of public diplomats. In addition to addressing principles and standards of public diplomacy practice, such a body could encourage and support academic attention to issues and events related to public diplomacy and provide venues for the presentation and sharing among scholars and practitioners of new developments and new knowledge.

Yet another matter that deserves attention is the career path of public diplomats. As the 2008 report of the U.S. Commission on Public Diplomacy showed (see Chapter Three), U.S. public diplomats face a significant "glass ceiling" in reaching the top levels of diplomacy. Indeed, never has a U.S. public diplomacy officer "risen to the Foreign Service personal rank of 'career ambassador,' the Service's top rung, in the decades the rank has existed."[102] What is standing in the way? That is a question that deserves serious study.

An evolving profile

No doubt, the new public diplomat has a plate full of challenges and opportunities ahead as the roles and responsibilities of the new public diplomat continue to expand and evolve as times and events warrant. The resiliency and the abilities of the men and women charged with carrying out the public diplomacy mission will be tested. One area that may claim greater attention in the future is what has been called the "militarization" of public diplomacy.

According to Copeland, for example, although the "more familiar, garden variety elements of public diplomacy—lobbying and advocacy; the strategic use of the media; building relationships with non-state actors; and managing networks of contacts"—have a crucial role in the new environment, military public diplomacy or "counterinsurgency"

[102] The United States Advisory Commission on U.S. Public Diplomacy, *Getting the People Part Right*, 35.

represents "the leading edge of public diplomacy tradecraft."[103] Indeed, Copeland sees a "convergence in thinking about counterinsurgency (COIN) and military public diplomacy [that] is unprecedented."[104] As a result, Copeland argued, the modern public diplomat must be "a high-functioning, well-educated, street-smart problem-solver, with an open mind, sharp instincts, a Blackberry and, when necessary... a Kevlar vest."[105]

Envisioning the new public diplomat as a guerilla in combat boots illustrates with some drama the multidimensional nature of a profession that continues to evolve. Such a portrait also suggests that the function of public diplomacy—and concomitantly the roles and responsibilities of the public diplomat—remain somewhat elusive. Just as clearly defining the function of public diplomacy will be an important step in advancing the discipline, so too will defining the specific roles and responsibilities of the public diplomat be an important step in advancing the profession. As Hemery observed, part of the difficulty in designing proper public diplomacy training programs for public diplomats is that '[t]he concept of public diplomacy is for many—even for enthusiasts—still a trifle blurred. It is difficult to generate a training programme of any intellectual coherence without clearly defined parameters."[106]

Public diplomats play a unique role in global society. As official representatives of their nations, they serve as the "faces" of their countries and the purveyors of their countries' views, values, policies, and ideals. But the public diplomat is more than a mouthpiece for his or her nation's foreign policies. The public diplomat is the steward of his or her nation's relationships with the people of the world.

---

[103] Daryl Copeland, "No Dangling Conversation: Portrait of the Public Diplomat," in *Engagement: Public Diplomacy in a Globalized World: A Collection of Essays and Case Studies.*

[104] Ibid.

[105] Ibid.; see also Daryl Copeland and Evan Potter, "Military Public Diplomacy Meets Political Counter-Insurgency: Two Sides of the Same Coin," paper presented at the annual meeting of the International Studies Association, March 27, 2008.

[106] John Hemery, "Training for Public Diplomacy," 208.

PART THREE

A WAY FORWARD

CHAPTER TEN

REBUILDING U.S. PUBLIC DIPLOMACY: LESSONS FROM THE FIELD

The 'lessons' of experience—of past history—are a necessary guide, of course.[1]

In contemplating a way forward for U.S. public diplomacy, it is important to ensure that the "lessons of experience" are not ignored. In that regard, Chapter Three identified important matters that must be addressed if public diplomacy is to realize its potential both as a strategic national resource and as an emerging profession. It is also important to ensure that those closest to the frontlines of American public diplomacy have a voice in the debate on U.S. public diplomacy's future.[2]

Toward that end, previous chapters have incorporated the findings of the *USIA Alumni Study* on specific issues related to public diplomacy concepts and practices. This chapter presents additional results of the study, which documented the collective views of America's public diplomats on steps that should be taken to rebuild U.S. public diplomacy in the years ahead.

The chapter first reports the public diplomats' views on the state of U.S. public diplomacy and its importance to the nation. It then reviews lessons learned from their decades of experience in the field. Finally, it outlines the public diplomacy specialists' recommendations for rebuilding U.S. public diplomacy. Although the survey focused on the men and women who served as public diplomats on behalf of the United States, the forward-looking results have implications for public diplomacy beyond U.S. borders.

---

[1] Henrikson, Alan K., "Diplomacy's Possible Futures," *The Hague Journal of Diplomacy* 1 (2006): 4.

[2] Ibid.

The state of U.S. public diplomacy

Nearly all (98 percent) USIA alumni indicated that they are deeply troubled by the state of U.S. public diplomacy, with similar numbers expressing extreme concern over America's diminished image in the world (98 percent) and the rise in global anti-Americanism (94 percent).

An overwhelming majority (88 percent) indicated they do not believe the United States is diplomatically prepared to address ideological threats to U.S. interests in the twenty-first century. Most important to the nation's lack of preparedness, they said, were government leaders' apparent lack of interest in and respect for the attitudes and interests of foreign publics. As one put it, "Not only are we not prepared, we don't seem to know what or how to do what is necessary to establish dialogues with countries we need to reach. Nor do we seem to care. Arrogance, self-righteousness and ignorance are a deadly combination."

Others perceived an over-emphasis on military resources and a lack of commitment on the part of U.S. officials to public diplomacy. As one put it, "We've sacrificed diplomacy to the U.S. military." Another said, "There is not sufficient understanding of or interest in public diplomacy on the part of senior officials and policy makers in the executive branch or in the Congress."

According to the former diplomats, public diplomacy's poor state also can be attributed to structural and operational problems created by the dissolution of the USIA and integration of public diplomacy into the State Department. As one put it, "[After the Cold War], we marched home and disarmed ourselves by dissolving the very mechanism that had been so successful in overcoming communist thought and pointing out the foolishness of tyranny. We kept the nukes, but tossed out our communication skills; and lacking these tools, we risk a slide back into the conflicts and threats of the past. Doesn't say much for our native wisdom or our ability to learn, does it?"

When asked to rate U.S. public diplomacy on a scale of 1 to 5 with 1 being excellent and 5 being poor, 83 percent rated U.S. public diplomacy today as marginal (43 percent) or poor (40 percent). These numbers stand in stark contrast with the ratings for public diplomacy during the Cold War, which 87 percent of USIA alumni rated as excellent (30 percent) or good (57 percent).

Table 10.1 The State of U.S. Public Diplomacy*

"How would you rate the U.S. government's public diplomacy during the Cold War?

Excellent	Good	Fair	Marginal	Poor
30%	57%	12%	1%	0%

"How would you rate the U.S. government's public diplomacy today?"

Excellent	Good	Fair	Marginal	Poor
0%	3%	15%	43%	40%

* The *USIA Alumni Study* (n=213; rounded percentages of respondents)

The importance of public diplomacy

The *USIA Alumni Study* posed the following question to America's public diplomats: Why is public diplomacy important to the United States today? The answer, according to USIA alumni, is because international understanding and support of America and its policies, ideals, and values is critical to its ability to protect and advance national interests. As one observed, "U.S. standing abroad is at a low ebb. That matters. We cannot achieve our national goals, including the marginalization of terrorists, without the understanding and support of people around the globe."

In addressing the importance of public diplomacy, the USIA alumni most frequently cited four factors:

1) the increasing importance of international relations in the twenty-first century ("The world is even more complex [than during the Cold War] and the U.S. needs all the friends it can have to live peacefully and successfully in it.");
2) the rising influence of nonstate actors in world affairs ("Publics increasingly influence the policies undertaken by their governments on everything from the importation of genetically modified foodstuffs to the treatment of copyrighted materials.");
3) growing anti-Americanism ("Perception of the United States as arrogant and self-serving is at its highest level in history."); and
4) heightened threats of terrorism ("There are weapons and terrorists to use them around the globe who disdain the United States and have access to a burgeoning youthful population that the nation has neglected, even ignored.").

Many of the USIA alumni cited a critical need for public diplomacy to address the damage to America's image abroad caused by the Bush administration. As one observed:

> The Bush administration has done such damage to our international reputation that it will take decades to repair it. They made more enemies than we have had in my lifetime and lost the trust and respect of allies and their populations to the extent that I believe other nations will feel for a very long time they cannot trust us, can get along without us, and that we deserve whatever happens to us. It will take decades of public diplomacy work to turn that around, if we ever get the chance.

Additionally, America's place and status in the world have changed, the USIA alumni said, such that "increasing global interdependence, the multiplication of power centers, and the emergence of new transnational threats make the United States increasingly vulnerable to the impact of events abroad." As one observed, "We may still be the only superpower, but new centers with prospects for exerting a serious impact on the welfare of Americans are developing (i.e., China, Iran, North Korea, Venezuela)."

Many of the practitioners pointed to America's diminished leadership position: "Our world image is in the gutter. Our policies are anathema to a majority of world peoples. Our allies don't trust us; our enemies hate and despise us. We are no longer a beacon of hope. We are seen as having betrayed our heritage of democracy and freedom. We are feared more than respected.... We can't lead when nobody wants to follow."

With respect to terrorism, the public diplomats identified new threats directed at the United States by nonstate actors with whom the nation is engaged in "a conflict of ideas." The "only way we can pursue terrorism effectively," said one, "is by developing friends and allies who will help us." Another of the former diplomats explained, "The world in many respects is far more dangerous than it was in the Cold War period because of the rise of nonstate bodies with access to sophisticated weaponry and who are far more effective in their public opinion efforts than the Soviets were. PD efforts need to be better tailored to deal with this new enemy."

The bottom line, summed up by one of the former diplomats, is that the nation needs to "show a continuing care for the good opinions of mankind." Another advised, "If we build bridges now, no matter what issue we face, we will find that prospects for collaboration with others are immensely improved." Importantly, "in the twenty-first century when public policy worldwide is heavily influenced by popular attitudes and behavior, U.S. programs to reach and engage a wide range of audiences are indispensable."

History's lessons

What specific lessons did USIA alumni learn that would be useful to U.S. public diplomacy officials today? In response to this question, the former public diplomats cited five key lessons:

Lesson One: Listen and learn. The public diplomacy specialists stressed that mutual understanding and respect between U.S. representatives and people abroad are critical factors in public diplomacy's success. As one observed, "Public diplomacy is *not* indoctrination." Rather, another said, "public diplomacy is as much about the publics we are engaging as ourselves. Just putting out a message is only part of the process, and a small part at that. There needs to be more true dialogue, to build an atmosphere of understanding and trust." Others emphasized the importance of "dialogue rather than monologue," stressing that "an imperialistic approach to public diplomacy is counterproductive."

The former diplomats advised today's public diplomacy officials to "show that public diplomacy is a two-way exchange." One said, "Don't just talk at people, ramping up the volume if they don't understand." Put more bluntly, "It is vital that we learn to 'shut up and listen'" and to "recognize that we don't have all the answers."

According to the USIA alumni, "'hard-sell' diplomacy simply does not work. If public diplomacy is meant to shove down the throats of the recipient foreigners the 'politically accepted party line of the day' then there is no use in pursuing public diplomacy any further." Another echoed, "You cannot shove ideas down people's throats. PD requires a diplomatic approach encompassing mutuality."

Lesson Two: Interact with local publics. Personal relations are the most important aspect of successful public diplomacy, according to the USIA alumni. As one put it, "Public diplomacy means person-to-person—in the marketplace, on the sidewalks and the officers' own homes.... Public diplomacy is personal." Others emphasized the importance of interactions with local opinion leaders: "As much day-to-day personal contact as possible with country nationals—opinion shapers primarily, of course—is the really vital element. And this doesn't mean a Karen Hughes-type honcho spending an hour at an orphanage (or whatever) and getting a lot of local TV play. Without this type of contact, the impression is one of remote arrogance, with utter disregard for the host country's interests and goals."

This story from one USIA veteran captures the sentiment expressed by many others:

> In the early days of USIA, there was an experienced PAO [public affairs officer in charge of public diplomacy] who was asked what kind of program he would set up if he had only $25 in his budget. 'I would take my most important contact out to lunch,' was the reply. Perhaps with the problems of today, the budgets, the bulging populations, and the urgency of our efforts, this answer is too simplistic. However, my message is that it is a direction public diplomacy should heed. It should deal with human beings as human products of their culture.

Lesson Three: Focus on long-term relationship-building rather than short-term "quick fixes." Public diplomacy is primarily a long-term enterprise, according to USIA alumni. "Good public diplomacy," they stressed, "requires sustained relationships of trust and mutual good will." As one said, public diplomacy is "about people-to-people. 'Hearts and minds' one at a time."

Expectations of immediate results are unrealistic, according to the USIA veterans. One observed, "There is seldom a quick fix for priority issues. Nothing can replace thoughtful, professional work across the board over time." Rather, "public diplomacy is incremental. It is neither a long-term process that will show results overnight nor one that is necessarily easy to measure precisely." In other words, "You cannot change attitudes overnight. That might take a whole generation." One of the former diplomats advised that "people worldwide are not stupid and should not be treated as recipients of 'quick I love you' programs."

The USIA officers explained that "public diplomacy is not primarily a communications function." Rather, "it is a relational function. It says to the people of the world that simply peaceful connection between Americans and foreign peoples is at the core of our relationship." In other words, "Public diplomacy is not a typical political tool. It takes time; throwing press releases at a problem won't solve it." Put another way, "Public diplomacy is *not* providing information. It *is* building relationships."

At the same time, they recognized the importance of managing the events of the day. As one explained, "Our long-term objectives for the

U.S. and USG [United States government] are most important, but PD officers must be skillful at dealing with short-term policy issues, and 'correcting the record,' too." But, "[w]hile it is important to 'manage' the daily news cycle, the true payoff for public diplomacy comes from long-term programs that foster deep associations with the U.S. and the things American."

Lesson Four: Tell the truth. According to the USIA alumni, ethics and values are important aspects of effective public diplomacy. As one said, "Credibility is hard-won and fragile." Numerous comments from the former diplomats focused on the need for honesty, advising that in dealing with foreign publics, U.S. officials should "tell the truth... warts and all." As one put it, "honesty and openness are the best attributes of a successful public diplomacy effort."

Others pointed to the consequences of failing to meet this mandate, counseling that "once caught not telling the truth, regaining credibility is very tough slogging." Put more simply, "Without credibility, PD is a failure."

Lesson Five: Use technology wisely. Although important to the future of public diplomacy, new media are not its salvation, cautioned the public diplomats. Rather, contemporary public diplomacy officials should "never believe that a program that is computer-driven or mass-produced can have the effect of a person-driven message." One suggested, "Virtual public diplomacy can never replace the handshake and personal greeting in the language of the host country contact." In other words, "Personal diplomacy still matters. Technology is a tool not a panacea."

In commenting on why traditional communication tools should not be abandoned, the USIA alumni also pointed to the diverse circumstances regarding access to and use of new media in various parts of the world. For example, "Sometimes low tech remains the way to go. While the Internet is obviously central to many public diplomacy information strategies, its importance is relatively less in the Third World. Tangible products that can actually be given out, such as pamphlets, magazines, or low-cost books, still have a very high impact."

At the same time, the diplomatic experts recognized the need to harness the potential of new media to communicate more effectively with foreign audiences in places where new media is accessible and popular. And, as one advised, they also recognized that much work must be done in this area:

> Make better use of Internet technologies than we are doing today. The rise of collaborative workflows and professional networking over the Web offers enormous opportunities to build millions of connections between Americans and publics overseas for business, professional, philanthropic, and social purposes. People worldwide are becoming chat-friends, Flckr buddies, Face networks, and Linked-In contacts, not faceless masses that can be manipulated by propagandists and demagogues. The State Department is woefully unprepared for this phenomenon.

Recommendations for going forward

In addition to specific lessons learned that would be helpful to contemporary public diplomacy officials, the USIA alumni were asked what recommendations they would give current and future administrations for improving the overall effectiveness of U.S. public diplomacy. Their responses are reflected in the following list of the top ten recommendations derived from their collective comments. The recommendations are annotated with representative responses from the public diplomacy experts.

1. Adopt a national diplomatic worldview that demonstrates respect for the attitudes and opinions of people abroad.
   - "Understand that a democratized, globalized world means publics matter more than foreign ministries."
   - "Project the United States as an integral part of this world, with humility and understanding for the views and values of other cultures and other political systems. Beware of projecting notions of American exceptionalism."
   - "It is high time to restore a dialogue and teamwork with other nations in shaping a common approach to the really fundamental problems the world faces: poverty, ignorance, disease and global warming."
   - "We are part of a global economy and need to be understood and respected in order to ensure our peace and prosperity."
2. Recognize and respect public diplomacy's role in protecting and advancing national interests.
   - "Public diplomacy is an indispensable element in the conduct of U.S. foreign affairs—co-equal with diplomatic, economic and security programs."
   - "Take it seriously and use it effectively."

- "Elevate the importance of public diplomacy."
- "Increasing global interdependence, the multiplication of power centers, and the emergence of new transnational threats make the U.S. increasingly vulnerable to the impact of events abroad. Public diplomacy is one of the few means we have at our disposal to mitigate negative reaction to our policies and actions."

3. Understand that good public diplomacy cannot overcome bad policy.
   - "Public diplomacy can be no better than the foreign policies of the United States."
   - "Public diplomacy has an opportunity to succeed only when U.S. policy seems fair, honest, and respectful of other cultures."
   - "No public diplomacy program will be effective without policies that reflect the needs and interests of the countries and not just the arrogance of U.S. power."
   - "No amount of clever PD can make a bad policy look good."
4. Incorporate public diplomacy into the foreign policy-making process.
   - "Don't treat public diplomacy as an afterthought, but make it as central to foreign policy as the substance of the policy."
   - "[Public diplomacy] needs to be an independent voice in decision-making about U.S. foreign policy and its presentation at every level of government."
   - "Those who deal with public diplomacy should be involved at the highest level with policy formation, not just in its execution."
5. Develop a public diplomacy operation that transcends administrations and is based on American as opposed to partisan political ideals and values.
   - "Public diplomacy is about the country, not about the government. It needs to engage and represent the full range of responsible opinion in the United States, not just views of the majority or of the current government."
   - "Public diplomacy refers not just to backing the U.S. party in power at the moment but is a furtherance of U.S. cultural values—what we stand for—long term."
   - "Keep the political appointees out of the public diplomacy field. They only muck up the effort with their political agendas."
   - "Create a new, nonideological public diplomacy agency."
6. Establish an *independent* public diplomacy entity that is part of the U.S. government.

- "There is a need for a unified and centralized structure for public diplomacy, government directed. Similar to USIA, but modernized. It *must* be separate from the State Department."
- "Most of what USIA learned in a forty-five-year existence cannot be transferred to State because the atmosphere there has always been unreceptive and continues to be. They just don't believe an information program plays a significant role in the formulation and execution of U.S. foreign policy, they never had appreciation for what USIA knew about public opinion in foreign countries, nor did they think it important."
- "In the State Department the importance of public diplomacy is lost and misunderstood—even at top levels."

7. Establish and sustain an active U.S. presence in local communities throughout the world.
   - "There is no substitute for boots on the ground. If you want people to understand you, you need interaction on their turf. You need seasoned, experienced, culturally/politically sensitive people *there*."
   - "You can't just shout at people from Washington."
   - "Nothing can replace a worldwide network of libraries, cultural centers and meeting space open to one and all for discussions and meaningful exchange of ideas. Our new 'fortress America' attack-hardened embassies are a PD disaster!"
   - "When I was a branch PAO [in charge of U.S. public diplomacy] in Johannesburg in the waning days of apartheid (although it appeared to be going strong at the time), many elderly black people told me how grateful they were to the United States for maintaining a library there, going back to the time of their youth. It was, in fact, the only one in the country for many years that blacks could use, and it was the place where they received much of the education they had. Just opening the door to all made a statement—and earned lasting good will—way beyond anything the USIS country plan could have predicted. This story is no doubt replicated, with variations, in other countries with other issues. By being ourselves as Americans—and by maintaining a strong presence over the long haul—our public diplomacy was an effective component of our foreign policy."
8. Provide adequate resources for public diplomacy to be successful over the long term.

- "We simply do not devote sufficient resources in terms of personnel and finances to public diplomacy."
- "There are no shortcuts now available to the United States. A serious long-range plan to rebuild USG PD from the ground up is needed. Large amounts of funding, well spent over at least twenty years is needed to recreate what USIA had. American and Foreign Service National employee staffing must be greatly enlarged. Language, area studies, and diplomacy skills must be given the highest priority for many years. Nothing can replace long-term flows and sincere personal interaction between the U.S. PD professionals, American and Foreign Service nationals, and their foreign counterparts. A whole new web of trust must be built from the ashes of USIA."
- "Public diplomacy is labor-intensive because nurturing purposeful relationships takes time. There are not enough officers to respond to Washington's endless dictates AND get out to meet people and establish meaningful relationships. USIA cut so many positions, it became impossible to be effective. We are still understaffed. Technology can help, but cannot replace an officer going out to meet people where they are—literally and figuratively."

9. View public diplomacy as a specialist function, and recruit and train accordingly.
   - "We have lost the experts who can conduct public diplomacy."
   - "Recognize public diplomacy as a unique discipline."
   - "Recruit motivated professionals. Provide them with ample training in foreign languages and management."
   - "Engage professional, trained public diplomacy [Foreign Service] officers, rather than relying on political appointees."
   - "I think Rice's admonition that everyone in State 'does' public diplomacy is nonsense. There's a reason for specialization."
10. Restore America's promise.
    - "I never thought, after nearly thirty years overseas, most of the time explaining the U.S. as the best thing going—a strong country of laws, justice and open, exciting achievement, that I would so despair of the future for America. Money and bravado do not make us a great nation. Honesty, openness, and concern for the least among us, at home and globally, have all but vanished from our national agenda."

- "The U.S. desperately needs to restore its credibility in the world."
- "Too much of the world misunderstands the U.S. and its goals."
- "Too much of the international community not only distrusts U.S. policy but suspects we're no longer true to our basic value structure, which has long been respected and is increasingly no longer believed to motivate our policy. It takes longer to recapture that respect than it does to lose it."
- "We are in increasing isolation. Power alone will not make a world where we can live comfortably and meaningfully. We must show what we stand for and believe and this includes a willingness to show we can understand what others stand for and believe."

A new start

The views of USIA alumni reported here contain valuable insights that should be integrated into discussions of how best to rebuild U.S. public diplomacy. The lessons—listen and learn, get involved locally, tell the truth, focus on long-term objectives, understand the limitations of new media—provide principles of practice that will be useful both in strategic planning and field operations. Recommendations on matters related to resources, structure, and operations similarly could help to improve the effectiveness of public diplomacy practices going forward.

The public diplomats' emphasis on the interpersonal dimensions of public diplomacy should receive special attention in the development of future U.S. public diplomacy initiatives. As the survey showed, public diplomacy at its core is about *human* relationships that must be established and nurtured over time. On this matter particularly, it will be important to remember—especially for those inclined to dismiss the recommendations of former USIA officers as reflecting the requirements of a different time—that, while the context in which public diplomacy is conducted may have changed, the fundamental tenets of good public diplomacy may not have changed all that much.

Perhaps most important in terms of clearing a path forward for U.S. public diplomacy is the practitioners' call for America's leaders to recognize the importance of people abroad to the nation's ability to protect and advance national and global interests. The *USIA Alumni Study* revealed a basic truth clearly understood by those who have served on the frontlines of American public diplomacy—before U.S. public diplomacy can be successfully rebuilt, America must regain a "decent respect for the opinions of man[and woman]kind."

CHAPTER ELEVEN

TEMPTING FATE: THE FUTURE OF U.S. PUBLIC DIPLOMACY

Whereof what's past is prologue, what to come, [i]n yours and my discharge.[1]

In the 2006 launch issue of *The Hague Journal of Diplomacy*, editors Jan Melissen and Paul Sharp observed that both "[t]hose who study diplomacy and diplomats themselves need to reflect more, and more explicitly, on what they do, why they do it, and why it is worth doing."[2] Melissen and Sharp acknowledged that such exploration may "raise hackles among those who believe that the value of diplomacy and diplomats is self-evident to those with eyes to see, and not worth explaining to those with limited vision."[3]

However, they continued, "principles of democratic accountability and marketable value require the increasingly rich variety of practitioners of diplomacy to demonstrate their value to other people as citizens and consumers."[4] Failure in this regard, they said, results "in others who are not endowed with much understanding of diplomacy imposing their conceptions of what such jobs should be."[5]

As this book reveals, U.S. officials' "limited vision" has substantially limited American public diplomacy's advancement both as a strategic national resource and as an emerging profession. At the same time, the inability of U.S. public diplomacy practitioners and scholars to make a convincing case for public diplomacy's place in the national strategy has contributed to its faltering state. Thus, if public diplomacy is to realize its potential (both in the United States and elsewhere), it is imperative that those who conduct and study public diplomacy provide a clearer picture of what it is and why it is important in protecting and advancing national and international interests.

---

[1] William Shakespeare, quote from *Tempest*, Act 2, Scene I, http://www.shakespeare-literature.com/The_Tempest/3.html (accessed January 20, 2009).

[2] Jan Melissen and Paul Sharp, "Editorial," *The Hague Journal of Diplomacy* 1 (2006): 1.

[3] Ibid.

[4] Ibid.

[5] Ibid.

Implications for theory and practice

The purpose of this study was to investigate the intellectual and practical development of public diplomacy, with a specific focus on U.S. public diplomacy, in an effort to identify factors that influenced public diplomacy's development in the past and examine issues that will be important to public diplomacy's advancement in the future. The study does not conclude with a proposal for a particular structural model or strategic approach to public diplomacy that should be adopted by foreign ministries throughout the world. Given the diversity of national needs and interests, the range of strategic objectives to which public diplomacy can contribute, and differing local conditions in various parts of the world, such an approach likely would limit rather than further public diplomacy's future potential. As others have observed, there is no "one-size-fits-all" public diplomacy.[6]

The study does conclude, however, that there is a critical need for clarity and agreement on fundamental aspects of public diplomacy that have stifled its development and may diminish its future. Of great concern is public diplomacy's identity crisis, which is exacerbated by the lack of a clear and coherent definition of public diplomacy and broad conceptual confusion about its purpose and value. While the adaptive nature of public diplomacy is an important quality in a dynamic environment, ignoring the need for greater clarity on matters related to public diplomacy's function and scope risks marginalizing public diplomacy's role in national strategy and opens the door to other fields (e.g., marketing) and functions (e.g., Defense) stepping in to assume greater authority over matters that are best handled by public diplomacy specialists. It also risks allowing others who do not understand public diplomacy to impose on public diplomats their conceptions of what public diplomacy should be.[7]

The study also concludes that the widely-accepted view of public diplomacy as a "power" resource has impeded public diplomacy's development both in theory and in practice. The quick adoption of a power-based model of public diplomacy by many scholars and practitioners appears to have stifled exploration of alternative theoretical

[6] See, e.g., Dan Sreeby, "Public Diplomacy: The Field Perspective," in *America's Dialogue with the World* ed. William P. Kiehl (Washington, DC: Public Diplomacy Council, 2006): 95.

[7] Jan Melissen and Paul Sharp, "Editorial": 1.

constructs and—as the post-9/11 U.S. experience demonstrates—contributed to failed strategies guided by a self-interested desire to gain power and influence in global affairs rather than a desire to enhance international understanding among world citizens and achieve shared goals and benefits.

In contemplating next steps in public diplomacy's theoretical and practical development, the relational framework proposed here lays out a promising way forward. The relational paradigm challenges practitioners and scholars to seriously contemplate "why they do" public diplomacy and "why it is worth doing." In rejecting a power-based model of public diplomacy, the book proposes a relational worldview that reflects intellectual trends in the field and addresses the need for communication symmetry and mutuality in public diplomacy practices.

In exploring the concept of nation branding and the evolving roles and responsibilities of the modern public diplomat, the book also focuses attention on what public diplomats "do" and the qualifications required to do it effectively. With regard to these matters, some have suggested that private sector expertise and resources are required in order for public diplomacy to be successful.

As an example, Gyorgy Szondi proposed that the integration of nation branding and public diplomacy could make public diplomacy "more strategic" and "facilitate strategic planning and co-ordination."[8] According to Szondi, a branding strategy also could "bring creativity and a breath of fresh air in reaching out to foreign publics," make public diplomacy "more results-oriented," and produce "more tangible results."[9] Additionally, Szondi said, a branding perspective could "improve public diplomats' communication skills and competencies, which are often poor."[10]

Such statements are curious in that they suggest that public diplomacy is not—or cannot be—all these things without "outside" counsel. In fact, in order to be successful, public diplomacy must be strategic. It must be coordinated with others whose activities influence a nation's international relations. It must be creative and innovative. It must be

[8] Gyorgy Szondi, "Public Diplomacy and Nation Branding: Conceptual and Practical Differences," *Discussion Papers in Diplomacy* (The Hague: Netherlands Institute of International Relations "Clingendael," 2008), 19.

[9] Ibid., 19–20.

[10] Ibid., 19.

results-oriented. It must produce tangible results. And, as the *USIA Alumni Study* showed, it must be conducted by experienced professionals who communicate well.

At the same time, it is recognized that public diplomacy is not always—perhaps not often—practiced strategically. Post-9/11 U.S. public diplomacy initiatives provide instructive examples. In three consecutive reports—in 2003, 2005, and again in 2006—the GAO reported that U.S. public diplomacy lacked both a strategic foundation and strategic direction.[11] Such findings indicate that U.S. officials have failed to engage in the strategic planning needed for public diplomacy to be effective, as well as to demonstrate its success. The national plan for U.S. public diplomacy and strategic communication released in 2007 provided little evidence of significant improvement.

But such findings do not mean that the U.S. government is *incapable* of developing a public diplomacy operation that could be successful both in improving America's image abroad and in enhancing the nation's relations with world citizens. Certainly, the USIA experience suggests otherwise. Rather, such findings indicate that U.S. officials have not made rebuilding public diplomacy a priority, nor have they provided the necessary leadership and resources required for public diplomacy to succeed.

On this point, a return to the 9/11 Commission Report is instructive. In examining the factors that contributed to the terrorist attacks in New York, Washington, and Pennsylvania, the Commission identified four kinds of failures: "in imagination, policy, capabilities and management."[12] Although the group essentially ignored diplomatic failings in the final report of their investigation, if they had taken a closer look at post-Cold War/pre-9/11 public diplomacy, they would have found that the same four failures applied.

Thus, in devising a way forward for U.S. public diplomacy, questions related to each—questions that remain unanswered more than eight years after 9/11—deserve special attention. As the Commission observed, in reflecting on past failures, "the United States should con-

---

[11] Government Accountability Office, *U.S. Public Diplomacy: State Department Elements Lack Certain Communication Elements and Face Consistent Challenges* (Washington, DC: 2006), http://www.gao.gov/new.items/d06707t.pdf (accessed on January 21, 2009).

[12] The 9/11 Commission, *The 9/11 Commission Report: Final Report of the National Commission on Terrorist Attacks Upon the United States* (New York: W. W. Norton & Company, 2003): 339.

sider *what to do*—the shape and objectives of a strategy" and "*how to do it*—organizing their government in a different way."[13]

In a world characterized by change, imagination may be one of the most important factors in determining public diplomacy's future success. Yet, U.S. public diplomacy *still* operates in a bureaucratic straightjacket that stifles rather than encourages innovation. In such an environment, how are public diplomats to imagine new threats and opportunities the nation will face in the years ahead? How are they to imagine new ways of thinking about and conducting public diplomacy?

The policy factor speaks to both the need for government leaders to consider the public implications of U.S. foreign policies and the need for public diplomats to have a voice in policy making. It also addresses the importance of public diplomacy objectives that reflect the growing participation of nonstate actors in matters related to policy. Why does public diplomacy *still* not have a permanent and respected role in U.S. foreign policy formulation?

Resources—human and otherwise—alone will not make public diplomacy successful. But inadequate resources undoubtedly will ensure its failure. Why have U.S. leaders in the White House and Congress *still* not provided needed resources and developed the capabilities required for public diplomacy to succeed?

Admittedly, an increasingly complex network of government agencies and private parties involved in activities related to U.S. public diplomacy creates a considerable management challenge for U.S. officials. Yet, many of the same problems faced today have existed for many years. Why have U.S. officials *still* not figured out how public diplomacy resources and operations are best managed—and by whom?

The "last three feet"

In refining the strategic direction of public diplomacy, rather than adopt one particular strategic approach, public diplomats would be better served by identifying *principles of practice* that contribute to public diplomacy's effectiveness in establishing and sustaining

[13] Ibid., 361.

beneficial relations with people abroad. In that respect, face-to-face interactions through cultural and educational initiatives and other activities are widely recognized as among the most effective strategies for covering what Edward R. Murrow called "the last three feet." Notable examples are the United States' Fulbright exchange programs and International Visitors Program,[14] and programs sponsored by the British Council, the cultural arm of the U.K. government whose goal is to encourage intercultural dialogue and "strengthen understanding and trust between and within different cultures."[15] Although such programs have received less attention historically than the information/advocacy components of public diplomacy,[16] their long-term relational focus reflects the philosophic framework that should guide public diplomacy going forward.

What makes these programs work? In a study of U.S. cultural exchange programs, Cynthia P. Schneider outlined the characteristics of what she called "best practices in cultural diplomacy": communicate some aspect of America's values; cater to the interests of the host country or region; offer pleasure, information, or expertise in the spirit of exchange and mutual respect; open doors between American diplomats and their host country; provide another dimension or alternative to the official presence of America in the country; form part of a long-term relationship and cultivation of ties; and be creative, flexible, and opportunistic.[17] The case examples from which these criteria were derived, Schneider noted, "testify that U.S. diplomats and NGOs understand the criteria of successful cultural diplomacy."[18]

Such studies illustrate the value of learning from past successes. In this regard, the *USIA Alumni Study* revealed principles of effective practice that will be useful going forward. Additional case studies in the United States and other parts of the world would deepen under-

---

[14] See, e.g., Sherry Lee Mueller, "Professional Exchanges, Citizen Diplomacy, and Credibility," in *America's Dialogue with the World*, ed. William P. Kiehl (Washington, DC: Public Diplomacy Council, 2006).

[15] British Council, "75 Years of Cultural Relations," http://www.britishcouncil.org/new/?tab=2 (accessed January 22, 2009).

[16] See, e.g., Nicholas Cull, *The Cold War and the United States Information Agency: American Propaganda and Public Diplomacy, 1945–1989* (Cambridge, UK: Cambridge University Press, 2008): 487–492.

[17] Cynthia P. Schneider, "Diplomacy that Works: 'Best Practices' in Cultural Diplomacy," unpublished paper, 2003.

[18] Ibid.

standing of strategic issues in public diplomacy—and provide much-needed evidence that public diplomacy works. As William P. Kiehl wrote in *America's Dialogue with the World*, "It will surprise many that there are a number of successful ways to bring about a dialogue between America and the world and that these methods have been in use for more than sixty years."[19]

Of course, as the USIA alumni and others have pointed out, there is a need to adapt (and employ new) public diplomacy strategies to meet the challenges of a new time. Changes in the global environment demand that diplomatic practices change, too. But the fundamental tenets of good public diplomacy should not be abandoned in efforts to "modernize."

While much has changed in diplomatic affairs, the human dimension of international relations has not. For that reason, as Jean-Robert Leguey-Feilleux observed, "the basic skills that make diplomacy what it is will remain indispensable, regardless of what new instruments or techniques may be invented: these skills are personal attributes, however acquired, enabling people of different races, cultures, and political affiliations to communicate and work together."[20]

The ends of diplomacy have not changed either. As Daryl Copeland reminded, "The search for the nonviolent resolution of differences through negotiation and compromise, and the promotion of cooperation for mutual gain are constant."[21] These fundamental truths should guide practitioners and scholars as they continue to refine the intellectual and practical dimensions of public diplomacy.

The second mandate

In reflecting on the ongoing discussion and debate concerning U.S. public diplomacy's future, one particular gap stands out—the "second

[19] William P. Kiehl, ed., *America's Dialogue with the World*, 4–5.

[20] Jean-Robert Leguey-Feilleux, *The Dynamics of Diplomacy* (Boulder, CO: Lynne Reinner Publishers, 2009): 362.

[21] Daryl Copeland, "Three Peas in Search of a Pod: A Personal Perspective on Public Diplomacy, Public Opinion Research and the Public Environment," in *Public Diplomacy: Practitioners, Policy Makers, and Public Opinion, A Report of the Public Diplomacy and World Public Opinion Forum* (Los Angeles: USC Center on Public Diplomacy and Washington, DC: Pew Research Center, 2006), 21.

mandate" to enhance *Americans'* understanding of the world and its citizens.[22]

Often overlooked in contemporary writings on public diplomacy is the fact that the legislation that guided U.S. public diplomacy's early development included "mutual" understanding as a goal of public diplomacy initiatives.[23] Former President Jimmy Carter reinforced this principle in a 1977 directive advising U.S. public diplomats to make "mutuality" a guiding principle of their work and adding a "second mandate" that required them to enhance *Americans'* understanding of the world and its citizens.[24]

Notwithstanding post-9/11 U.S. public diplomacy efforts, which for the most part did not reflect principles of mutuality, the *USIA Alumni Study* indicated that mutuality was considered by USIA officers to be a hallmark of their work in their field. Indeed, there was considerable recognition that public diplomacy, in order to be effective, must be a "two-way" street.

However, while mutuality may have characterized the work of public diplomats working abroad, there has been little effort to carry out the "second mandate" at home. One reason, according to veteran USIA officer Fred Coffey, is that "there were never enough resources to do both."[25] Others have suggested that the *domestic* mandate simply didn't resonate with *Foreign* Service officers.[26]

As a result, while U.S. educational and exchange programs have made substantial contributions to a limited number of Americans' understanding of foreign cultures and peoples, overall efforts to create real and broad-based mutual understanding—i.e., among *both* foreign publics and Americans—have been more limited. Surprisingly, there is scant mention of this in the literature on U.S. public diplomacy.

This oversight may be particularly important in the years ahead, as U.S. leaders continue to combat growing anti-Americanism throughout the world.[27] As Andrew Kohut and Bruce Stokes reported in

---

[22] See Hans N. Tuch, *Communicating with the World: U.S. Public Diplomacy Overseas* (New York: St Martin's Press, 1990), 32.

[23] See David I. Hitchcock, Jr., "U.S. Public Diplomacy," *Significant Issues Series X, Number 17* (Washington, DC: The Center for Strategic Studies, 1988), 26.

[24] Ibid.

[25] Personal interview, March 21, 2007.

[26] Personal interview, William Mauer, March 22, 2007.

[27] See, e.g., *Global Public Opinion in the Bush Years (2001–2008), The Pew Global Attitudes Project* (Washington, DC: Pew Research Center, 2008).

America Against the World: How We Are Different and Why We Are Disliked, "American exceptionalism and anti-Americanism are inextricably related."[28]

According to Kohut and Stokes, their study of how Americans' views and values differ from those of other publics found that "the default position of the average American is to ignore the rest of the world."[29] Not only do "Americans underestimate their interdependence with the rest of the world," they discovered, but "[i]ndividualism inclines Americans to believe that they do not need the rest of the world."[30] The consequence, Kohut and Stokes pointed out, is that Americans' "[r]elative lack of interest in foreign countries and events results in little awareness of the new phenomenon of global connectedness."[31] The risk going forward," they said, "is that Americans will ignore the lessons of history, which teach that hubris, and the inattentiveness to others that so often accompanies it, can lead to trouble."[32]

The practical implications of such findings for public diplomacy are significant. As history shows, the lack of a domestic constituency for public diplomacy contributed to its demise after the Cold War, and the lack of broad-based domestic support has similarly impeded public diplomacy's advancement since 9/11. If a domestic constituency for public diplomacy is not developed going forward, the marginalization of public diplomacy by U.S. officials is likely to continue. As Kohut and Stokes observed, "Americans' indifference toward many foreign policy questions [has] the effect of giving U.S. leaders far greater leeway in shaping foreign policy than in shaping its domestic counterparts."[33]

In addressing such concerns, it will be important to examine the legislative underpinnings of U.S. public diplomacy. For example, the Smith-Mundt Act of 1948, which prohibits the dissemination of materials developed for people abroad within the United States, has contributed to the information deficit among Americans about their country's involvement overseas. Despite its noble purpose—to protect U.S. citizens from government "propaganda"—the law has effectively ensured that Americans know little about what their government is doing and

[28] Andrew Kohut and Bruce Stokes, *America Against the World: How We Are Different and Why We Are Disliked* (New York: Henry Holt and Company, 2006), 225.
[29] Ibid., 221.
[30] Ibid., xv.
[31] Ibid., 222.
[32] Andrew Kohut and Bruce Stokes, *America Against the World*, 222.
[33] Ibid.

talking about with people abroad. Perhaps more importantly, because they have been kept in the dark about what public diplomacy entails, they have little recognition of its importance to national interests.

While there are competing views on whether Smith-Mundt should be repealed, there is broad recognition that changes are needed in terms of what and how the U.S. government communicates with U.S. citizens on matters related to foreign policy.[34] Clearly, the time has come to revisit legislative mandates that were developed before the age of the Internet and that continue to affect contemporary public diplomacy policies and practices.

Tempting fate

In examining the history of public diplomacy during the Cold War, Nicholas Cull concluded that the "United States is at its heart a skeptical participant in public diplomacy."[35] Pointing to "a longstanding and pervasive suspicion of government information and an associated reluctance to spend money on such works," Cull observed that public diplomacy has been "justified only in an emergency when the call of 'national security' has trumped natural reticence."[36]

A similar conclusion might be drawn from the nation's involvement in public diplomacy after 9/11. In the immediate aftermath of the terrorist attacks, new public diplomacy activities were undertaken in the Middle East. Yet, U.S. policymakers' enthusiasm for public diplomacy has since waned. Both the meager funds afforded the function and an apparent lack of interest on the part of policymakers in rebuilding American public diplomacy suggest that U.S. leaders do not yet recognize either the increasing influence of foreign *publics* in international relations or public diplomacy's unique and important role in the protection and advancement of national and international interests.

What will it take for U.S. leaders to fully understand that America's relations with the people of the world really matter—and, because they really matter, those relations will require considerably more attention than they have been given in recent years? Although the answer to

[34] See, e.g., *The Report on the Smith-Mundt Symposium of January 13, 2009* (Washington, DC: Armstrong Insights Group, LLC, 2009).
[35] Nicholas J. Cull, *The Cold War and the United States Information Agency*, 499.
[36] Ibid.

this question is uncertain, history likely will show that a confluence of world events (rather than foresight on the part of U.S. leaders) will be most consequential to public diplomacy's advancement in the new century. Two major occurrences already point in that direction. First, 9/11—an unprecedented act of terrorism on U.S. soil by nonstate actors, which illustrated the importance of tending to U.S. relations with people abroad. Then, in 2008, an economic crisis that demonstrated with striking clarity just how interconnected and interdependent the world has become.

In addressing the latter, *New York Times* columnist Thomas Friedman wrote that once the financial crisis was over, the world would be one in which global economies would be more intimately tied together than ever before. "We're all connected and nobody is in charge," he said.[37] "It will be a world in which America will not be able to scratch its ear, let alone roll over in bed, without thinking about the impact on other countries and economies. And it will be a world in which multilateral diplomacy and regulation will no longer be a choice. It will be a reality and a necessity."[38] The bottom line, as Friedman observed, is: "We are all partners now."[39]

America's new president seems to agree. During his run for the White House, Barack Obama frequently addressed the need for America to mend its relations with world citizens. More recently, as president, he has presented a more respectful America to the world and signaled the country's intentions to reengage in global affairs. Certainly, the fact that he gave his first interview as president to the Arabic news service Al-Arabiya was a welcome sign in the Middle East that he wants to improve U.S. relations with the Muslim world. His June 2009 speech in Cairo, which focused on the need for nations and peoples to work together to address common challenges, further reinforced the idea of an America ready to stand by and work with those who share the nation's hopes for a more peaceful and prosperous world for all its citizens.

Notwithstanding the president's unprecedented popularity with people at home and abroad, however, it will take more than words to reverse the course of public diplomacy's fate. It will take the president's

[37] Thomas L. Friedman, "The Great Iceland Meltdown," *The New York Times*, October 19, 2008.

[38] Ibid.

[39] Ibid.

leadership both in charting a new course for the country that reflects a "decent respect for the opinions of mankind" and in providing the direction and resources needed to *show* the people of the world that America is not the self-centered, arrogant, power-hungry nation many believe it to be.

It will take a commitment by Secretary of State Hillary Clinton to make public diplomacy a priority in U.S. diplomatic affairs. And it will take the leadership of the under secretary of state for public diplomacy and public affairs to ensure that America's public diplomats have the direction and autonomy needed to carry out their mandate.

Although it is too early to tell what the Obama administration might mean for U.S. public diplomacy, as hope arrived in Washington, so, too, did a renewed sense of possibility for public diplomacy's future. Clearly, the new president in both his words and actions has signaled a new era in America's international relations. And he has given people both at home and abroad a profound sense of optimism concerning America's engagement in the world. But time alone will tell whether Obama's legacy will include the development of a new U.S. public diplomacy that will transcend his administration and sustain America's relations with foreign publics in the years ahead.

In a 1994 *Foreign Affairs* article, Walter Lacquer made a passionate plea to "save" public diplomacy from the apathy he perceived on the part of the Clinton administration toward the USIA. Although he lost that fight (with the dismantling of the agency), he accurately predicted what it might take for U.S. leaders to recognize the importance of international relations to the United States. In the long shadows of 9/11, his words seem eerily prescient: "There is always the possibility that a major international crisis will have a salutary effect, doing away with the delusions about the state of the world, generating greater awareness of the dangers facing America, and putting an end to lethargy and indifference."[40]

As the future of U.S. public diplomacy continues to be debated, the wisdom of Lacquer's counsel remains clear:

> [I]t is only a question of time until it is accepted that the United States got its priorities wrong in the conduct of its foreign policies and the choice of its instruments. There will always be room for diplomacy but in

[40] Walter Lacquer, "Save Public Diplomacy: Broadcasting America's Message Matters," *Foreign Affairs* 73, no. 5 (September/October 1994): 24.

> its present form it is largely an eighteenth-century relic that badly needs rethinking and refashioning. The limits of military and economic power have become all too obvious of late.... Perhaps in the future, those who failed to accept the importance of public diplomacy will think of various excuses to justify their misjudgment. But this will be of little help, for in this field there is no room for rush programs to make good the neglect of many years. A price will have to be paid: races that were run, will not be rerun, because at the time too many people in Washington overslept.[41]

The events of 9/11 provided the wake-up call needed for U.S. leaders—and the leaders of other nations—to see the consequences of inaction with regard to public diplomacy. Yet, as memories of that day have faded, so too has the motivation to create the critical infrastructure required to strategically manage the United States' relationships with the people of the world and to provide the resources needed for public diplomacy to be successful.

In the meantime, the global "war on terror" goes on and America's tattered relations with foreign publics, while improving under the Obama administration, are still torn. The question, then, that should be posed to America's president and his cabinet today is this: When the next wake-up call comes, will you be caught napping, too?

[41] Ibid.

APPENDICES

APPENDIX ONE

ABOUT THE *USIA ALUMNI STUDY*

In June of 2007, a 15-page questionnaire was mailed to 441 members of the USIA Alumni Association.[1] A reminder post card was sent two weeks later. Completed questionnaires were received from 213 members, for a response rate of 48 percent.

Of the USIA alumni responding, the average age was 73. The youngest participant was 44; the oldest was 93. A total of 169 of the respondents were male, 43 were female, and one did not respond to this item.

The survey participants worked in U.S. public diplomacy for an average of 25 years. The shortest time reported was less than 1 year; the longest time was 66 years. The majority of survey participants came from the senior ranks of the U.S. Foreign Service, with 45 percent reporting Senior Foreign Service (SFS) as their top rank of service and 27 percent reporting their highest rank as FS01.

Table A1 *USIA Alumni Study*: Highest Rank of Service

Rank	% Respondents*
Senior Foreign Service	45%
FS-01 or higher	27%
FS-02	9%
FS-03	5%
FS-04	2%
FS-05	1%
Senior Executive Service	1%
GS-15	3%
GS-14	3%
GS-13	2%
GS-12	1%
GS-11	0%

* Rounded percentage of respondents; n = 213

[1] The United States Information Agency Alumni Association subsequently changed its name to Public Diplomacy Alumni Association.

Table A2 *USIA Alumni Study*: Service in Various Regions of the World

Region	% Respondents*	Mean # Years**
Africa	33%	1.93
Europe	53%	4.79
Near East	17%	.94
South Asia	25%	1.03
Western Hemisphere	38%	3.19
Washington, DC	76%	8.37
Other	19%	.96

* Rounded percentages of respondents; n = 213
** Numeric average between 0 years of service and the highest number of years of service in the respective regions

The majority of participants left government service after the end of the Cold War, with 41 percent retiring during public diplomacy's steep decline in the last decade of the 20th century and an additional 17 percent retiring after the dissolution of the USIA. Twenty-nine percent of the respondents retired between 1980 and 1989 and 12 percent retired before 1979. Three participants (1 percent) reported that they are still working in the State Department.

The former diplomats reported service abroad in Europe (53 percent), the Western Hemisphere (38 percent), East Asia (34 percent) and Africa (33 percent). Fewer reported service in South Asia (25 percent) and the Near East (17 percent). A sizable majority (76 percent) also reported service in Washington, DC.

More than two-thirds (67 percent) of the respondents reported experience in information programs; the same number (67 percent) reported experience in cultural and educational exchange programs; about half (53 percent) reported experience in management; and just over one-fourth (28 percent) reported experience in international broadcasting.

The language expertise of the former diplomats was extensive, with many respondents reporting fluency in multiple languages. When asked in what foreign languages they were able to communicate, the USIA alumni listed 54 languages, including French (50 percent), Spanish (41 percent), German (27 percent), Portuguese (19 percent), Russian (12 percent), Italian (9 percent), Serbo-Croatian (8 percent), Thai (7 percent), Japanese (7 percent), Polish (7 percent), Romanian (5 percent), Vietnamese (5 percent), and Greek (5 percent).

Table A3 *USIA Alumni Study*: Service in Public Diplomacy Areas

Area	% Respondents*	Mean # Years**
Information Programs	67%	7.53
Cultural/Educational Exchange Programs	67%	7.53
International Broadcasting	28%	2.69
Management	53%	5.56
Other	28%	1.84

* Rounded percentages of respondents; n = 213
** Numeric average of all responses between 0 years of service and the highest number of years of service in the respective areas

Table A4 *USIA Alumni Study*: Foreign Language Proficiencies*

Afrikaans	<1%	Arabic	6%	Bengali	1%
Burmese	1%	Cambodian	1%	Cantonese	<1%
Catalan	1%	Chinese	8%	Czech	3%
Danish	1%	Dutch	1%	Estonian	<1%
Farsi	2%	Finnish	2%	French	50%
German	27%	Greek	5%	Hausa	<1%
Hebrew	1%	Hindi	2%	Hungarian	3%
Icelandic	<1%	Indonesian	3%	Italian	9%
Japanese	7%	Kikongo	<1%	Korean	3%
Krio	<1%	Lao	2%	Lingala	<1%
Macedonian	<1%	Norwegian	2%	Persian	<1%
Polish	7%	Portuguese	19%	Quechua	<1%
Romanian	5%	Russian	12%	Serbo-Croatian	8%
Setswana	<1%	Shona	<1%	Sinhala	<1%
Slovenian	1%	Spanish	41%	Swahili	2%
Swedish	1%	Taiwanese	<1%	Tamil	<1%
Thai	7%	Turkish	3%	Ukranian	<1%
Urdu	2%	Vietnamese	5%	Zulu	<1%

* Rounded percentages reflect respondents indicating an ability to communicate in the language; n = 213

APPENDIX TWO

U.S. NATIONAL STRATEGY FOR PUBLIC DIPLOMACY AND STRATEGIC COMMUNICATION

Strategic Communication and Public Diplomacy Policy Coordinating Committee (PCC)

We will lead the cause of freedom, justice, and hope, because both our values and our interests demand it. We believe in the timeless truth: To whom much is given, much is required. We also know that nations with free, healthy, prosperous people will be sources of stability, not breeding grounds for extremists and hate and terror. By making the world more hopeful, we make the world more peaceful—and by helping others, the American people must understand we help ourselves.

President Bush at the White House Summit on Malaria
December 14, 2006

MISSION AND PRIORITIES

The strength, success and security of the United States of America rest on our commitment to certain fundamental values and principles. These values gave birth to our nation, and govern our actions in the world. We believe all individuals, men and women, are equal and entitled to basic human rights, including freedom of speech, worship and political participation. While the forms of government will vary, we believe all people deserve to live in just societies that protect individual and common rights, fight corruption and are governed by the rule of law. Across the world, America seeks to work with other governments and nations in a spirit of partnership that supports human dignity and fosters peace and progress.

The National Security Strategy of the United States establishes eight national security objectives:

- To champion human dignity;
- To strengthen alliances against terrorism;
- To defuse regional conflicts;
- To prevent threats from weapons of mass destruction;
- To encourage global economic growth;
- To expand the circle of development;
- To cooperate with other centers of global power; and
- To transform America's national security institutions to meet the challenges and opportunities of the twenty-first century.

Public diplomacy and strategic communication should always strive to support our nation's fundamental values and national security objectives. All communication and public diplomacy activities should:

- Underscore our commitment to freedom, human rights and the dignity and equality of every human being;
- Reach out to those who share our ideals;
- Support those who struggle for freedom and democracy; and
- Counter those who espouse ideologies of hate and oppression.

STRATEGIC OBJECTIVES

The United States Government seeks to partner with nations and peoples across the world in ways that result in a better life for all of the world's citizens. As a multicultural nation founded by immigrants, America respects people of different cultures, backgrounds and faiths. We seek to be a partner for progress, prosperity and peace around the world.

We have established three strategic objectives to govern America's public diplomacy and strategic communication with foreign audiences:

I. *America must offer a positive vision of hope and opportunity that is rooted in our most basic values*

These values include our deep belief in freedom, and the dignity and equality of every person. We believe all people deserve to live in just societies that are governed by the rule of law and free from corruption or intimidation. We believe people should be able to speak their minds, protest peacefully, worship freely and participate in choosing their government. We want all people, boys and girls, to be educated, because we know education expands opportunity and we believe those who are educated are more likely to be responsible citizens, tolerant and respectful of each other's differences. We want to expand the circle of prosperity so that people throughout the world can earn a living and provide for their families. America has long been a beacon of hope and opportunity for people across the world and we must continue to be that beacon of hope for a better life.

II. *With our partners, we seek to isolate and marginalize violent extremists who threaten the freedom and peace sought by civilized people of every nation, culture and faith*

We can achieve this goal by:

- Promoting democratization and good governance as a path to a positive future, in secure and pluralistic societies;

- Actively engaging Muslim communities and amplifying mainstream Muslim voices;
- Isolating and discrediting terrorist leaders, facilitators, and organizations;
- De-legitimizing terror as an acceptable tactic to achieve political ends; and
- Demonstrating that the West is open to all religions and is not in conflict with any faith.

III. *America must work to nurture common interests and values between Americans and peoples of different countries, cultures and faiths across the world*

Far more unites us as human beings than divides us. Especially at a time of war and common threats, America must actively nurture common interests and values. We have shared interests in expanding economic opportunity, promoting peaceful resolution of conflicts, enhancing scientific collaboration, fighting diseases that respect no border, and protecting our common environment. A cornerstone of American policy and public diplomacy must be to identify, highlight and nurture common interests and values.

STRATEGIC AUDIENCES

Successful public diplomacy and strategic communication must address both mass audiences and specific target audiences. Certain media such as television, radio and the internet, as well as press and public affairs operations, reach a broad public. But public diplomacy efforts are also directed at narrower, more discrete groups, especially those that because of their expertise, stature, or leadership roles influence the decisions and opinions of others. Opinion leaders in foreign societies can be effective partners in advancing our broader public diplomacy goals. We need to tailor our public diplomacy and communication programs to specific audiences, using the most appropriate and effective media available. Those specific audiences include:

I. *Key Influencers*

"Key Influencers" are those whose views can have a ripple effect throughout society. They include clerics, educators, journalists, women leaders, business and labor leaders, political leaders, scientists and military personnel. Our public diplomacy programs and efforts should engage these key influencers, and especially encourage and empower them to speak out against the forces of violent extremism and in favor of peaceful resolution of disputes, tolerance and freedom.

II. *Vulnerable Populations*

Our public diplomacy and strategic communication must take into account demographic characteristics of different societies, and focus especially on those groups most vulnerable to extremist ideology:

> Youth—A top public diplomacy priority should be reaching out to young people—the voters, entrepreneurs, and leaders of tomorrow. Many of our traditional public diplomacy programs, however, have not directly reached this demographic group, which makes up more than 50% of populations in the Middle East and elsewhere. We need to employ education and exchange programs as well as Internet and other forms of communication to reach this audience.

Women and Girls—Numerous studies have shown that when women are educated and empowered, they become the most effective agents of social change, progress and prosperity. Improving the educational and economic opportunities of women can have a profound impact on overall social stability, economic development and human rights. Educating women in developing countries helps improve overall family health, reduce illiteracy and stabilize communities. Of the 70 million people who are illiterate in the broader Middle East, more than two-thirds are women. Promoting education for women and girls in these societies is critical to their long-term success and to the advancement of liberty and opportunity.

Minorities—We need to reach out to marginalized groups such as indigenous populations, as well as racial and religious minorities who often do not have equal educational or economic opportunities. America also has great expertise and experience in helping develop opportunities for persons with disabilities; this should be shared more widely with countries across the world.

III. *Mass Audiences*

With increasing numbers of people across the world getting their news and information primarily from television, America must expand its presence on international broadcasts. USG broadcasting entities of the Broadcasting Board of Governors provide direct channels to mass audiences worldwide through television, radio and VOA's web site. We are rapidly developing improved capabilities to employ the power of Internet and other new technologies. USG officials in Washington and abroad are engaging more actively than ever with foreign media, including television and radio as well as print. Outreach through foreign media should be considered a basic work requirement for USG officials to the greatest extent possible. With mass audiences worldwide now receiving much of their news via television, all USG officials should make appearances on television news and information shows a special priority.

PUBLIC DIPLOMACY PRIORITIES

To achieve our mission, we have established the following priorities for public diplomacy programs and activities:

- **Expand education and exchange programs**
  The U.S. government should continue its recent trend of increasing funding for critical exchange programs, perhaps the single most effective public diplomacy tool of the last fifty years. Exchange programs should emphasize students (future leaders of society) and key influencers in society (clerics, women, journalists, business, scientists, government, military and political leaders) whose exchange experience can impact wider segments of society. The impact of exchanges should also be amplified through use of technology and media; both USG and private broadcasting should be invited and encouraged to produce documentaries and news coverage of exchange programs.

  English language teaching is a priority program and should be expanded. Learning English provides a skill that helps young people improve their lives and job prospects, and helps counter extremism by opening a window to a wider world of knowledge. English language programs are among the most effective ways to reach young people before they are old enough to participate in exchange programs, and are particularly effective at expanding the horizons of young people from disadvantaged neighborhoods.

  Agencies should also actively partner with the private sector to increase exchange and education opportunities through internships, mentoring and education programs in countries where they operate. Finally, agencies and embassies should partner with those who have a mutual interest in encouraging travel to the United States including the higher education community, travel and tourism industry, and business, scientific and technology communities.
- **Modernize communications**
  In an era when mass media, especially television, reaches mass audiences in an unprecedented way, United States government officials must significantly expand their presence and appearances on foreign media. United States Ambassadors should be the "voice" of

America as well as its official representative and should make regular appearances on major foreign media, explaining U.S. policies, values and views. The new State Department regional "hub" operations, designed to provide language trained spokesmen and more aggressive booking of American officials on regional media, should be continued and expanded beyond current locations in London, Brussels and Dubai. High ranking officials, subject experts and employees with foreign language capabilities should be identified, encouraged and rewarded for making appearances on international media. Interviews and appearances on foreign media should be a priority, not an afterthought, as part of international travel by high ranking government officials. All agencies and embassies must also increase use of new technologies, including creative use of the internet, web chats, blogs and video story-telling opportunities on the Internet to highlight American policies and programs. The United States government should continue to expand the National Security Language Initiative to encourage more young Americans to learn critical foreign languages.

- **Promote the "diplomacy of deeds"**
America's deeds—providing health care, education, economic opportunity, food and shelter, training for political participation, help after disasters—can communicate our values and beliefs far more effectively than all of our words. Yet too few people (including those in our own country) know the tremendous impact Americans are making on lives around the world every day, through government programs, private and charitable programs, and the contributions of individual Americans. These programs should be continued and expanded, especially in the areas people across the world care most about: health, education and economic opportunity. Health and science diplomacy (HIV/AIDs, malaria, avian influenza, military clinics, hospital ships, cancer detection and awareness, natural disaster prevention and scientific discoveries) have particular resonance and should be a priority for all embassies and agencies with health and science programs. All agencies and embassies should make a major commitment to more aggressively tell the story of how these programs are helping people improve their lives and opportunities. Partnerships with the private sector, foundations, and religious and charitable organizations should also be encouraged through events like the White House Summit on Malaria to increase coordination

and expand effectiveness and visibility. America should also demonstrate respect for local culture, art and history across the world through expanded arts and cultural partnerships and support for the Ambassador's Fund for Cultural Preservation.

INTERAGENCY COORDINATION

The Policy Coordinating Committee (PCC) on Public Diplomacy and Strategic Communication led by the Under Secretary for Public Diplomacy and Public Affairs is the overall mechanism by which we coordinate our public diplomacy across the interagency community. To help accomplish our mission, the PCC will establish the following structures:

I. **Counterterrorism Communications Center headquartered at the Department of State**, with the core mission of developing messages and strategies to discredit terrorists and their ideology.

II. **Interagency Crisis Communication Team**
The National Security Council will initiate an interagency conference call immediately upon major breaking news that might have an impact on our efforts against violent extremism to coordinate message points. Call participants should include, at a minimum:
- White House Communications Office
- NSC Senior Communications Director/Spokesman
- White House Press Secretary
- State Department Public Diplomacy and Public Affairs
- Defense Department Public Affairs

Following the response decision, a conference call will be conducted with public affairs and communication representatives from relevant agencies to refine and coordinate unified messaging. The resulting message from the Counterterrorism Communications Center and appropriate official statements will be relayed to Cabinet secretaries, ambassadors and the military chain of command through the Rapid Response Unit at the State Department.

III. **Regular Monitoring of Implementation**
The Public Diplomacy and Strategic Communication PCC will meet regularly to review progress in implementing this communication strategy.

INITIAL COMMUNICATION ACTIVITIES

All segments of the USG have a role in public diplomacy and global communication. To ensure that we maximize the overall effectiveness of the USG to communicate around the world, each agency and embassy should:

I. *Develop an agency-specific plan to implement the public diplomacy/strategic communication objectives in this document*

Agency plans should:

- Identify two or three key programs/policies which the agency will highlight to support the overall public diplomacy/strategic communication goals
- Identify target audiences
- Assign responsibility and outline specific plans for communicating key programs and policies to the target audiences through speeches, foreign travel, media interviews, etc.
- Identify:
  - NGO and private sector partners with whom the agency works
  - Subject matter experts who can explain and advocate U.S. policy
  - Workers who speak foreign languages and could translate/participate in interviews
- Recommend envoys to advance public diplomacy efforts
- Outline current activities and programs that can be linked to support global public diplomacy
- Develop criteria to evaluate effectiveness

II. *Basic Information Sharing*

The State Department has created a new "Public Diplomacy Briefing Book" that is available via internal internet to update all USG officials on regional and country-specific policies, official statements and key messages. The briefing book should be a part of briefing and preparation for all USG officials prior to foreign travel so our messages are clear and consistent. All agencies should also assist in collecting and transmitting timely material to be featured on appropriate websites:

- Compelling stories (including pictures and videotape if possible) of how American programs are impacting people's lives. Interviews of those receiving health care, collaborating on scientific research and innovation, or participating in English language and exchange programs should be provided and featured on the State Department's "Partnership for a Better Life" website.
- A database of digital images and videos should be developed in conjunction with search engine technology.
- Material should include quotes in print and on video that represent mainstream Muslim views and rejection of terrorists/extremism.
- Best practices should be identified and shared through agency websites.

Audience Analysis: Understanding foreign public opinion is vital to successful communication. The USG should create a central repository of information and analysis of public opinion in different countries so we can better understand how citizens of other countries view us and what values and interests we have in common. Such information is currently collected by a number of different agencies (BBG, State Department INR, DOD, USAID, some individual embassies) as well as private sector organizations such as Gallup and PEW. Accurate, up-to-date information should be housed in one central location for interagency submissions and access. Information from this central repository should be available to all senior government communicators, and to the new Counterterrorism Communications Center, to help develop and monitor the effectiveness of messages.

III. *Proactive Media Booking*

The State Department's new regional media hubs in London, Brussels and Dubai are equipped to support messaging and booking of senior USG officials abroad to project American viewpoints.

NEEDED RESOURCES

Funding

The U.S. is engaged in an international struggle of ideas and ideologies, which requires a more extensive, sophisticated use of communications and public diplomacy programs to gain support for U.S. policies abroad. To effectively wage this struggle, public diplomacy must be treated—along with defense, homeland security and intelligence—as a national security priority in terms of resources. We must continue to significantly increase funding for all public diplomacy and strategic communication programs, but, specifically, we need urgent funding for priority programs such as people-to-people exchanges, English language summer and after-school programs for young people in strategic areas, science outreach projects, and new media outreach to keep up with evolving audiences and technology. Increased support for Public Diplomacy programming is vitally important to confront today's global challenges and the threat that terrorism poses to free peoples everywhere.

Congressional approval of FY2007 supplemental funding of $50 million for public diplomacy is an important first step towards providing the resources required for this effort. This supplemental funding will support priority programs in key countries in the effort to counter violent extremism, including a major new summer program offering English language teaching for young people ages 8–14 and increased digital outreach in critical languages.

CONCLUSION

Public diplomacy is, at its core, about making America's diplomacy public and communicating America's views, values and policies in effective ways to audiences across the world. Public diplomacy promotes linkages between the American people and the rest of the world by reminding diverse populations of our common interests and values. Some of America's most effective public diplomacy is communicated not through words but through our deeds, as we invest in people through education, health care and the opportunity for greater economic and political participation. Public diplomacy also seeks to isolate and marginalize extremists and their ideology. In all these ways, public diplomacy is "waging peace," working to bring about conditions that lead to a better life for people across the world and make it more difficult for extremism to take root.

ATTACHMENT A

ACTION PLAN FOR STRATEGIC OBJECTIVES

I. *Reinforce a Positive Vision of Hope and Opportunity*

A. *Seek opportunities to link programs and policies with America's values*

Examples

1. America sponsors scholarships for girls because we believe all children, boys and girls, are equal and equally deserving of the right to an education to improve their prospects in life.
2. America sponsors workshops on workers' rights because we believe all human beings are entitled to basic rights and fair treatment by their employers.
3. America provides development and disaster assistance to respond to human needs and suffering, regardless of culture, beliefs or nationality.
4. America issues reports on human rights, religious freedom and trafficking in persons because we believe all people everywhere should be able to worship as they wish and no person anywhere should be sold into slavery.
5. America is advocating greater freedom of expression and political participation in the Middle East because we believe those are the rights of all people, everywhere.
6. America is partnering with countries across the world to fight terrorism because it threatens the right of all people everywhere to live in security and peace.
7. America collaborates with scientists worldwide because shared knowledge and innovation can benefit all mankind.

B. *Emphasize the diplomacy of deeds in all of America's development and disaster assistance*

Across the world, America feeds the poor, educates the illiterate, cares for the sick and responds to disasters. Yet often, the USG engages in so many different development projects that we get minimal recognition for any of them. Public affairs staff should identify the one or two development programs with the most impact and resonance in each specific country and work to drive home the message.

Example
Eradicating malaria is a top priority in a number of African countries. While we participate in many other programs, we should make sure every high-profile visitor, every ambassadorial event, every communication from American officials in these countries includes an update on our activities to wipe out malaria. New approaches should be developed to highlight progress: a chart at the front door of the embassy or consular office posts the growing number of lives saved; a regular radio update calls attention to milestones, the ambassador devotes the first paragraph of every speech to a progress report on fighting malaria. The USG needs to communicate in all we say and do that America is committed to partnering with people of each country to wipe out malaria.

1. **Spotlight ways in which American assistance is helping real people achieve better lives; collect and share success stories.**

Example
Public affairs staff should videotape compelling stories from participants in USG programs (women in a literacy class who can now help their children with homework, farmers who make more money because of the improved quality of their crops, girls who are attending school for the first time, science students interacting with U.S. scientists to push the envelope of knowledge) and post them to appropriate web sites. A series of vignettes could be collected on CD or shared in a podcast so they can be made available to local teachers, the media, and others.

Highlight and suggest ways for media to "cover" exchange programs—perhaps by partnering with a local radio or television station who interview participants regularly or produce a documentary or news report. U.S. government broadcasting should likewise be encouraged to cover America's development assistance, education and exchange programs with feature programs and interviews with recipients.

2. **Use Personal Examples in Communication.**

- Speechwriters should incorporate appropriate personal anecdotes to demonstrate America's core values in remarks given by officials.
- Encourage journalists to report stories of how United States' programs, education and trade have benefited citizens and their families.

3. **Establish plans for high-profile assistance in cases of major disaster that include strategic communication and public diplomacy.** USAID and military response to major disasters should be immediate and highly visible. Special priority should be placed on allowing press from the affected country and international media access to cover that assistance. When events are catastrophic (2005 tsunami, Pakistan earthquake, Lebanon destruction post-Israeli/Hezbollah war), highly visible presidential-level, private-sector teams should be recruited to raise private money and highlight the American's people's generosity and support for those affected.
4. **Facilitate contributions (coordinated by USG through state.gov website) from the American people for specific disaster relief opportunities.**

C. *Broaden the reach of strategic communication by including all USG officials, high-profile Americans, the business sector and the education sector*

1. **All senior USG officials should add at least one public diplomacy event in every country they visit when traveling on official USG business.**
   All Cabinet Secretaries should also participate in media interviews with foreign media (not merely foreign-based U.S. correspondents, but foreign television, radio and newspapers), and those media interviews should be strategically scheduled at the front end of the travel schedule to have the maximum impact, not as an afterthought.

Examples
- Appear on a highly rated television news or interview show
- Participate in a school program
- Visit a cultural site with local relevance
- Visit a health, science or education project the USG is sponsoring and highlight ways it is improving local lives

2. **Designate and commission "Special American Envoys" to help promote American values.**
These high-level representatives would reflect the diversity of America, should represent different fields (sports, health, science, music, acting) and could attract substantial news coverage/interest overseas.
3. **Engage more private sector partners.**
Agencies and embassies should identify and reach out to institutions, industries, foundations and private sector entities, especially those with a shared interest in attracting people to America and improving America's relations with people in specific countries.

Examples
- Travel and Tourism Industry
- Higher Education Community
- American Business and Labor Communities
- Provide government funding to develop public-private partnerships to advertise America as a higher education and tourism destination.
- Build coalitions of private sector disaster response partners similar to those assembled in Lebanon, Guatemala and Pakistan.
- Embassies should encourage American companies with operations in their countries to provide internships, education programs and exchange opportunities to help develop their work force and introduce more people to America; companies should be encouraged to partner with the embassy in sponsoring cultural and sports programs that foster interaction and respect between cultures.

4. **Encourage Americans themselves to be citizen diplomats.**

Examples
- Better links/information should be placed on U.S. Government web sites to help citizens understand cultural differences and show respect for other cultures
- American youth should be encouraged to learn critical languages
- Students should be encouraged to study world geography/history/culture
- Encourage Americans to become host families for exchange students and foreign visitors
- Encourage Americans to donate to global relief efforts that reinforce U.S. assistance programs.
- Evaluate and expand Department of Education partnerships in foreign countries.

II. *Isolate and Undermine Violent Extremists*

The U.S. government needs to communicate more effectively, clearly and consistently to rebut terrorists' propaganda and undermine extremist ideology. To improve this effort, the State Department is in the process of establishing an interagency "Counterterrorism Communications Center" working with the Department's Rapid Response Unit to develop and deliver a proactive, coordinated USG message. This command center will have as its core function developing messages to undermine and marginalize extremist ideology and propaganda. The Counterterrorism Communications Center will also aggressively rebut and efficiently respond to actions and statements by terrorist groups and leaders across the world. It will actively seek opportunities to respond to breaking news, rebut negative messages and counter erroneous reporting. Appropriate agencies will detail experts to help support the work of the center. The center will be led by a Senior Foreign Service communication professional reporting directly to the Under Secretary for Public Diplomacy and Public Affairs; the deputy director will be a senior military officer from the Department of Defense. Working sub-groups are currently examining different aspects of the ideological struggle, including: terrorists' use of the Internet, television programming, publishing and alternative technologies. These working groups will make ongoing recommendations to the Policy Coordinating Committee for action.

A. *Place strategic focus on critical countries in the ideological war against terror*

"Pilot Counties" have been designated to more intensely concentrate our public diplomacy efforts and resources in the ideological war through interagency-coordinated and country-specific plans that take advantage of all elements of national power. Each pilot country has written a plan outlining strategic goals, target audiences, and the programs/means to reach those audiences to undermine support for terrorism. Pilot countries have proposed additional programs and activities that will be implemented as funding becomes available. Pilot country projects are expected to facilitate best practices that can be applied more broadly to public diplomacy in other areas.

B. *Identify and engage key influencers whose views have a ripple effect throughout society*

Such influencers include clerics, educators, journalists, physicians, women leaders, business leaders, scientists, and military personnel. Every appropriate diplomatic tool available should be used to nurture engagement, foster common values and interests with these influential individuals and encourage them to speak out against the extremists.

Examples
- Specialized exchange programs
- Academic and professional conferences
- Journalist workshops
- Embassy cultural events
- Military-to-military training and exchanges

1. **Religious Leaders**—The unique role of religion in the current war on terror requires that greater efforts be made to engage in dialogue with the leaders of faith-based communities. Moral and religious leaders such as clerics, imams, rabbis, monks and priests can foster tolerance and mutual respect among religions and their followers.

   USG officials should seek opportunities to participate in events that resonate with local populations, including visits to important religious and cultural sites and hosting events such as Iftar dinners to demonstrate respect for different faiths.

   Special efforts should be made by USG officials to highlight mainstream Muslim voices that condemn extremist violence.

Examples
- Quote mainstream voices in speeches or interviews
- Suggest individuals who condemn violence for media appearances
- Feature them in editorials/opinion pieces
- Feature them on USG broadcasting programs
- Sponsor interfaith programs and conferences featuring a diversity of mainstream voices.
- Encourage television programming on "faith matters" featuring guests who offer mainstream views of Islam, Christianity, Judaism and other faiths.
- Encourage foundations/think tanks/NGOs/universities to include mainstream views on Islam when sponsoring conferences and publishing academic articles.

2. **Youth Audience**—Because they are a sustainable force and will play a role for many years to come, more resources should be devoted to and specific outreach plans developed for specific segments of the youth audience, including early, middle, high school, university and young professionals.

Examples
- Sports diplomacy
- After school and summer youth enrichment programs
- Youth ambassador programs
- English language teaching programs
- Pre-college counseling and exam prep
- High school/college exchanges
- Cultural performances and collaboration
- Broadcasts tailored to young people with a mix of music and news
- Greater use of emerging media such as podcasts, webzines, etc.

3. **Women and Girls**—Educating and empowering women and girls should be a priority and programs should be significantly expanded.

Examples
- Establish women's centers that include computer training and democracy education
- Provide micro-finance grants and loans so women can start small in-home businesses
- Offer literacy programs that include information on nutrition and health
- Sponsor business mentoring conferences and exchanges
- Increase efforts against trafficking in persons
- Build networks of women scientists

4. **Minority Groups**—Special outreach should be directed to members of minority groups and indigenous people who often do not have full access to education and capital.

Example
Martin Luther King scholarships are awarded in Colombia to African-Colombian students to promote the pursuit of higher education.

C. *Undermine violent extremism by fostering a climate of openness and respect for religious diversity*

1. Support Muslim-Americans' efforts to be a "bridge" between American and Muslim communities worldwide.

Examples
- Send teams of Muslim-Americans to Muslim communities abroad to engage in citizen dialogue.
- Sponsor "town hall meetings" between Muslim-American communities and Muslim audiences worldwide, suggest regular programs on USG broadcasting.
- Encourage the development of documentaries, reality shows, soap operas and other television shows that feature American families living in the Middle East and Middle Eastern families living in America.
- Engage the Muslim-American scientific community

D. *Foster grassroots worldwide condemnation against terror; make suicide bombing a matter of shame, not honor*

1. Encourage world leaders, especially leaders of diverse faith communities, to state clearly that no cause, no complaint and no grievance can ever justify the murder of innocents.
2. Cultivate partnerships with allied governments who are proactively engaged in the war on terror. Strengthen efforts, share appropriate information and reinforce themes to cooperatively and comprehensively respond. Host and attend workshops, conferences and events to promote best practices and share ideas.
3. Highlight the human cost of terror. Where culturally appropriate, foster awareness of the victims of terror and highlight the human loss inflicted on the families and communities of victims.

Examples
- Encourage leaders of all faiths to speak out against suicide bombings; explain it violates the tenets of all faiths, including Christianity, Islam and Judaism.
- Encourage members of religious congregations to begin grassroots movements against terror.
- Remind audiences that violent extremism is rejected by the vast majority of Muslims around the world.
- Remind audiences that the victims of terror are often innocent children and women; they have come from more than 90 nations and many of them are Muslims.

E. *Focus on the type of ideology and society the extremists want to impose on others throughout the world, especially Islamic nations*

The extremists have stated on numerous occasions that their goal is to create and impose a unified, dictatorial state on the proud and currently sovereign nations of the diverse Islamic world. The majority of civilized people do not want to live in the type of society the violent extremists seek. The best example is the society that was imposed by the Taliban in Afghanistan. Books were burned, music was banned; cultural icons were destroyed; girls were not allowed to go to school or learn to read; and women were not allowed to work—even if their husbands had been killed and they had no means of support. Freedom of expression and worship were not allowed; in fact, faith practices were so strictly proscribed that men could be punished if their beards were not the exact, appropriate length.

F. *Confront Hate Speech*

Aggressively confront speech that encourages hate or incites violence and inflames misunderstandings around the world.

Examples
- Encourage tolerance in textbooks.
- Work with UNESCO and other international organizations to condemn hate speech and eliminate it from textbooks.

III. *Nurture and Project Common Interests and Values*

Americans and people of different countries, cultures and faiths across the world share many common values and interests. America believes in the dignity and value of every human being in the world. We respect the historical and cultural roots of other political and social systems, even as we uphold the inalienable and fundamental human rights of every human being. Emphasizing these common interests and values must be an integral part of all USG communications.

A. *Each agency should identify and build on areas in which their expertise/mandate corresponds with a common interest of the world*

> **Example**
> America has a shared interest with the people of the world in protecting and improving our environment/confronting climate change. Through participation in international conferences, interviews, and outreach programs, communicate America's common interest in improving our environment. Make sure all our officials frame their message by stating that we want to partner with other countries in ways that advance our common interest in improving the world's environment.

B. *Develop active, agency-specific alumni networks of current and former official guests, speakers, professional exchanges and study programs as resources for outreach*

> **Examples**
> – Cultivate long-term relationships with participants and encourage collaboration on proposed initiatives to strengthen relationships.
> – Encourage professional networking among individuals and share networks with agencies engaged in parallel programs.

C. *Greater focus should be placed on three major areas that human beings across the world care most about: health, education and economic opportunity*

1. *Health*

Further commit America to working in partnership with other nations to eradicate preventable diseases. Convene conferences to focus/track progress and publicize major initiatives and encourage greater collaboration between government agencies (including DOD, HHS, USAID, VA) and foundations, NGOs, health care organizations (doctors/nurses/hospitals/pharmaceuticals) and religious congregations.

American health programs that reinforce this goal include:

- President's Emergency Plan for AIDS Relief
- Avian flu response
- Malaria programs and summit

- Health diplomacy and training of medical professionals in the Americas
- Increased emphasis on maternal/infant mortality and immunization programs
- Efforts to improve water quality and supplies
- Military hospital ships, which are highly visible and should be deployed strategically to support public diplomacy
- Middle East breast cancer initiative

Further partnerships should be developed, and medical and science diplomacy envoys recruited to help champion America's commitment to better health for the people of the world.

2. *Education*
Every effort should be made throughout the USG to expand educational programs across the board, ranging from English teaching, teacher training, student exchanges, medical and science education exchanges, literacy training of all types, establishment of virtual science libraries (e.g. Iraq). Recent efforts such as the creation of major new after-school and summer English language training programs should be significantly expanded.

Example
English language teaching offers youth a job-related skill and improves their economic prospects, while opening a window to our shared values and the wider world of information. By hosting summer and after-school programs, we can reach young people in their own countries, before they are old enough to travel to America on exchange programs.

3. *Economic Opportunity*
America's support for micro-loans, job training, literacy and trade should be highlighted as examples of America's desire to improve prosperity for people across the world.

D. *Expand private sector linkages*

Encourage international professional exchanges, ask companies to sponsor internship opportunities and joint professional projects.

E. *Sharing the best of American culture mitigates negative images and misunderstanding*

Foster private sector partnerships to significantly expand cultural, sports, musical and artistic and scientific exchanges. Sports activities forge a common bond and teach teamwork, discipline, respect for others and abiding by rules. Art and culture are a shared language that taps into the range of human emotions and reminds us of our common humanity. Shared arts and cultural appreciation can help bridge political and policy differences. U.S. science and technology are widely respected in the Muslim world, and offer a promising entry point for engaging citizens and society.

Examples

- Global Cultural Initiative—USG will work with private sector partners to enhance exchanges of art, film, dance and music and share expertise in arts management.
- Islamic World Science Partnerships—USG will help build public-private partnerships in science collaboration, focusing on education, youth and women.

ATTACHMENT B

GENERAL COMMUNICATION GUIDELINES

Demonstrate respect. The most comprehensive survey we have conducted shows the number one thing the United States can do to improve public perception of our country is to demonstrate respect for other countries' culture and contributions; this is especially true in many Islamic countries. United States officials can demonstrate respect by: visiting important historic and cultural sites during foreign travel; actively scheduling "listening" events and opportunities to interact with foreign publics and listen to their point of view; planning events that demonstrate respect for different cultural and faith traditions; inviting respected local authors, historians, poets, musicians, etc to appear at USG sponsored events; and attending important cultural and historical events in other countries.

Use humility. The history of our own country is one of constantly striving and many times failing to live up to our own noble values. Our society is not perfect, and we should not be afraid to admit that we face many challenges and struggle to live up to our own ideals.

Use caution when dealing with faith issues in the public square. Government officials should be extremely cautious and if possible, avoid using religious language, because it can mean different things and is easily misconstrued. The extremists are murderers who pervert religion, members of a cult that promotes death and destruction rather than legitimate practitioners of any faith. When it is necessary to make a point that involves Islam, for instance, quote Muslim voices themselves. Also, avoid characterizing people of any faith as "moderate"—this is a political word which, when extended to the world of faith, can imply these individuals are less than devout and faithful. The terms "mainstream" or "majority" are preferable. Finally, avoid phrases such as the "Muslim community" that imply it is monolithic; Muslim communities, like other faith communities, are diverse.

Create platforms where divergent ideas are encouraged and freely and openly debated. Support conferences sponsored by think tanks and foundations and intellectual publications that foster debates. Seek to empower/highlight Muslim voices that speak out against terror and violence, even when they do not agree with every aspect of U.S. foreign policy.

Use good pictures and images. Well-choreographed pictures and images convey emotion and/or action as well as a convincing story.

Suggestions:

- Before any event, think through a desired picture that would best capture and tell the story of the event.
- Where should the photo be taken—what is the background? The background should help convey where you are—the country, the city, the building, the environment. Should there be a flag in the background? Is there a banner behind or in front of the podium? Is a recognizable part of the building visible? What part of the building is recognizable? E.g., capture I.M. Pei's Pyramid as your background for an event at the Louvre rather than an unrecognizable column inside.
- Who should be in the picture? The principal along with those who are the focus of the event should be in the picture to help convey the story. Musicians? Youth? Government officials? E.g., if the Ambassador and State Minister for Education are speaking at a Fulbright event, make sure to get shots not just of the officials speaking but with Fulbright grantees in the photo.
- What is the action or the emotion? Are they dancing? Talking? Listening? Learning? Enthusiastic? Include props if that helps convey the story. E.g., if the Ambassador is meeting with 4th graders to give out books, the photo should include students holding the books, youth reading, pointing to a picture in the book, etc.
- The photographer should think through the location for the photo with all of the technical considerations in mind—not shooting into the sun, not in front of reflective glass or a mirror, not in shade or shadows, etc. The key people who need to be included in the shot should be identified.
- Look for the action or emotion. For action shots, get a tight shot rather than wide. A tight shot will convey more emotion in addition to the story. E.g., for a U.S. military big band in town with swing dancers, rather than capturing the whole crowd, pick out one couple in full enthusiastic swing dancing in front of a large U.S. flag and banner of the event so the country and occasion are conveyed.

Develop a communication strategy to support public diplomacy events and policy developments. Carefully consider the target audience, desired goals and objectives, and the key messages to effectively reach target audiences, as well as how results will be measured. The "ABCDE" communication process model that follows is an example of a planning tool that can be used to think through the message and the best way to deliver it to a target audience.

ATTACHMENT C

CORE MESSAGES—GENERAL

- As a diverse, multi-cultural nation founded by immigrants, America includes and respects people of different nations, cultures and faiths.
- America seeks to be a partner for progress, prosperity and peace.
- The American government wants to work in partnership with nations and peoples across the world in ways that result in a better life for all the world's citizens.
- Because we believe all people are equal and equally valuable, we believe people everywhere should be free to speak their mind, to participate in their government, to worship as their conscience dictates, to assemble freely and to pursue opportunity, economic, political and creative.
- While we do not expect every country to shape its government like that of the United States, we believe that citizens should be able to participate in choosing their governments and that those governments should be accountable to their citizens. We believe all people want to live in societies that are just, governed by the rule of law, and not corrupt.
- We believe in universal education, with equal opportunity to learn for girls as well as boys.
- We believe in open markets and free trade to foster economic opportunity so all people have the ability to have productive jobs and provide for their families.
- As a nation where people are free to worship as their conscience dictates, we respect all faiths. Many Muslims live, work and worship freely in America and are an important part of American society.

CORE MESSAGES—SPECIFIC TO THE WAR ON TERROR

- All major world faiths, including Islam, Christianity, Judaism, Hinduism and Buddhism, teach that life is precious and that the taking of innocent life is wrong.
- The violent extremists we face in the war against terror do not represent, but instead pervert, Islam by advocating the mass murder of innocents—and most of their victims have been fellow Muslims.
- No grievance and no cause—no matter how legitimate they are—can ever justify acts of terror.
- Violent extremism is rejected by the majority of civilized people of all faiths.
- The majority of people of all faiths do not want to live in the type of society the violent extremists seek.
- The struggle against violent extremism should unite the nations and citizens of the world because terrorism threatens all the communities of the world. Acts of terror have brought tragedy, destruction, death and terrible grief to innocent people from Indonesia to Morocco, Spain to Jordan, England to India and Egypt. The victims of September 11th were citizens of more than 90 different countries and adherents of many faiths, including Christianity, Judaism and Islam.
- Terrorist attacks began long before the U.S. acted to remove the Taliban regime that was harboring al Qaeda in Afghanistan, or to remove Saddam Hussein's brutal regime from power in Iraq. The violent extremists, such as those who were responsible for the mass murder plot targeting airplanes in London in 2006, have long targeted innocent people. Their agenda is to impose a Taliban-like regime on the many proud and sovereign nations of the Islamic world, and they have nothing but intolerance for all those who do not share their extremist beliefs—including fellow Muslims.
- Through their indiscriminate killing of innocent people, the violent extremists have repeatedly shown their contempt for human life, regardless of race, ethnicity or religion.
- We saw the type of society the extremists seek in the Taliban rule of Afghanistan. Books were burned, music was banned, cultural icons were destroyed. Little girls were not allowed to go to school or learn

to read, and women were not allowed to work to support themselves even if they were widowed and had no other means of support.

- The difference between democratic values and the type of society that the violent extremists want is stark:
  - Freedom vs. tyranny
  - Tolerance and respect for differences vs. intolerance for any diversity
  - Religious freedom vs. state-imposed requirements of worship
  - Freedom of speech vs. imprisonment for differing views
  - Freedom to associate vs. restrictions on leaving your home
  - Education for all vs. no education for girls, limited education for boys
  - Accountable governments with citizen participation vs. unelected, self-declared leaders
- The violent extremists have killed thousands of Muslims, as well as innocent women, children and the elderly over the past several decades. The bombings of a wedding celebration in Jordan, bus passengers in London, and day laborers in Baghdad who were trying to earn money to support their families, are examples of cruelly calculated terrorist murders.
- The fight against terrorism is a concerted fight for values and principles that are universal. Much more unites us as citizens of the world than divides us. Across all borders, we share a common humanity. While the color of our skin, the language we speak, or the way we worship may be different, people everywhere aspire to speak their minds, participate in their society, worship freely, live in security, and pursue education, jobs and greater opportunities for their families.
- The ideology of the violent extremists uses a perverted religiosity to attempt to justify murder, terror, and violence. Yet such actions are always abhorrent and always wrong, and the international community, the interfaith community and decent men and women everywhere must speak out against those who advocate hate, violence and terrorism. We call on leaders of all faiths to work for mutual respect and understanding and to send a clear message: that killing oneself and murdering innocent people is always wrong.
- As an international community, we must foster debate, encourage education and provide information, to help people learn and make decisions for themselves, because we believe most people every-

where, of every faith, will choose freedom over tyranny and tolerance over intolerance.

- Despite al Qaeda's repeated attempts to characterize the world as being in the midst of a clash of civilizations, the simple fact is that the international community—east and west, north and south—has come together in unprecedented ways to confront common threats and ease human suffering. America is doing its part, working in partnership with countries throughout the Islamic world to improve the lives of Muslims. America is the largest bilateral donor of food and health aid to the Palestinian people. Americans were the largest providers of help to Muslims affected by the tsunami in Indonesia and the earthquake in Pakistan. We provide funds for Muslim girls and boys to go to school, for Muslim women to learn English, and for Muslim young people to get training for jobs. And in Afghanistan and Iraq, we are working in partnership with democratically elected Muslim leaders to provide freedom and security for Muslim populations that were brutally repressed under the Taliban and Saddam Hussein.
- As we look forward, we seek to work in a spirit of partnership with people and nations across the world to confront this ideology of hate and foster a climate of hope and opportunity. The U.S. is far from perfect, yet we believe the noble ideals of freedom and justice that guide us are right and true for human beings everywhere. We want to work in partnership with nations throughout the world in ways that will result in a more peaceful and prosperous world, and a better life for all people.

ATTACHMENT D

ADDITIONAL COMMUNICATION VEHICLES

USG Broadcasting

Consistent with the BBG's statutory mandate to operate in accordance with the highest standards of professional journalism and to safeguard the editorial integrity and independence of its broadcast organizations, as well as the BBG Strategic Plan for 2008–2013, the Broadcasting Board of Governors shall:

- Review existing strategies and resources in order to focus BBG efforts on the critical priority countries for U.S. foreign policy. Means of signal delivery (television, FM radio, internet, etc.) should vary according to audience demographics, media habits, trends, etc. Decisions should be made on the basis of thorough audience research and U.S. national priorities.
- Build upon BBG's reach and impact within the Islamic World, including augmentation of news gathering, reporting and programming for Alhurra TV and Radio Sawa, Radio Farda, etc.
- BBG's various programs should broaden and deepen overall coverage of Islam and foster interfaith dialogue, including discussion of Islam and modernity and Islam and democracy, ensuring the participation of mainstream Muslim voices.
- Help audiences in authoritarian countries understand the principles and practices of democratic, free and just societies.
- Engage the world in a conversation about America, including the presentation of accurate and comprehensive information to counter misinformation and disinformation about the United States, its policies, and culture, as well as the use of interactive dialogues with key audiences, such as youth.
- Broaden cooperation with U.S. public diplomacy, including playing an active role in the interagency strategic planning; facilitating the exchange of relevant data, including survey results and polling data, with other government agencies; and developing partnerships with like-minded institutes and foundations outside the government.

BBG should consider covering newsworthy events sponsored by government agencies, such as exchange programs, health care, scientific collaboration, and education initiatives.

Non-BBG Activities

Narrowcasting: In response to changing user habits and the dramatically different media landscape, new web-based approaches must be developed and expanded by all agencies. The interagency community should collaborate with technology professionals to identify recommendations on current trends and the most effective ways of reaching youth audiences.

Examples

- **Internet Outreach:** Pod casts, web chats, SMS text messaging, blogs, and other web-based programs are being developed and expanded to share U.S. foreign policy messages with audiences around the world. Additional capacity has been added to broadcast live events, such as the President's State of the Union address, in more languages worldwide.
- **Digital Outreach Team:** A new unit at the State Department engages on blogs and web chats in Arabic to correct misrepresentations of U.S. policy.
- **Democracy Dialogues:** A new interactive, web-based discussion of the principles of democracy has been launched. Every two months, a different theme is featured.
- **"Partnership for a Better Life:"** A website to provide a visual gateway to stories of individuals and institutions benefiting from U.S. foreign aid has been established, building on President Bush's State of the Union message that: "For people everywhere, America is a partner for a better life." Our ambassadors are strongly encouraged to highlight ways the American government and people are improving the lives of people in their host countries.

ATTACHMENT E

EVALUATION AND ACCOUNTABILITY

As Edward R. Murrow once observed, no cash register ever rings when a mind is changed. The impact of information and education programs that touch the emotions, beliefs, intellects and allegiances of diverse audiences around the world is often difficult to gauge, especially when many public diplomacy activities may only produce long-term, rather than immediate, impact.

Nevertheless, all United States government agencies must build evaluation and measurement into strategic communication and public diplomacy program design. They must examine the effectiveness and impact of their efforts. While we cannot prove that additional USG appearances on television will change minds, we can track the growing number of interviews, the time allotted to representing America's point of view, and whether our key messages were in fact conveyed. Participants in our exchange and education programs can and should be interviewed to find out what aspects were most effective; speakers should be evaluated for quality and effectiveness in presenting American values and beliefs.

Evaluation should measure progress toward the achievement of goals, allowing managers to adjust methods and means, and make informed decisions about resources. Performance measurement and evaluation ensure accountability and transparency so that stakeholders, including the American public, can justify program expenditures as a prudent use of taxpayer funds.

The Policy Coordinating Committee should implement its evaluation and measurement strategy as follows:

- **Establish a culture of measurement:** The PCC will communicate to all departments and agencies the importance and value of evaluations and performance measurement using common standards and comparable data that support the three strategic imperatives. Increased commitment to data collection and reporting will help improve communication and public diplomacy programming and more effectively demonstrate the impact of our collective efforts.

- **Establish common core performance indicators:** The PCC will analyze the performance indicators submitted by departments and agencies with a view to approve a uniform set of relevant core indicators for use in all agencies. Individual agencies will then create sub-indictors to comprehensively evaluate supporting internal efforts. This will provide greater focus and coherence across agencies and bureaus, standardize and streamline processes for the field, and ensure data collection supports both processes.
- **Establish mechanisms for data collection:** Each individual agency and department shall allocate resources, establish indicators, and deploy mechanisms to gather relevant data. This evaluation process will be used to establish baselines and track the impact of public diplomacy programs and activities.
- **The PCC will conduct periodic agency-specific reviews** of public diplomacy and strategic communication efforts to validate successful programs, recommend the continuation of activities, and direct resources.

INDEX

Diplomatic Studies

Series Editor
Jan Melissen, *Netherlands Institute of International Relations 'Clingendael'*

1. Lloyd, L. *Diplomacy with a Difference.* The Commonwealth Office of High Commissioner, 1880-2006. 2008. ISBN 978 90 04 15497 1
2. Bátora, J. *Foreign Ministries and the Information Revolution.* Going Virtual? 2008. ISBN 978 90 04 16900 5
3. Berridge, G.R. *British Diplomacy in Turkey, 1583 to the present.* A study in the evolution of the resident embassy. 2009. ISBN 978 90 04 17639 3
4. Fitzpatrick, K.R. *The Future of U.S. Public Diplomacy.* An Uncertain Fate. 2010. ISBN 978 90 04 17720 8